Where the River Narrows

Classic French & Nostalgic Québécois
Recipes From St. Lawrence Restaurant

JEAN-CHRISTOPHE POIRIER
with **JOIE ALVARO KENT**

appetite
by RANDOM HOUSE

Appetite by Random House® and colophon are registered trademarks of Penguin Random House LLC.

Library and Archives of Canada Cataloguing in Publication is available upon request.

ISBN: 9780525611189
eBook ISBN: 9780525611196

Cover and book design by Jennifer Griffiths
Written with Joie Alvaro Kent
Photography by Brit Gill, except page 148
Photo on page 8 by Amy Ho
Photos on pages 2, 5, and 6 courtesy of the author
Printed in China

Published in Canada by Appetite by Random House®, a division of Penguin Random House LLC.

www.penguinrandomhouse.ca

10 9 8 7 6 5 4 3 2 1

appetite
by RANDOM HOUSE

To Dara, Aïla, and Florence.

LEFT: JOIE ALVARO KENT, WRITER

MIDDLE: J-C AND FAMILY AT
GLORIOUS ORGANICS FARM

RIGHT: BRIT GILL, PHOTOGRAPHER

CONTENTS

CHAPTER 1

QUÉBEC

CHAPTER 2

CLASSIC FRENCH

CHAPTER 3

ST. LAWRENCE

CHAPTER 4
HOME COOKING

FOREWORD

BY DEREK DAMMANN

"THE RESTAURANT IS called 'Ask for Luigi'? Who's that?"

"It's where I work now. I think you'd like it."

"Can I get a table for two?"

"We don't take reservations."

"No reservations . . . you're my sister. Who does this guy think he is?"

Something as simple as a hot meal can take over so much of your life, but your professional views on it change dramatically as you mature. Ego-driven and complicated multi-course extravaganzas make way for simpler fare; thoughtful, regional, and emotional, overflowing with finesse. A dish of eggs and anchovies was the first thing I tasted at Ask for Luigi, a tiny Italian restaurant where J-C was the chef. It was an epiphany, best enjoyed with a touch of anger. Not for any reason other than it was delicious and oh so clever. Damn you, J-C, for coming up with it.

J-C is, if you haven't figured it out yet, from Québec. A magical place that I now call home. In fact, I more than likely moved here just as he was leaving. I didn't know him then; we weren't buddies nor colleagues. I'll be completely honest; I know very little about his career. Which is actually great, since I don't have to wax poetic about which ranks he came up through to "be the chef he is today." What I can say is that J-C comes from the world of *grande cuisine*. Today, we have inherited a world of *petite cuisine*. There are ten to eighteen small and tepid portions. The focus is on presentation, rather than eating. But for J-C, food is about generosity and this is reflected on his plate as well. Kitchens have become more systematic and are not such emotional spaces anymore.

Sauces are mere droplets out of bottles on the pass. Instead, he embraces the stoves like a passionate concert pianist, roasting a duck and extracting the sauce out of the chopped-up carcass. There is a great quote by Marco Pierre White that says, "If you've been given opportunities, then you have to create opportunities. If you are given knowledge, share your knowledge. If you were born with talent, show your talent off." From the humble beginnings in a time where you went to work to learn your craft, in a time where there was no such thing as a celebrity chef, J-C is an ambassador of his trade, giving people an insight into his world. Allowing them to buy into his dream, and that dream is to feed people to the best of his abilities.

Most of my knowledge of Québec, like a lot of kids who grew up on the West Coast, was championed by my French and History teachers in high school. Outside of that, it was my mother yammering on about Céline Dion, and the usual culinary stereotypes that often define a nation. England's is meat pies, fish 'n' chips, cup o' tea. Canada lends itself to back bacon, doughnuts, and stubby beers. Québec is beaver tails, poutine, and maple syrup. While all of these ring true, if each country is a culinary heavyweight in its own right, Québec is the ringleader in Canada. It's the one that shoots the person out of the cannon, it's the one that crams twelve clowns into a tiny car, it's the one that puts its head in the lion's mouth. Insanity and intrigue around every corner—but the one thing Québec has that makes it truly unique is its regionality. There is no denying the food culture has been heavily influenced by French traditions, but recent decades have seen truly French cuisine phased out in favour of revisited Québécois classics. Québec has boasted a strong sense of self and a well-developed culinary identity for longer than most Canadian regions, thanks to a strong, provincially protected agriculture industry. Everything is a work in progress, but thanks to great chefs like J-C, the province is pushing forward and showcasing the limitless potential.

So, who do I think this guy is?

When I think of tenacity and dedication to his craft, J-C and St. Lawrence are the benchmark. Like a swan floating gracefully across a pristine lake, the frantic legs invisible under a beautiful, smooth sheen. Moving slowly and deliberately with great attention, J-C demonstrates the importance of regional French cuisine and proves that if you are a really good cook, you can go back in time. This book, *Where the River Narrows*, is a fascinating glimpse into what makes St. Lawrence tick, filled with invaluable lessons of respect, responsibility, and delicious food. This cookbook will inspire you, but remember that cooking is a philosophy, it's not a recipe.

In a very strange time full of energy and opportunity, the culinary world is wide open for interpretation. J-C demonstrates the importance of taking ten steps backwards before taking one giant leap forward, understanding and sharing how sophistication and restraint can shape you personally and professionally. He is truly on an artist's journey, creating his own intimate snapshot of our culinary landscape.

DEREK DAMMANN

INTRODUCTION

4:45 p.m. Pre-shift staff meeting's in the bag, and everyone's starting to gear up for doors opening in fifteen minutes. Holy shit, eighty-five covers on a Tuesday night. Even after twenty-five years in the industry, I still get butterflies before the first guests arrive. David cues up "Thunderstruck" by AC/DC on the sound system and cranks it super loud. For five minutes, every single team member goes a little apeshit, screaming "YEAH!" at the tops of their lungs—we're all amped. Then, just as abruptly as it began, the music dies, and we all settle into that familiar groove. We've blown off some of the pre-game stress; it's still there, but at least it's a little more controlled and less chaotic now. Above all, though, we stay grounded because we have faith in our system at St. Lawrence, faith in each other, faith that everyone's station is looking good, faith that we're all serious enough to be ready. It's the calm before the storm. Bon service, tout le monde. *It's go time.*

I can't say that cooking has always been my calling. When I was a kid, I spent most of my time playing team sports, but eating has always my true passion. I loved—and still love—the ritual of sitting at a table and having a hearty meal with family and friends. It was as if a deep understanding of the power of food ran through my veins from a very early age; I could see how it brings people together and gives everyone something to talk about.

We didn't dine at restaurants very often while I was growing up in Saint-Jérôme, Québec. I discovered that part of my culinary journey much later. But we always had something good to eat on the table at home because my mother was incredibly creative with the budget. The food that came out of her kitchen was traditional, healthy, and seasonal. And, damn, could Mom ever throw a party. I remember so many epic dinners with Dad's soccer friends—those nights were always off the hook. Six-year-old me would stare wide-eyed at the *méchoui*, the spit-roasted lamb stuffed with pounds of butter and spices (and I mean ridiculously huge amounts of butter). Everyone would fight for the *mignonettes* (testicles), but I'd grab a giant leg bone. It was huge for a little kid, kind of like something out of *The Flintstones*, and I'd sit in the corner chewing on that massive piece of lamb, loving every bite.

Spending time outdoors was a big part of my childhood, and foraging fiddleheads with my father was the adventure that I looked forward to the most. We'd come back home to sauté them simply in butter with chopped garlic; I'll never forget how impressed I was to taste something so delicious that we'd just picked ourselves in the forest.

For most of his life, my paternal grandfather had a small *cabane à sucre* (sugar shack) in the woods, accessible only by foot or by Ski-Doo. With seven sisters and two brothers in my dad's family, it was always a big deal when all his siblings and their families got together. Our annual sugar shack reunion was, by far, one of my favourite family gatherings. All my cousins and I would run from tree to tree, screaming at the top of our lungs when we were lucky enough to find maple sap in the buckets. And watching my grandfather reduce that liquid into amazing maple syrup was the most magical thing ever.

Admittedly, the teenage years were tough for me. I didn't know a lot about myself, who I was or what I liked. For the most part, I was incredibly confused about what I should do with my life. But I did know one thing for sure: I could never be stuck in a job where I'd be chained to a desk. I needed to move, to always be active. My closest friends pushed me to take the one-year course in *hôtellerie* to become a cook. A bunch of my buddies and I were sharing a house together at the time, and I was always the one who'd meal plan, cook, and grill for us all. Who knows—maybe they were leveraging the prospect of better meals! Regardless, a career in cooking seemed like a natural fit for me, so I told myself, "Why not give it a shot?"

I spent a year training in classical French cooking techniques, and decided to take my first kitchen job at Les Remparts in Old Montréal. A true old-school French restaurant, its menu featured dishes like veal sweetbreads with grapes, venison with chestnuts and salsify, *coq au vin*, *côte de veau* with chanterelles and *vin jaune*, lobster ravioli with bisque, poached pears in Riesling, and *mousse au chocolat* with *crème chantilly*. I was immediately hooked.

The physical aspect of cooking is what really drew me in, and I saw the kitchen brigade as being very much like a sports team. I believe that good cooking, at least in a restaurant, demands being in good physical condition. The long hours, stress, and abuse your body endures on an everyday basis are huge factors, and a person has to deeply love cooking to dedicate themselves to it. Is it a good way to live? I don't have the answer to that. But I can confess that I was all in from day one and became obsessed with food and this profession right away.

Midway through service, and we're all hustling. I'm on the pass slicing and plating pâté en croûte, *then dressing an endive salad, then putting the finishing touches on a* ballotine de canard *so that it's ready to send. A sprinkle of Maldon salt on one plate, a drizzle of olive oil on another. Damn, almost missed wiping off that little drop of* sauce vin rouge. *Landen's busy plating on the other side of the pass, making sure that sauces are strained, clean, the right consistency, and properly seasoned. Jules is firing a pork chop for table 31, searing it in a cast-iron pan before resting it for at least ten minutes. Timing is everything. Margaux is next to me, prepping plates of bread and* cretons *for the new arrivals who just sat down while she's juggling bills coming in for dessert—*tarte au citron *for bar 10. The chits keep on coming, but we're in it to win it. Every night.*

I've got to tip my hat to Chef Normand Laprise. Learning how to survive the storm and understanding that a smooth sea never made a good sailor were two of my biggest lessons from the time I spent in his kitchen at Toqué!. Such immaculate organization and precision, and—oh my god!—the produce coming in was of a quality that I'd never seen before. It was a 180-degree shift from the classic French cuisine I'd been immersed in. It was refreshing and exciting, and the corresponding intensity, standards, expectations, and stress levels were also very high. I learned right away that I had to change my mindset, to never complain, and to start doing more than what was expected of me. No other restaurant or chef has had such a meaningful impact on my cooking philosophy and career.

After just shy of two years at Toqué!, an all-too-familiar feeling started to surface. I'd progressed on the line from garde-manger to meat station, to chef de partie entremetier, and to chef de partie saucier, but something was missing. Out of the blue, I decided to quit—I do things like this sometimes. Woke up and said to myself "I'm done," with no real plans for what might come next. But I knew I wanted to get the hell out of Québec, out of my comfort zone, and so I moved out west.

Chef Rob Feenie's newly opened restaurant Lumière is what drew me to Vancouver, British Columbia; lucky for me, the chef de cuisine was Québécois. That French connection was my in. I sold everything I owned, packed one bag and all my knives, and relocated across the country, leaving my family, friends, and girlfriend behind. At the time, I could barely speak English. My English vocabulary was literally no more than "hello," "thank you," and "goodbye." Talk about being a fish out of water. And if I thought Toqué! was busy, Lumière launched the definition of "being in the weeds" straight into the stratosphere.

Lumière was different from Toqué!, smaller in size but with triple the workload and only half as many cooks in the kitchen. We had an à la carte menu, a tasting menu, a vegetarian tasting menu, and on top of that, a bar menu for what was essentially a second restaurant attached to Lumière's dining room. Chef Feenie had won *Iron Chef* that year against Chef Morimoto; as a result, we were the hot spot in Vancouver, and we were slammed every night.

I spent six out of seven days each week at work, sixteen hours a day. Yet, despite that, I enjoyed my time at Lumière. So many great cooks came out of that kitchen—lots of us are now chefs and restaurateurs. Working shoulder to shoulder with people for long hours in a high-pressure environment is like going to war every night, knowing you need each other to win it. It forges a strong bond, and all the cooks I met at Lumière remain my close friends. But although we put out excellent food together and I learned a lot in Chef Feenie's kitchen, my biggest takeaway from Lumière was what I learned about myself.

At some point in a cook's career comes the dark time when you're not sure if you want to keep pursuing this madness. You see everyone around you—except for your fellow cooks—working fewer hours and making way more money. And if your life partner doesn't work in the industry, then you've got huge problems on your shoulders because they'll never understand why you're doing this to yourself. Being on the line at Lumière, I realized that no matter how difficult it was to play at a high level and how mentally hard it was to know that I'd be missing important moments in my family's and friends' lives, I was too invested in my career. There was no going back to something else. I loved working hard to reach

a goal and the incredible sense of accomplishment I felt upon reaching it. Oddly enough, I loved the pressure too. After Lumière, I wanted to be a chef more than anything.

Front of house is in full gear now. Our manager Julie's polishing plates because we're running out. Happens all the time because we're a little restaurant and don't have that much tableware. Sarah's killing it behind the bar, making a French 75 and pouring glasses of Sancerre. Booze sales are gonna be good

tonight. Robert Charlebois is next up on the playlist—
"J't'aime comme un fou" from what I can hear over
the guests' conversations, Christophe's favourite.
David's running empty plates to the dishpit.
Christophe's running desserts for table 37. Next turn's
about to get seated—kitchen's gonna get hit again
soon. Every night feels like a Saturday night these
days; I've gotta shut up and remember that this is a
good problem to have. "Dig deep, everyone," I say to
the crew. "It's almost over. We're gonna get it done."

Over the next ten years, I tried to figure out what my career was going to look like; that process involved a lot of wandering and soul searching. I checked out of Vancouver for a while, taking a step back to spend about fourteen months travelling through South America. It was a search for perspective, not only on my work but on my life. I started in Chile, went up to

Peru, up again to Ecuador, back down to Bolivia, into Argentina, and completed the loop by ending up in the south of Chile before making my way back home. Everything I owned was in my backpack. No keys, no attachments whatsoever, no responsibilities, except making sure I had something to eat every day. Travelling through these countries, having pared back my life in such an extreme way made me appreciate the value of living simply. With that clarity, I was ready

to come back and attack the next few years with a more complete sense of purpose.

There were lots of stops and starts, lots of forks in the road. Along the way, I opened some award-winning restaurants and grew up as a businessperson; those heights of success were tempered by a ton of sacrifices, as well as some pretty significant failures and kicks in the teeth. I chalk it up to impatience. Young cooks—myself included—always want to be good at their craft right away. They've got something to prove, whether it's to the outside world, to their fellow chefs, or to themselves. When they walk into a restaurant as a finished product, see the kitchen running so smoothly and see the dishes coming out, they think to themselves, "Hell yeah, I want this." So they apply for a job, join the team, and become part of the process—and then quit after realizing how damn hard it is. In my experience, true success doesn't come overnight. Back then, I didn't understand that it takes twenty to twenty-five years in the industry before you can really put your finger on your true direction.

A life-changing meal that my now-wife, Dara, and I had at L'Ami Jean in Paris crystallized my approach to owning a restaurant. It took everything I thought I knew about being a chef and turned it on its head. Knowing I'd be going full tilt after opening St. Lawrence, I took the opportunity to grab some much-needed downtime in 2016 and stole away with Dara for my very first trip to France—at last. I immediately felt like I was home, and the entire trip was like a dream. On our second day in Paris, I proposed to the woman of my life in front of Basilique du Sacré-Coeur—seriously, the best day ever. We strolled through the city without a care in the world, hopping from restaurant to restaurant, but there was one spot I knew I had to hit: L'Ami Jean, a tiny bistro in the seventh *arrondissement* with a crazy chef who made phenomenal food. Everything I'd heard about it was true, and our dinner was better than I could have imagined.

What impressed me most was the electric presence of chef/owner Stéphane Jégo. He was in the kitchen with his team: cooking, plating, expediting, and yelling at everyone in a good way, with passion. Chef Jégo was possessed by the passion of a chef with high expectations who wants things done his way, the *right* way. I was spellbound and I couldn't stop watching him work. These days, you don't often see chefs on the line anymore; for that matter, you don't even see them in their restaurants very often. It's all about media and appearances, with so-called glamour becoming more important than everyday cooking tasks.

I loved L'Ami Jean so much that I cancelled my reservation at Le Chateaubriand two weeks later and went back for a second meal. Chef Jégo was on the line once again, working his ass off and yelling, *"Allez, allez! Service! Plus vite! On y va!"* Dining at L'Ami Jean was so inspiring that I wanted to follow in Chef Jégo's footsteps. I wanted to be a chef who led by example and actions, who was in the kitchen every day with his crew, on the front line so all the customers could see and feel the passion, dedication, care, and sacrifice. That day, I decided to attack St. Lawrence just like that and be the Stéphane Jégo of Vancouver. I was me again, with all my dreams, my beliefs, and my energy. I had a plan with a clear vision.

Fuck, it's 10:15 and we're still pushing out mains. But we can see the light at the end of the tunnel now; it's that point in the night when everyone takes a big deep breath. J'ai jamais vu un service qui ne se termine pas—I've never seen a service that doesn't end. It will be over soon, then we clean, reorganize, plan the next day, and finally get to go home. But there's a few more plates to go. Remember, guys: we're only as good as our last plate.

Unmistakably, St. Lawrence is my baby, my passion project, the most honest reflection of who I am as a person and my career as a cook. It is beyond special to me. Rooted in tradition, history, and authenticity, it has soul and, more importantly, a story to tell. St. Lawrence is about Québec, about old-school classic French cooking, but also about the nostalgic memories of home. It's completely outside the box for Vancouverites, a French restaurant unlike anything they've ever experienced, with dishes on the menu that they'd normally have to travel to Québec or Europe to taste.

When you step into St. Lawrence, you don't feel like you're in Vancouver at all—it's like you've been transported to a little bistro in *le vieux Montréal* or a little town in France—and that's exactly what I wanted. We've been successful right from the beginning. Our guests love us, and the media has been squarely on our side. With St. Lawrence, I've found my purpose. My mission is to represent my Québécois culture outside of Québec, and to make sure that the old French classics and techniques aren't forgotten. Today, I'm 100 percent dedicated to this restaurant. It's an extension of my home. That's where you'll find me most of the time, cooking and mastering my craft, enjoying life.

Where the River Narrows appropriately represents Québec itself—the phrase is a direct translation of the Algonquin word "*kebec,*" referencing the area around Québec City where the St. Lawrence River is hemmed in by towering cliffs. This beautiful name for my home province that's so close to my heart reminds me of the countless hours spent standing on the banks of Lac Carré with my dad, fishing for trout and walleye. But it also captures how my culinary inspiration has distilled over the course of my career, narrowing to focus squarely on the rich culinary culture that runs through my veins. And that's what I hope to share with you in this book. Thank you for reading it.

JEAN-CHRISTOPHE

HOW TO USE THIS COOKBOOK

THERE'S SOMETHING IN this book for everyone who loves to cook, whether it's at home or in a restaurant kitchen. Above all, I'd like to help people realize it's not that difficult to get back to the basics of French cookery. So many people are scared of attempting to make French food. Sure, you can spend three days on all the steps for a complex dish, but you can also spend ten minutes to cook something that's easy and delicious.

At its best, French food is simple, highlighting a main ingredient with sauces and condiments. Even making stocks and sauces is easier than you think, and you can freeze them to use later, cutting down your prep time for any given dish.

Unlike many cookbooks, this book wasn't written around the seasons; rather, it traces my personal culinary journey, highlighting memorable moments, people, and dishes throughout my life thus far. Keep this in mind when choosing the recipes you'd like to try. For example, it probably isn't the best idea to make a raspberry custard tart in the middle of February. It's wiser to wait and tackle this dessert in July, when berry season is in full swing.

Please read the book, chapter, and recipe introductions first, instead of skipping straight to the recipes like most people do. It's important that you gain a feel for my approach to cooking in order to understand how and why each step is done. This book contains the concepts, philosophies, flavours, and recipes that I like. It's perfect for me, but that doesn't mean it has to be perfect for you. I believe that when it comes to recipes, the goal is to make it the first time just as I've suggested. The second time around, you can adjust a few things that might not work for you and start to introduce your own touch. By the third kick at the can, you should be ready to make the dish your own, adding or removing components, seasoning to your personal preference, plating it differently, and so on. Play around within the parameters of a dish, and don't be afraid to change things up to suit your palate. Cook with emotion, logic, and love.

I like things with soul that tell old stories, things that are a little rundown because they've been around a long time. I hope my cookbook will become exactly that for you over time: well loved and well used, adorned with sticky notes marking favourite recipes and handwritten notes in the margins. It should be messy, splattered with stains from bubbling pots, torn, and maybe even a little bit smelly from being too close to the stove.

ELEMENTALS

LET'S FACE IT: cooking French food is technical. But all the technique in the world won't matter if your ingredients aren't top-notch. They may be a little more expensive, but they make an exponential difference to the quality of your cooking.

BUTTER

There is no butter like the butter in France. End of story, full stop. Now that we've gotten that fact out of the way, I'd say that not everyone has tasted good cultured butter. We're pretty lucky here in Canada to have good butter available from Québec, Ontario, and PEI. Yes, it's a little on the pricier side, but it's higher quality and you'll be using smaller quantities of it. It's not the butter you'd throw into a pan for searing a piece of meat; it's the butter you're going to spread on a piece of hot bread, fresh out of the oven. Good butter really shines when you use it to finish a dish, making butter sauce for steamed fish, mounting a sauce with it, and glazing vegetables like carrots, turnips, or asparagus in a pan with white wine or vegetable stock or water. For cooking and baking, I generally use good-quality unsalted butter. This enables me to control the salt content of the dish myself, rather than leaving it to a particular butter manufacturer's salt ratio.

FLOUR

I try not to have too many types of flour in my own home kitchen. If you keep too many different kinds in your pantry, I feel that they'll go bad before you have a chance to use them. For pretty much any cooking or baking recipe, you'll be good to go with a high-quality organic all-purpose flour. I make a lot of pasta, so I also have a lot of 00 and semolina flour on hand. For people who love baking bread, whole wheat, buckwheat, and red fife flours are other solid options.

OILS

I'm pretty picky when it comes to oil. I keep grapeseed oil next to my stove for general cooking because it's flavourless and perfectly neutral, and it has the highest smoking point. If you heat olive oil too much, it burns and gives your finished dish an unpalatable acrid taste. For salad dressing, I like first-press canola oil, which is almost fluorescent yellow and has a wonderful flavour. Don't settle for overprocessed canola oil; it has zero flavour and colour. Far too often, people make salad dressing by mixing poor-quality canola oil with olive oil to add flavour when, in reality, good-quality first-press canola oil is all you need. Bear in mind that olive oil can be spicy, bitter, and/or grassy, and using too much of it in a salad dressing can add too much "character." Dressing made with 100% olive oil might ruin your salad; instead, it's better to just finish your salad with olive oil.

Top-notch grapeseed oil, first-press canola oil, and extra-virgin olive oil all definitely have a price tag, and it's up to you whether you want to spend the money. But I highly recommend trying each of them once. When you start incorporating good-quality oils into your pantry, you'll realize what you've been settling for. You won't know what you've been missing until you taste the difference. If, after the great experiment, you decide that the extra expense isn't for you, just go back to the shitty one.

SALT

Diamond Crystal kosher salt is the standard in all my recipes because of its grain. To me, salt is salt—it's the way it has been manipulated that makes the difference. Diamond Crystal has a grain that's easier to control; this is especially important to me because I use my fingers to season food, and I need to be able to feel the salt. Table salt on the other hand is much too fine, and I can't feel it in my fingertips or sprinkle it properly.

Maldon sea salt is my go-to for finishing a dish. It's the first layer of salt that's skimmed off during the evaporation process, resulting in very thin, delicate flakes that are inconsistent in size and have a fantastic crunch. There's nothing like Maldon in terms of the texture it provides and the little salty bursts that pop up throughout your dish. Some bites are more intensely salty, some are a bit milder, and the variation makes it fun to eat. Sel de Guérande, or *sel gris*, is commonly used in France as a finishing salt, but I think it's too wet and doesn't have a pleasant mouthfeel.

VINEGARS

Think of it this way—there's a big difference when it comes to $7 olive oil versus $25 olive oil, and the same goes for vinegar. If you spend $15 on a bottle instead of $5, you'll get something wonderful. Top-quality vinegar is more flavourful, which invariably means you'll end up needing to use less of it, thus helping you to stretch a more expensive bottle.

My default all-purpose vinegar is red wine vinegar. I quite like the flavour of sherry vinegar, especially for finishing lentils, which love a lot of fat and vinegar. I also keep a good balsamic vinegar on hand: it doesn't have a super-high acidity, and it's nice and sweet. When I'm dressing a salad, I usually drizzle in a little bit of good-quality balsamic and squeeze in the juice of half a lemon to brighten it up.

Apple cider vinegar is also pretty key, and I generally use it in place of white wine vinegar. It's used a lot in Québécois cuisine, as well as dishes from Brittany and Normandy in France—all regions that grow a lot of apples. Just as my mom and most Québécois do, I always keep apple cider vinegar in my pantry. It's perfect for making pickles or finishing baked beans to balance out the sweetness.

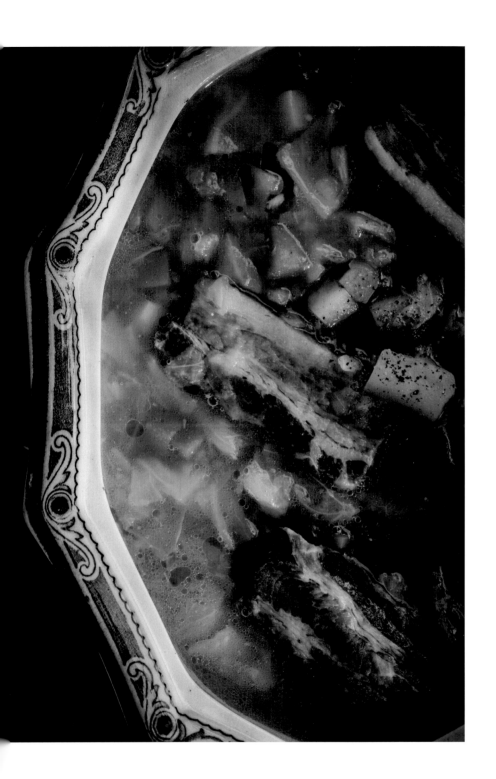

QUÉBEC

EVERYONE ALWAYS ASKS, "What's the difference between French food and Québécois food?" Let's not forget that Québec *is* French. Both our language and our cuisine are direct links to that part of our tradition. But when the British tried to invade, they also added their culinary influence to the mix with dishes like meat pie and split pea soup with ham hock.

Historically speaking, Québec was a poorer blue-collar province, and its more rustic-style food reflects that. Affordable ingredients were the foundation for simple, hearty meals, especially in stick-to-your-ribs wintertime dishes centred on potatoes, cabbage, and pork. Yet despite our struggles, Québécois people are excessive, bold, and full of personality, and our ebullience is mirrored in the way we eat. We're irreverent in the face of culinary rules, breaking them and turning them on their heads to make them our own.

The way I cook today is very much influenced by childhood memories of my mother's kitchen in Saint-Jérôme, Québec. She was an impressive cook, making everything from scratch. Although her meals aren't as elaborate today as they once were, one standby dish she still enjoys preparing is *potée de boeuf* (beef stew). Mom always used a shoulder cut of beef and tons of vegetables: cabbage, quartered leeks, turnips, rutabaga, and potatoes. From this gargantuan one-pot meal, she would feed our entire family; everyone would be stuffed, and we'd still have leftovers for lunch days afterward. The recipes in this chapter are dishes that I grew up on, that are close to my heart and are my take on classic Québécois food.

Cretons

Yield: 1 TERRINE
Preparation time: 30 MINUTES
Cooking time: 2¼ HOURS +
OVERNIGHT CHILLING

What you'll need:

Terrine mould, 10 inches by
3 inches by 3 inches deep (25.5 cm
by 7.5 cm by 7.5 cm)

1 pound (450 g) pork back fat,
diced into ¼-inch (5 mm) cubes

½ cup (125 mL) water

2 tablespoons (30 g) unsalted butter

1½ cups (250 g) diced onions

1 tablespoon (10 g) roughly
chopped garlic

1.7 pounds (750 g) ground pork

1 cup (75 g) diced white bread

1⅓ cups (325 mL) homogenized
milk (3.25% milk fat)

¼ teaspoon (1 g) ground cloves

1 teaspoon (3 g) ground cinnamon

1¼ teaspoons (3 g) freshly ground
nutmeg

1 tablespoon + 1 teaspoon (15 g)
kosher salt

1 teaspoon (2 g) freshly cracked
black pepper

Toasted sourdough bread slices, for
serving

French's mustard, for serving

There was a time when restaurants always brought complimentary bread and butter or olive oil to the table as a gracious way to begin a meal. Alas, they eventually began charging for it rather than giving it away—me included—with the rationale that bread isn't cheap and butter is even more expensive. A few years ago, my wife and I were lucky enough to spend a couple of weeks in France, where every single restaurant offered their guests bread with either rillettes *or butter. I'd forgotten how much this simple gesture makes you feel welcome and relaxed, and it solidified my need to bring that sense of hospitality to my restaurant in Vancouver.*

In a medium saucepan on low heat, gently cook the back fat and water until melted, about 45 minutes. Remove from the heat and strain into a small bowl, reserving some of the liquid fat for sweating the onions and garlic and layering over the cretons later on. The remaining cubed bits are the *fonte*, which will be added to the cretons mix.

In a frying pan on medium heat, melt the butter with 1 tablespoon (15 g) of the liquid pork fat. Sweat the onions and garlic, stirring often, until the onions are translucent but without colouration, about 15 minutes. Add the ground pork and cook, breaking it up with a wooden spoon as it cooks. When the ground pork is almost fully cooked, about 15 minutes, stir in the *fonte*, bread, milk, cloves, cinnamon, nutmeg, salt, and pepper. Lower the heat to low and cook for 1 hour or longer, until all the liquid has evaporated. Turn off the heat and let cool completely. Have a taste and adjust the seasoning if needed.

Transfer the mixture to a food processor and pulse for 10 seconds to ensure the cretons are nice and smooth. Line the inside of the terrine mould with plastic wrap. Using an offset spatula, spread the cretons evenly in the mould, and cover with a layer of the reserved liquid pork fat. Refrigerate overnight.

The next day, unmould the cretons by pulling the plastic wrap out of the terrine. Serve yourself a nice big slice, because you deserve it, along with a thick slice of toast slathered with butter and yellow mustard. Trashy French's classic yellow mustard is a must. Nothing else will do. Trust me.

✦

Jambon Persillé à l'Ancienne

Ham Hock and Parsley Terrine

Yield: 8 TO 10 PORTIONS
Preparation time: 50 MINUTES
Cooking time: 2½ HOURS +
OVERNIGHT RESTING

Jambon persillé, or parsley-coated ham, has been around for a long time. A traditional dish in France's Burgundy region, this humble ham hock terrine, made with fairly inexpensive ingredients, eventually found its place on the Québécois family table. It's also known as Easter ham and often appears as part of an Easter or Mother's Day feast. Occasionally, it's even made in the form of a rillette that you can spread on a nice piece of bread. Serve this terrine with some Dijon mustard, cornichons, maybe pickled eggs, and definitely sliced baguette.

1 ham hock

1 pig trotter

1 onion, peeled and quartered

1 carrot, peeled and cut into large chunks

1 stalk celery, cut into large chunks

1 bulb garlic, halved horizontally

2 bay leaves

1 sprig thyme

2 tablespoons (30 mL) white wine vinegar

1 teaspoon (5 mL) black peppercorns

2 sheets gelatin, soaked in cold water

2 tablespoons (30 mL) grainy Dijon mustard

1 to 2 grates of freshly grated nutmeg

Kosher salt and freshly cracked black pepper, to taste

2 shallots, peeled and finely chopped

½ cup (125 mL) dry white wine

1 bunch (50 g) fresh flat-leaf parsley, leaves stripped and finely chopped

Sauce Ravigote (page 21), to serve

To a large stockpot, add the ham hock, trotter, vegetables, herbs, vinegar, and peppercorns. Add enough water to cover. Bring to a simmer on medium-high heat, then lower the heat to low and simmer gently, regularly skimming off any impurities that come to the surface, for 2½ hours or until the meat is falling off the bones. Using a slotted spoon, transfer the meat to a baking sheet and let stand at room temperature until cool enough to handle.

Meanwhile, strain the cooking liquid through a fine tamis (see tip) and discard the vegetables and herbs. Skim off any fat from the surface of the liquid and pour the stock into a large pot. Bring it to a boil and reduce it to 4 cups (1 L). Taste the stock for saltiness (from the ham hocks)—it should have the same seasoning level as a soup. Add salt if needed, or add water if it's too salty. Add the soaked gelatin sheets and stir until dissolved.

Using your hands, remove the fat, bones, and skin from the ham hock meat. Remove any bones and cartilage from the trotters, but keep the skin—that's the good stuff. Cut the hock meat into roughly ½-inch (1 cm) pieces (you don't have to be too precise). Chop the trotter skin and meat into pieces the same size. You should have about 1.3 pounds (600 g) of meat in total. Transfer all the chopped meat and skin to a large bowl. Mix in the mustard, nutmeg, salt, and pepper until fully combined. Set aside in the refrigerator.

In a small saucepan, bring the shallots and wine to a simmer on medium-high heat and reduce until there's almost no liquid left. Transfer to a bowl and let cool completely at room temperature. Mix in the parsley.

continued

Brush the inside of a small salad bowl with a bit of water (this makes it easier for the plastic wrap to stick), then line it with plastic wrap. Brush the plastic wrap with water and adhere a generous layer of the parsley-shallot mixture all around the inside of the bowl.

Add the rest of the parsley-shallot mixture to the chopped meat and mix well. Add the meat to the bowl, taking care not to push it down too much; you need to leave gaps where the liquid can penetrate. Pour the stock over the ham until the bowl is full. (You'll likely have some stock left over. Make sure you freeze it for another use—good stock is worth its weight in gold.) Cover the bowl with plastic wrap and refrigerate overnight.

To serve, unmould the dome of *jambon persillé* onto a plate. Place it in the centre of your table with a knife for people to cut slices. Serve the ravigote vinaigrette alongside in a gravy boat.

TIP *A tamis is a drum-shaped kitchen utensil with an open top and a flat mesh bottom that acts as a strainer, and the mesh is available in different gauges. It's a cook's secret weapon for sifting clumpy dry ingredients and making super-silky-smooth purées.*

VARIATION *If you aren't using the pig trotter, you'll need to add two to three more sheets of gelatin to the reduced stock—this will help gel the liquid.*

⚜

SAUCE RAVIGOTE

Ravigote Vinaigrette

Yield: 2 CUPS (500 ML)
Preparation time: 30 MINUTES
Cooking time: 9 MINUTES

2 large eggs, room temperature

¼ cup (65 mL) chopped fresh flat-leaf parsley leaves

1 small shallot, peeled and finely diced

3 tablespoons (45 mL) chopped fresh tarragon leaves

3 tablespoons (45 mL) chopped fresh chives

3 tablespoons (45 mL) chopped fresh chervil

1 tablespoon (15 mL) chopped capers

1 clove garlic

3 tablespoons (45 mL) sherry vinegar

1 tablespoon (15 mL) Dijon mustard

1 teaspoon (3 g) kosher salt

¼ (0.5 g) teaspoon freshly cracked black pepper

Pinch cayenne pepper

½ cup (125 mL) grapeseed oil

½ cup (125 mL) extra-virgin olive oil

Prepare an ice bath. In a small pot on high heat, cook your eggs in boiling water for 9 minutes, then transfer them into the ice bath to stop the cooking. Peel the eggs and finely chop them.

In a small bowl, place the parsley, shallot, tarragon, chives, chervil, and capers. Using a Microplane, grate the clove of garlic into the bowl. Mix to combine, and reserve.

Next step is to emulsify your vinaigrette. In the bowl of your stand mixer with the whisk attachment (or in a medium bowl if whisking by hand), add the sherry vinegar, mustard, salt, pepper, and cayenne pepper. In a separate small bowl, mix the grapeseed oil and extra-virgin olive oil together. While mixing at medium speed, slowly drizzle the oil mixture into the vinegar mixture to create an emulsion. Pour the emulsified vinaigrette into the bowl with the herbs and shallot, and stir to combine. Taste and make sure the seasoning is perfect to you.

⚜

Soupe aux Petits Pois

Yellow Pea Soup

Yield: 6 PORTIONS

Preparation time: 30 MINUTES +
6 HOURS OR OVERNIGHT SOAKING

Cooking time: 1¼ TO 1¾ HOURS

❧ *Traditional split pea soup, c'est le top of Québécois comfort food in my opinion. Popular nationwide but spread via Québécois cuisine, it's a must-have at the sugar shack when the maple syrup is running. The authentic version is always made with whole dried yellow peas; you'll need to soak them if you want to go that route. For the ultimate pro move, you could also simmer a ham hock until it's fall-off-the-bone tender, use the ham stock instead of chicken stock, and chop up the ham meat before adding it to the soup. It's time-consuming but totally worth it. Here, however, I propose a simpler and faster version. The finishing drizzle of maple syrup, bourbon, and parsley is the perfect twist, providing a boost of flavour.*

2 cups (450 g) dried yellow split peas

2 tablespoons (30 g) duck fat or unsalted butter

6 ounces (175 g) smoked bacon, finely diced

3 shallots, finely diced

2 stalks celery, finely diced

2 small carrots, peeled and finely diced

1 cup (250 mL) of your favourite beer (drink the rest)

6 cups (1.5 L) Chicken Stock (page 308, or store-bought), ham hock stock, or water

1 tablespoon (10 g) kosher salt

½ teaspoon (1 g) freshly cracked black pepper

2 sprigs thyme

1 bay leaf

1 tablespoon (15 mL) finely chopped fresh flat-leaf parsley

2 tablespoons (30 mL) maple syrup

2 tablespoons (30 mL) bourbon

Soak the peas in cold water at room temperature for at least 6 hours or overnight. Drain just before you're ready to make the soup.

In a large pot on medium heat, melt the duck fat. Sweat the bacon, stirring often, for 3 minutes, then add the shallots, celery, and carrots. Stir often and pay attention: you want to see light colouration, about 10 minutes. Add the drained peas and stir for 1 minute to heat them up. Have a sip of your beer and deglaze the pot with 1 cup (250 mL) of it. Reduce until there's almost no liquid left, then stir in the chicken stock, salt, pepper, thyme, and bay leaf. Bring to a simmer on medium-high heat, then lower the heat to low, cover tightly, and simmer for 60 to 90 minutes or until the peas are fully cooked. Discard the thyme and bay leaf.

Transfer one-third of the soup (2 cups/500 mL) to a blender and purée. Stir the purée back into the pot and add water if the soup is too thick. Taste the soup and make sure the seasoning is to your liking.

In a small bowl, combine the parsley, maple syrup, and bourbon. Portion the soup into individual bowls and drizzle some of the parsley magic garnish on top.

Drink more beer.

VARIATION *You can add diced foie gras and chunks of ham hock to the soup, warmed through with it at the end, for a more decadent version.*

✦

Soupe à L'Oignon

Onion Soup

Yield: 6 PORTIONS
Preparation time: 45 MINUTES
Cooking time: 2½ HOURS

8 large yellow onions, peeled and halved, divided

½ cup (125 mL) grapeseed oil, divided

3 sprigs thyme

2 cloves garlic, smashed

1 bay leaf

8 cups (2 L) Chicken Stock (page 308, or store-bought) or water

1 tablespoon + 1 teaspoon (16 g) kosher salt

¼ cup (55 g) unsalted butter, cubed

⅓ cup (55 g) all-purpose flour

2 tablespoons (30 mL) cognac or brandy

¼ cup (60 mL) dry white wine

1 cup (250 mL) dark beer from Québec

2 tablespoons (30 mL) Worcestershire sauce

Freshly cracked black pepper

Croutons (recipe follows), to garnish

12 slices (11 ounces/300 g) Gruyère cheese

12 slices (11 ounces/300 g) Emmenthal cheese

Soupe à l'oignon has always been one of my favourite things for lunch on a cold winter day. My mom's French onion soup was absolutely killer; I remember her making it after cross-country skiing mornings with the family. I'm totally convinced that the secret is to be generous with the cheese. And I'm not a huge fan of soft caramelized onions in my soup—personal preference, but I like the onions to have more texture. Yet I still want that caramelized flavour in the broth. That's why I divide the onions into two batches, cooking one slowly on low heat, and the other quickly on high heat.

The first step is to make a caramelized onion stock. Slice four of the onions ½ inch (1 cm) thick. In a large pot on high heat, heat ¼ cup (60 mL) of the oil until smoking hot. Add the sliced onions and cook, stirring, for 5 minutes. Lower the heat to medium-low and add the thyme, garlic, and bay leaf. Continue slowly cooking the onions, stirring occasionally, until they are dark golden and nicely caramelized. Done properly, the caramelization process will take 1 hour or more.

Once the caramelized onions are ready, pour in the stock and bring to a simmer on medium-high heat, then lower the heat to low and cook gently for 15 to 20 minutes, until the liquid has taken on the flavour of the onions. Remove from the heat and strain the liquid through a tamis, pushing on the onions with the back of a wooden spoon to extract as much liquid as possible. Reserve the caramelized onion broth and discard the mashed onions. All we want is the flavour of caramelized onions in the broth, not the softened onions themselves.

Slice the remaining onions to the same ½-inch (1 cm) thickness. In the same large pot on high heat, heat the remaining oil. Add the onions and cook, stirring. We want to brown them more quickly than the first batch; just make sure you don't burn them—stay close and stir often. Sprinkle in 1 tablespoon of the salt; it will help to break down the onions and release their moisture.

After 15 to 20 minutes, lower the heat to medium. Stir in the butter until it melts, then sprinkle the flour on top and stir until fully incorporated.

continued

Deglaze with the cognac, then the wine, and finally the beer. Reduce the liquid by half. Stir in the caramelized onion stock, bring to a simmer, cover, and simmer gently for 30 minutes, stirring once in a while. Stir in the Worcestershire sauce and pepper. Taste for seasoning and add more salt if needed.

Preheat your broiler, with the rack in the top position. Place six onion soup bowls on a baking sheet and ladle the onion soup into them, leaving a bit of space for croutons and cheese. Add a handful of croutons to each bowl and top with two slices of Gruyère and two slices of Emmenthal. Broil until the cheese is melted, caramelized, and bubbly. Wait a few minutes before taking your first bite, as the soup will be nuclear hot.

⚜

CROUTONS

Yield: 3 CUPS (750 ML)

Preparation time: 10 MINUTES

Cooking time: 15 TO 20 MINUTES + 15 MINUTES COOLING

¼ cup (60 mL) melted unsalted butter

2 cloves garlic, grated

3 cups (750 mL) ¾-inch (2 cm) torn sourdough bread chunks

Big pinch kosher salt

Freshly cracked black pepper, to taste

Preheat your oven to 375°F (190°C), with the rack in the centre position.

In a small bowl, mix the butter with the garlic. Place the bread chunks on a baking sheet, drizzle with the melted butter mixture, and season with the salt and pepper, then toss until well combined. Bake, tossing occasionally, until golden brown, 15 to 20 minutes. Let the croutons cool completely.

Store leftover croutons in an airtight container for up to 3 days. When ready to use, warm them up in a 350°F (180°C) oven for 5 minutes.

⚜

FOR AS LONG as I can remember, Mom was always busy in the kitchen. She and Dad hosted guests a lot, and they were generous and hospitable to a fault. Long before it was a thing and way before people even used the word, Mom stocked our fridge and pantry with organic ingredients. She belonged to a co-op that milled flour from grain she bought from them directly. Milk came from my uncle's farm not too far from our house in St-Croix. He'd give it to us unpasteurised, and Mom would transform it into the fattiest, most delicious yogurt ever. Our next-door neighbour raised geese, so Mom cooked with goose eggs quite often. Another guy down the road sold rabbit, so we ate a lot of rabbit at home. Even today, rabbit is something I always have on my St. Lawrence menu—I love it.

Whenever I talk to a young cook about how they'd prepare rabbit, they usually answer with something like deboning it, rolling it into a roulade or ballotine, cooking it sous vide, and then slicing a tiny precious portion for service. Forget that. I'd rather put a whole rabbit on my cutting board, chop it into six pieces with a big-ass cleaver, sear it in a cast-iron pan, deglaze with white wine, add a big spoonful of Dijon mustard, and throw it into the oven for a slow braise. To me, that's more what cooking really is. Rustic and generous with love and respect for the ingredients.

See, beyond the preparation for any feast, big or small—which itself is a wonderful experience—is the joy you get from giving, and from seeing the guests around your table happy. That's at the heart of Québec's *cabane à sucre* tradition. Visiting a sugar shack usually involves early afternoon Sunday brunch, either indoors or outside depending on how big the sugar shack is. And the table is always heaving with food. Québécois are a little extreme when it comes to that. We feed you until you can't even move.

There's always baked ham. Eggs poached in maple syrup. Side dishes coming out of your eyes: baked beans, different kinds of pickled cucumbers, pickled beets, pickled eggs, and pickled onions. Bacon and sausages too, because pork is delicious and more is more. *Grand-pères dans le sirop d'érable*, which are dumplings cooked in maple syrup. A giant pitcher of maple syrup on the table that you grab and pour all over everything. Loads of desserts like *tarte au sucre*, maple pie, and *pouding chômeur*. *Sucre à la crème*, which is maple toffee. And, without question, *tire sur la neige*, maple syrup that's boiled down, poured out on snow to cool into maple taffy, and wound onto popsicle sticks. My cousins and I went nuts for this as kids, and my two daughters love it just as much today.

Over the top, you say? Hell yeah. It's what true Québécois *joie de vivre* is all about.

Chaudrée au Blé d'Inde et Palourdes

Corn and Clam Chowder

Yield: 4 PORTIONS

Preparation time: 30 MINUTES + 1 HOUR SOAKING

Cooking time: 35 TO 40 MINUTES

Improving on the New England version of clam chowder, we Québécois love to add corn to ours. Sure I'm biased, but I definitely prefer it that way. Corn is one of the top vegetables in the province, and it's often paired with potatoes. When corn is in peak season and at its best, it adds sweetness and a crunchy element to the chowder that I really like. If you don't happen to have chicken stock handy, you could boil the corncobs in water along with yellow onions, garlic, peppercorns, and thyme to make a simple corn stock that will intensify the flavour of your chowder. Serve with soda crackers spread with salted butter.

1.7 pounds (750 g) Manila or littleneck clams

2 tablespoons (30 mL) grapeseed oil

1 shallot, sliced

1 clove garlic, crushed

1 sprig thyme

1 bay leaf

¾ cup (175 mL) dry white wine

¼ cup (55 g) unsalted butter

1 large yellow onion, finely diced

3 cloves garlic, finely chopped

4 tablespoons (40 g) all-purpose flour

5 slices (5 ounces/150 g) smoked bacon, cooked and chopped

Kernels from 4 fresh corn ears (about 2 cups/500 mL)

8 fingerling potatoes, cut into coins

2½ cups (625 mL) Chicken Stock (page 308, or store-bought)

2½ cups (625 mL) homogenized milk (3.25% milk fat)

1 cup (250 mL) heavy or whipping cream (35% milk fat)

1 tablespoon (10 g) kosher salt

Juice of ½ lemon

2 tablespoons (30 mL) finely chopped fresh flat-leaf parsley leaves

Put the clams in a bowl and soak under cold running water for 1 hour to remove any sand. Remove the clams from the water and rinse them one more time. Make sure all the clams are tightly closed, and discard any that don't close right away when tapped.

In a large pot on medium heat, heat the oil. Sweat the shallot and crushed garlic, stirring often, until soft, about 2 minutes. Add the thyme, bay leaf, and wine and cook for 1 minute to cook off the alcohol taste of the wine. Add the clams, cover with a tight lid, and cook for 3 to 4 minutes or until the clams open. Make sure not to overcook them or they'll be quite tough. Discard any clams that didn't open.

Drain the clam nectar into a bowl and reserve for the soup. Once the clams are cool enough to handle, remove the muscles from the shells, keeping a few clams in the shells for presentation, and reserve them in a bowl in the fridge.

In a large saucepan on medium heat, melt the butter. Sweat the onion and finely chopped garlic, stirring often and reducing the heat if need be—you want the onion and garlic fully cooked but without colouration—about 8 to 10 minutes. Stir in the flour and cook for another 2 minutes. Add the bacon, corn kernels, potatoes, stock, milk, cream, and salt. Bring to a gentle simmer, then lower the heat and cook for 20 minutes, stirring occasionally, until the potatoes and corn are fully cooked. Add the clam nectar and meat to the pot and cook for 1 to 2 minutes, until the clams are warmed. Remove from the heat and stir in the lemon juice and parsley. Portion the soup into individual bowls and arrange a couple of clam shells atop each bowl.

Huîtres au Four à la Florentine

Baked Oysters à la Florentine

Yield: 8 OYSTERS (2 PER PERSON)
Preparation time: 45 MINUTES
Cooking time: 30 MINUTES

Preparing a main ingredient à la Florentine—*poached eggs or chicken, for example—means your dish will include spinach and a cream sauce. I realize that not everyone is a fan of oysters, but they suddenly become much more popular when baked and gratinéed with cheese. Oysters à la Florentine is basically the same as Oysters Rockefeller. I've opted to use large oysters from the West Coast and serve two per person, but you can definitely use smaller oysters and serve six per person. It's the perfect party dish, because you can get all your prep done and even assemble the oysters before your guests arrive. All that's left to do is pop them into the oven before serving them* à la minute. *They're a wonderful pre-dinner* amuse bouche *on a beautiful sunny day, and obviously pair very well with a glass of champagne.*

Oysters:

8 Beach Angel or other large oysters

2 cups (500 mL) water

Spinach:

3 tablespoons (45 g) unsalted butter

2 small shallots, thinly sliced

2 cloves garlic, finely chopped

6 cups (175 g) spinach, stems removed

Kosher salt and freshly cracked black pepper, to taste

FOR THE OYSTERS: Thoroughly scrub the oysters under cold running water to remove any dirt. In a large saucepan on medium-high heat, bring the water to a boil and add the oysters, curved side down. Lower the heat to a simmer, cover, and steam until the oyster shells pop open slightly and the flesh is just slightly set, about 4 to 5 minutes. Remove the oysters immediately and shuck them to remove the meat and stop the cooking. Strain 2 tablespoons (30 mL) of the oyster liquor and set aside to add to the Mornay sauce. Reserve the bottom curved shells for serving. Place the oyster meat in a bowl and let it cool at room temperature, then carefully slice each oyster widthwise into three even pieces.

FOR THE SPINACH: Line a baking sheet with paper towels and set aside. In a large sauté pan on medium heat, melt the butter. Add the shallots and garlic, and gently cook while stirring, for 2 minutes, until soft but without colouration. Add the spinach and toss to coat, wilting it quickly. Season with salt and pepper. Transfer the spinach to the lined baking sheet and let cool, then squeeze out all the excess water with your hands. Set aside.

FOR THE MORNAY SAUCE: In a small pot on medium-low heat, warm up the milk. In a second small pot on medium heat, melt the butter and stir in the flour as soon as the butter starts to foam. Whisking constantly, cook for 2 minutes. (This is called making a roux, which is used to add texture and richness to your sauce.) Now drizzle in a little of the warmed milk,

continued

Mornay Sauce:

1 cup (250 mL) homogenized milk (3.25% milk fat)

2 tablespoons (30 g) unsalted butter

2 tablespoons (20 g) all-purpose flour

½ teaspoon (2 g) kosher salt

1 to 2 grates of freshly grated nutmeg

¼ cup (30 g) finely grated Gruyère cheese

¼ cup (30 g) finely grated Parmesan cheese

2 tablespoons (30 mL) reserved oyster liquor, strained

2 egg yolks

Assembly and Garnish:

4 tablespoons (30 g) toasted breadcrumbs

Finely grated Parmesan cheese

Coarse salt, for plating

whisking until a thick paste forms. Lower the heat and gradually pour in the remaining milk while continuing to whisk. Simmer very gently for 4 minutes, stirring often so the milk doesn't burn at the bottom of the pot. Strain through a fine tamis. Season with the salt and nutmeg, and stir in the Gruyère and Parmesan cheeses, the reserved oyster liquor, and the egg yolks.

TO ASSEMBLE AND GARNISH: Preheat your oven to 375°F (190°C), with the rack in the centre position.

Bunch up some foil on a baking sheet to make eight nests for the oysters (you could also use a bed of coarse salt). Place each reserved oyster shell on a nest. Spoon 1 tablespoon (15 mL) of the spinach mixture into the bottom of each shell. Place one sliced oyster atop the spinach in each shell and spoon the Mornay sauce over top, spreading it out until the sauce is flush with the edges of the shell. Sprinkle the breadcrumbs and some Parmesan on top.

Bake the oysters for 10 to 12 minutes or until you see a slight bubbling around the edges of the shells. Remove the pan from the oven and set the broiler to high. Return the pan to the centre rack and broil to caramelize the tops, about 10 seconds—be careful not to burn them. Remove from the oven and let rest for 2 minutes before serving.

To keep the oysters balanced on the plate, spread out a shallow bed of coarse salt and nestle the oysters into it to hold them upright. You'd be surprised how many people try to eat the salt—save them the unpleasant surprise and tell them what it is beforehand!

VARIATION *Whisk one batch of Hollandaise Sauce (page 307) and the juice of half a lemon into the warm Mornay sauce before spooning it over the oysters.*

⚜

Bisque de Homard Thermidor

Lobster Bisque Thermidor

Yield: 6 PORTIONS
Preparation time: 45 MINUTES
Cooking time: 1½ HOURS

This rich, velvety soup captures all the flavours of the classic Lobster Thermidor in a bowl. When it comes to selecting cheeses, I always go the extra mile to find a Québec cheese that suits a particular dish. I like using Louis d'Or cheese for its nutty and floral notes in both aroma and taste—the same characteristics as Gruyère.

Two 1.5-pound (675 g) live lobsters

3 tablespoons (45 g) unsalted butter

2 shallots, sliced

2 cloves garlic, crushed

1 stalk celery, thinly sliced

1 bulb fennel, thinly sliced, fronds reserved for garnish

½ teaspoon (2 mL) fennel seeds

2 sprigs tarragon

2 sprigs thyme

2 tablespoons (30 mL) tomato paste

3 tablespoons (45 mL) cognac

1 cup (250 mL) white vermouth (preferably Noilly Prat) or dry white wine

6 cups (1.5 L) Fish Stock (page 312, or store-bought) or water

1 cup (250 mL) clam broth (store-bought)

¼ cup (50 g) long-grain white rice

1 cup (250 mL) heavy or whipping cream (35% milk fat)

1 cup (250 mL) grated Louis d'Or or Gruyère cheese

1 tablespoon (15 mL) Dijon mustard

Kosher salt, cayenne pepper, and fresh lemon juice, to taste

Fill a large pot with salted water and bring to a raging boil on high heat. Butcher your lobsters humanely (see tip). Place the lobsters in the pot, cover, and return to a boil, then lower the heat to a gentle boil and cook until the lobsters turn bright red, about 9 minutes. Meanwhile, prepare an ice bath. Transfer the lobsters to the ice bath to stop the cooking.

When the lobsters are cool enough to touch, place them on a baking sheet and remove the meat from the tail, claws, and knuckles. Reserve the shells and, most importantly, the bodies and all the juices that were released onto the pan. Dice the lobster meat and reserve it in the fridge. Remove the gills from each side of the lobster heads and cut the bodies into smaller pieces.

In a large saucepan on medium heat, melt the butter. Sweat the shallots, garlic, celery, and fennel for 5 minutes, stirring often. Increase the heat to medium-high, stir in the lobster shells, bodies, and juices, and cook for 5 minutes, stirring occasionally. Stir in the fennel seeds, tarragon, thyme, and tomato paste, and cook for 3 minutes, stirring once or twice. Pour in the cognac, use a long match to light it, and flambé to cook off the alcohol. When the flames die down, add the vermouth and reduce by half. Pour in the fish stock and clam broth. Bring to a simmer, then lower the heat to low, cover, and cook for 30 minutes.

Strain the lobster broth through a fine tamis into a medium bowl, pressing down on the solids to extract as much liquid as possible.

Clean the large saucepan and pour the broth back in, along with the rice and cream. Stir to combine, bring to a gentle simmer on medium heat, then lower the heat to low, cover, and cook until the rice is extremely soft, about 20 minutes.

continued

Transfer the broth and rice mixture to a blender and blend on high speed for 1 minute or until smooth. Add the cheese and mustard, and blend for 1 minute.

Pass the bisque through a fine tamis back into the pan. Adjust the seasoning with salt, if needed, and stir in cayenne and lemon juice to cut the richness. Add the lobster meat and let stand, covered, for a few minutes to warm through. Serve immediately in warmed bowls.

TIP *To butcher a lobster humanely, firmly hold it belly down on a cutting board. Position the tip of your chef's knife between the lobster's eyes and swiftly insert it in one clean motion through the shell and the brain, ensuring that the lobster doesn't suffer.*

TIP *As a rule of thumb, the timing for boiling lobster is around 6 minutes for the first pound (450 g) plus about 3 minutes for each additional ½ pound (225 g).*

Saucisses Cocktail

Sausages in Maple Syrup

Yield: 10 TO 12 PEOPLE

Preparation time: 10 MINUTES +
12 HOURS MARINATING

Cooking time: 20 MINUTES

1 cup (250 mL) maple syrup

¼ cup (65 mL) soy sauce

¼ cup (65 mL) water

½ cup (125 mL) ketchup

2 tablespoons (30 mL)
Worcestershire sauce

2 tablespoons (30 mL) Dijon
mustard

2 tablespoons (30 mL) bourbon or
cognac

2 cloves garlic, chopped

Freshly cracked black pepper

2.2 pounds (1 kg) smoked hot-dog
sausages cut into thirds, or, if you
feel like it, my breakfast sausages
(see recipe)

You could buy the sausages like we do in Québec when preparing this dish, or you can opt to make the breakfast sausages yourself. If you don't have a sausage stuffer, you can form the meat into small meatballs or patties instead, as making sausages is time consuming. Just don't call them cocktail sausages.

In a medium bowl, mix together all the ingredients except the sausages. Pour this marinade into a large resealable plastic bag and add the sausages, mixing until they are well-coated. Chill in the refrigerator for 12 hours.

Preheat your oven to 400°F (205°C), with the rack in the centre position.

Transfer the marinated sausages to a large baking dish and bake for 15 minutes, uncovered. Place the sausages and half of the sauce into a large sauté pan. Cook on high heat to reduce the liquid by half, stirring often until the sausages are glazed and shiny, about 5 minutes. Put the sausages and sauce in a serving bowl and serve with toothpicks.

⚜

SAUCISSES À DÉJEUNER

Breakfast Sausage

Yield: ABOUT 25 TO 30 LITTLE
SAUSAGES OR LITTLE
MEATBALLS

Preparation time: 30 MINUTES

2 pounds (900 g) ground pork, preferably shoulder meat

1 tablespoon (11 g) kosher salt

3 tablespoons (40 g) maple syrup

2 teaspoons (3 g) fresh sage, finely chopped

2 cloves garlic, peeled and chopped

½ teaspoon (1 g) freshly cracked black pepper

½ teaspoon (1 g) Épices à Pâté (page 294)

2 bundles lamb casings, if making links

In a large mixing bowl, combine the pork, salt, maple syrup, sage, garlic, black pepper, and épices à pâté. Mix thoroughly with your hands. In a small frying pan, heat up some grapeseed oil on medium heat and fry a small test patty. Taste and adjust the seasoning if needed.

If you're game for sausage making, load the meat mixture into the sausage stuffer. Slide the casing onto the stuffing tube and get to work. Press your thumb and forefinger together on the casing every 1½ inches (3.5 cm) while twisting, and give it 3 to 4 turns before moving on to the next sausage. Be patient—it takes practice, but it's a great skill to master.

✛

Les Carrés de Fondus aux Parmesan

Parmesan Cheese Croquettes

Yield: **48 CROQUETTES**

Preparation time: **15 MINUTES +
3 TO 24 HOURS CHILLING**

Cooking time: **15 MINUTES**

Mom always used to serve these with salad when I was a kid, but hers were usually store-bought. Though you'll end up with more croquettes than needed when making this recipe, it's easier to prep a large batch all in one go and then freeze the extras after breading them. Serve the croquettes with the condiments of your choice or with a simple green salad.

What you'll need:

6 by 8-inch (15 by 20 cm) baking pan

2½ cups (625 mL) homogenized milk (3.25% milk fat)

¾ cup (170 g) unsalted butter

1 cup (150 g) all-purpose flour

Pinch kosher salt

Pinch freshly cracked black pepper

Pinch cayenne pepper

1 to 2 grates of freshly grated nutmeg

2 egg yolks

1½ cups (150 g) freshly grated Parmesan cheese

1 cup (100 g) grated Gruyère cheese

1 cup (150 g) all-purpose flour

2 eggs, beaten

1 cup (250 mL) breadcrumbs

12 cups (3 L) canola or vegetable oil

Line the baking pan with plastic wrap or lightly oil it.

In a small pot on medium heat, warm up the milk until it's almost simmering. In a medium saucepan on medium heat, melt the butter. Stir in the flour and cook, stirring, for 5 minutes to make a roux, ensuring that it doesn't take on any colouration. Slowly pour in the hot milk while whisking constantly until the mixture becomes smooth and thick. Season with the salt, pepper, cayenne, and nutmeg. Lower the heat to the minimum and add the egg yolks, whisking constantly. Cook for 1 minute, without simmering or boiling. Turn off the heat and gradually whisk in the Parmesan and Gruyère.

Pour the mixture into the prepared pan to a depth of ¾ inch (2 cm). Place a layer of plastic wrap directly on the surface of the béchamel to prevent it from forming a skin. Refrigerate for several hours, until fully set—or, better yet, a full day.

Unmould the béchamel and, using a hot knife, slice it into 1-inch (2.5 cm) squares. Now to bread the squares. Set up a little station for yourself with three bowls: the first with the flour, the second with the beaten eggs, and the third with the breadcrumbs. Coat a square with flour, then dip it in the egg mixture, and finally coat it in breadcrumbs. Make sure each square is coated evenly. (To freeze the croquettes you're not cooking right away, put in an airtight container and keep for up to 3 months. Put directly in the fryer from frozen, cook until golden brown, and finish in a 350°F (180°C) oven for 8 to 10 minutes.)

Preheat your oven to 350°F (180°C), with the rack in the centre position. Line a baking sheet with parchment paper.

continued

In a deep fryer or a large pot, heat the oil to 375°F (190°C). Working in batches of six to eight squares at a time to avoid crowding and cooling the oil too quickly, use a slotted spoon to slowly lower the breaded squares into the oil. Cook until golden brown, 2 to 3 minutes. Insert the tip of a paring knife into the centre of a square and make sure it's hot by testing the temperature of the tip of the knife against your lower lip. If it's not hot enough, transfer the squares to the prepared baking sheet and finish them in the oven for 4 to 5 minutes.

TIP *In general, it's important that milk doesn't reach the boiling point when cooking to avoid having it curdle and changing its delicate taste and texture. Keep it just below a gentle simmer; you're aiming for the point where it looks like it's forming a skin on top.*

Once the béchamel is portioned, put the squares in the freezer for 30 minutes to firm up before breading them. This will make your task easier and much less messy.

⚜

Les Fèves au Lard

Baked Beans with Maple Syrup

Yield: 15 PORTIONS

Preparation time: 30 MINUTES + OVERNIGHT SOAKING

Cooking time: 2 TO 2¼ HOURS

Les fèves au lard, *also called* bines *in Québec, is a truly traditional side dish. These days, it's mostly eaten for breakfast or in the* cabanes à sucre *across the province, but it was originally a main dish that belonged to the countryside—hearty, stick-to-your-ribs sustenance for pioneers, hunters, and travellers. Some establishments, like La Binerie Mont-Royal, have made it their specialty dish. This simple plate of slow-baked beans with maple syrup and a piece of salted lard became very popular with lumberjacks hundreds of years ago. It filled them up, warming them from the inside out, and gave them the energy to work outside during cold Québec winters. Me, I just find it tasty as hell; once I start eating it, I can't stop.* Les fèves au lard *were always part of my family's holiday feasts, and they always bring back good memories.*

What you'll need:

Three 1-quart (1 L) Mason jars

4 cups dried navy beans (about 2 pounds/900 g)

4 cups (1 L) cold water, for cooking

1 cup (250 mL) maple syrup

½ cup (125 mL) ketchup

½ cup (125 mL) blackstrap molasses

12 ounces (350 g) salted pork or smoked bacon, rind removed, diced

2 medium onions, finely chopped

1 bulb garlic, cloves finely chopped

1 tablespoon (15 mL) baking soda

1 tablespoon (12 g) kosher salt

1 teaspoon (2 g) freshly cracked black pepper

2 tablespoons (30 mL) Dijon mustard

1 tablespoon (15 mL) Worcestershire sauce

3 tablespoons (45 mL) apple cider vinegar

Place the beans in a large bowl and cover with the cold water. Let soak overnight at room temperature.

The next day, preheat your oven to 325°F (160°C), with the rack in the centre position.

Drain the water from the beans and place them in a large ovenproof pot. Add all the ingredients except the vinegar (acid will toughen the beans, so it's best to add vinegar at the end). Cover tightly and bring to a simmer on high heat, then transfer to the oven. Bake for 1½ hours. Uncover and bake for 30 to 45 minutes to let the liquid evaporate and dry the beans a little. Remove from the oven, stir in the vinegar, and taste for seasoning.

I like to preserve the baked beans in Mason jars. To do that, sterilize the jars by putting them in the 325°F (160°C) oven for 10 minutes. Transfer the baked beans into the jars, wipe off the rims, seal with the lids, and submerge the jars in a large pot of boiling water. Boil the jars for about 1 hour; within this time, the lids will pop and become slightly convex. Remove the jars from the pot and let them cool on the counter. Once sealed, the beans will keep for 6 months in a cool, dark cupboard or for up to 1 year in the fridge.

TIP *Adding baking soda to the cooking liquid gives you more tender beans in a shorter cooking time.*

Jambon au Sirop d'Érable

Maple Ham

Yield: 8 TO 10 PORTIONS

Preparation time: 15 MINUTES

Cooking time: 2 TO 2½ HOURS
FOR BOILING + 2½ HOURS FOR
ROASTING

Ham:

½ bone-in gammon ham (cured but not cooked), about 6.5 to 9 pounds (3 to 4 kg)

9 ounces (250 g) good organic hay (optional)

15 black peppercorns

10 juniper berries

8 whole cloves

5 bay leaves

3 sprigs thyme

3 sprigs rosemary

3 whole shallots, peeled

2 large carrots

1 bulb garlic, unpeeled, sliced in half horizontally

Glaze:

1¼ cups (300 mL) dry apple cider

¾ cup (175 mL) maple syrup

⅓ cup + 1 tablespoon (80 g) firmly packed brown sugar

2 tablespoons (30 mL) Dijon mustard

➤ *There are two ways you can go about making this recipe. You can buy a cured uncooked ham and cook it yourself, which will give you a less sweet, and more savoury ham, especially if you add the hay. Or you can save a lot of time by buying a quality cooked and lightly smoked ham and skipping directly to the roasting and glazing step. You'll still end up with a great result.*

TIP *Organic hay is usually easy enough to find at a pet store, or you could ask your friendly local farmer for some. It is optional, but will give a unique taste to your ham.*

FOR THE HAM: Choose a pot large enough to comfortably fit the ham and line the bottom with a layer of hay (if using). Nestle the ham on top. Add the spices, herbs, and vegetables, then completely cover the ham with more hay. Fill the pot with enough water to just cover the ham and hay. Bring to a gentle simmer on medium heat. Continue simmering until the ham is tender and a meat thermometer inserted in the centre registers 160°F (71°C), up to 2½ hours depending on the size of your ham. Use 15 minutes per pound (450 g) as a rough guideline.

Transfer the ham to a baking sheet and let cool at room temperature for 30 minutes. Discard the cooking liquid.

Preheat your oven to 325°F (160°C), with the rack in the centre position.

Using a knife, remove the skin from the ham and shave off some of the fat to even it out. Discard the skin and excess fat. Score the remaining fat all around the ham. Transfer the ham to a baking dish.

FOR THE GLAZE: In a small saucepan on medium heat, stir together the cider, maple syrup, brown sugar, and mustard. Bring to a simmer.

Pour the glaze over the ham and baste it. Roast for 2 to 2½ hours, basting the ham every 20 minutes, until the ham is tender and almost falling off the bone. You should be able to insert a knife blade all the way through the meat without any resistance, and the liquid should be reduced and thickened. Slice and serve.

⚜

Cuisses de Canard Confit, Ail, et Flageolets

Duck Confit, Roasted Garlic, and Flageolet Beans

Yield: 4 PORTIONS

Preparation time: 30 MINUTES +
24 HOURS CURING AND SOAKING

Cooking time: 2¼ HOURS

Confit de Canard:

1 teaspoon (5 mL) juniper berries

2 bay leaves

2 sprigs thyme, leaves only

1 sprig rosemary, leaves only

2 tablespoons (20 g) kosher salt
(approx., see tip)

4 bone-in, skin-on duck legs (about
4.5 pounds/2 kg total)

6 cups (1.5 L) duck fat

Roasted Garlic:

1 bulb garlic, broken into cloves
(unpeeled)

3 tablespoons (45 g) unsalted butter

Kosher salt and freshly cracked
black pepper, to taste

Beans:

1 cup (200 g) dried flageolet beans,
soaked in water overnight

Bouquet garni of rosemary, thyme,
and bay leaf (see tip)

4 cups (1 L) Chicken Stock (page 308,
or store-bought) or water

Kosher salt and freshly cracked
black pepper

2 tablespoons (30 mL) grapeseed oil

3.5 ounces (100 g) smoked bacon,
cut into lardons

2 tablespoons (30 mL) red wine
vinegar

Finishing:

1 teaspoon (5 mL) finely chopped
fresh savory (optional)

In the days before refrigerators, cooking and storing duck in its own fat was a means of preservation. It's a fantastic prep method that makes the meat silky and tender, and you can keep it in the fridge for a full year after it's cooked. In this recipe, you can substitute cannellini or even navy beans if flageolet beans are hard to come by. Larger beans are preferable, though, so they don't break down too much while braising.

TIP *To figure out how much salt to use, you'll need to know the total weight of your duck in grams. If you only know pounds, divide that by 2.2, then multiply by 1,000 to get the weight in grams. Now multiply that weight by 1.5% (or 0.015) to get the amount of salt in grams. If you want to measure your salt in tablespoons, you'll need 1 tablespoon for every 10 grams. If all that is too much math for you, just use 2 tablespoons in this recipe and call it a day.*

Translated as "garnished bouquet," a bouquet garni is a small bundle of herbs tied together with butcher's twine or unwaxed kitchen string. It mirrors the profile of herbs used in the dish and infuses subtle flavour in soups, braises, and stocks. The bouquet garni is removed before the finished dish is served.

FOR THE CONFIT DE CANARD: Using a mortar and pestle, grind the berries, then add the bay leaves, thyme, and rosemary, and crush the herbs for a few seconds. Add the salt and mix all the ingredients together.

Place the duck legs in a medium bowl and season them liberally with the herbed salt. Cover with plastic wrap and chill for 24 hours in the fridge. (Make sure to soak the beans at the same time.)

The next day, preheat your oven to 300°F (150°C), with the rack in the centre position.

Remove the duck legs from the fridge, rinse off the salt, and pat dry. Using the tip of a paring knife, make small pricks all over the skin to help the fat render.

In a heavy-bottomed, ovenproof pot or Dutch oven on medium heat, melt the duck fat and heat to 195°F (90°C). Carefully place the duck legs in the hot fat and return to 195°F (90°C), then cover with a lid or foil and

continued

transfer the pot to the oven. Roast until the duck is very tender and there's no resistance when pulling the bones, about 1½ to 2 hours. Make sure the fat never boils or even simmers, or the duck will overcook. Remove from the oven and let the meat cool in the fat.

FOR THE ROASTED GARLIC: Place the garlic cloves and butter in the centre of a square of foil and season with salt and pepper. Wrap the foil loosely around the garlic and seal it. Roast alongside the duck for 30 to 45 minutes, until tender and creamy. Set aside.

FOR THE BEANS: While the duck is roasting, place the beans and bouquet garni in a large saucepan. Cover with the stock and bring to a gentle simmer on medium-high heat. Lower the heat and simmer gently, uncovered, for 45 to 60 minutes, until the beans are fully cooked and creamy but still hold their shape. Discard the bouquet garni and season the beans with a few generous pinches of salt and pepper.

In a medium sauté pan on high heat, heat the oil. Pan-fry the bacon until browned and crispy. Drain off the excess fat and add the bacon and vinegar to the beans.

TO FINISH: Carefully remove the duck legs from the fat and set aside on a baking sheet. Strain the duck fat through a tamis into a large bowl, leaving any cloudy liquid behind. (To store, place the legs in a deep airtight container and pour the strained fat over top until it covers the legs by 1 inch (2.5 cm). Cover and refrigerate for up to 1 year. Even if you're not storing the duck itself, make sure to keep the duck fat in the fridge for other uses, such as frying potatoes or sautéing greens—it's literally flavour overload.)

To serve, preheat your oven to 350°F (180°C), with the rack in the centre position.

Heat a large non-stick pan on medium-high heat. (You won't need to add any fat, as the skin has plenty.) Place the duck legs in the pan, skin side down, and lower the heat to medium-low. This process makes the skin very crispy. I like to cover the legs with a square of parchment paper and put another pan on top to gently press them; it's also helpful as the fat from the legs has a tendency to splash. Cook until the skin is golden brown and crispy, around 10 minutes. If the skin of the duck legs is ready but the meat is not hot enough, pop them in the oven for about 10 minutes.

Scoop the beans and some of the liquid into a serving dish and top with the confit duck legs. Sprinkle with the fresh savory. Place the roasted garlic cloves all around the dish so your guests can squeeze out the beautiful garlic purée as a condiment.

⚜

Ragoût de Boulettes et Pattes de Cochon

Pork Shank and Meatball Stew

Yield: 6 PORTIONS
Preparation time: 1 HOUR
Cooking time: 3 TO 4 HOURS

➤ *Nothing screams Christmas more than* ragoût de boulettes et pattes de cochon. *You're almost 100% guaranteed that this traditional dish will be on any Québec family's table during the holiday season. If not, it's because they're feeling lazy. Making the dish does take a bit of time, but it's delicious—and who doesn't like meatballs? So I encourage you to make it and enjoy the process. Your guests will love you for it. Serve with boiled nugget potatoes and pearl onions, a few gherkins on a plate with marinated beets, and some Dijon mustard on the side, if you like.*

Pork Shank:

1 pork shank (skin on), cured and smoked

2 onions, peeled and halved

1 bulb garlic, halved horizontally

1 teaspoon (5 mL) juniper berries

4 whole cloves

2 bay leaves

1 cinnamon stick

Meatballs:

⅓ cup (40 g) breadcrumbs or panko

3 tablespoons (45 mL) homogenized milk (3.25% milk fat)

1 shallot, finely chopped

1 large clove garlic, finely chopped

1.1 pounds (500 g) ground pork

1 egg, lightly beaten

1½ teaspoons (7 mL) Dijon mustard

1½ teaspoons (5 g) kosher salt

¼ teaspoon (1 g) ground cinnamon

¼ teaspoon (1 g) ground cloves

¼ teaspoon (1 g) ground nutmeg

FOR THE PORK SHANK: Place the pork shank in a large stockpot and add the onions, garlic, and spices. Add enough cold water to cover, and bring to a simmer on medium-high heat. Lower the heat, cover, and simmer gently for 2 to 3 hours, until the meat is just falling off the bones.

Using a slotted spoon, transfer the pork shank to a baking sheet. Let cool. Strain the cooking liquid through a tamis, pour into a large pot, and reduce to 4 cups (1 L) on medium-low heat to concentrate the flavours and make a bouillon. Taste and make sure it isn't too salty. If it is, add water (or, even better, unsalted chicken stock).

Once the shank is cool enough to handle, remove and discard the bones, fat, and cartilage. You should have about 7 to 8 ounces (200 to 250 g) of meat, depending on the size of the pork shank. Shred the pork into pieces that are as small as possible. Set aside.

FOR THE MEATBALLS: Preheat your oven to 400°F (200°C), with the rack in the centre position. Line a baking sheet with parchment paper.

In a large mixing bowl, soak the breadcrumbs in the milk for a few minutes. Add the shallot, garlic, pork, egg, mustard, salt, cinnamon, cloves, and nutmeg. Mix gently with your hands to distribute the seasoning, but don't overwork the mixture or your meatballs will be too dense and tough. At this point, it's a good idea to cook a small patty to make sure the meat is seasoned properly, then adjust to taste.

Using a small (15 mL) ice cream scoop or a tablespoon, portion the meat mixture and transfer to the prepared baking sheet. Using your hands, form the portions into small meatballs. You'll end up with 20 to 25 meatballs,

continued

Sauce:

½ cup (75 g) all-purpose flour

⅓ cup (75 g) unsalted butter, divided

1 tablespoon (8 g) cornstarch

4 cups (1 L) bouillon from the pork shank

Kosher salt and freshly cracked black pepper, to taste

Maple syrup (optional)

Apple cider vinegar (optional)

give or take, which you'll place perfectly lined up on the pan. Bake for 15 minutes, until golden brown. Set aside.

FOR THE SAUCE: Place the flour in a sauté pan on medium heat. Using a wooden spoon, stir the flour until it turns light brown, about 15 minutes. Once the flour starts browning, it happens fast, and the trick to the sauce is getting the perfect colour for the flour—not too pale and not too dark. Sift the flour through a fine tamis. You'll need about ½ cup of toasted flour per litre of stock.

In a medium saucepan on medium heat, melt 4 tablespoons (60 g) of the butter. Stir in the toasted flour and the cornstarch. Cook for 1 minute. While whisking constantly, gradually add a few ladles of the reserved pork bouillon at a time until fully incorporated, with no lumps. Bring to a simmer and cook for 10 minutes, continuing to whisk constantly. The sauce should be thick like a gravy. If it gets too thick, add water; if it's too thin, add more cornstarch diluted in a bit of water. Turn off the heat, whisk in the remaining butter, taste, and season with salt and pepper. If the flavour of the toasted flour is too bitter for your liking, add a touch of maple syrup and a bit of cider vinegar to balance it out.

Stir the reserved shredded pork and meatballs into the sauce and cook on medium heat until heated through.

TIP *Bouillon is a clear seasoned broth without any solid ingredients. Sure, you could cheat by using bouillon cubes, but these are crammed full of sodium—homemade is always worth the effort when it comes to flavour.*

⚜

Longe de Cerf et Sauce au Thé de Maman

Venison Loin with My Mom's Tea Sauce

Yield: 4 PORTIONS

Preparation time: 15 MINUTES +
30 MINUTES CURING

Cooking time: 30 MINUTES

🌿 *Eating wild game meat is part of the Canadian identity, and both hunting and fishing seasons in Québec are a huge deal. In Europe, people expect to see wild game on the menu in high-end restaurants. Yet somehow, in most of Canada, we aren't allowed to serve it, and there's a lot of talk about the cruelty aspect of hunting. Sure, I agree that bad hunting and fishing practices do exist, but there are also bad practices in farming; all of these issues need to be addressed. When hunted ethically, wild meat is the purest meat you'll ever eat; some of the best meals I've had were made with wild game. I remember Mom always had a pot of tea right beside the stove to deglaze her cast-iron pan after searing steaks for dinner. Even though it was surprisingly delicious, I always thought the sauce tasted odd and outside of the box—that is, until I had it with game meat, and the combination suddenly made sense. The tea sauce is more like a jus than a thick sauce, as there isn't any starch to bind it. I like serving this dish with Pomme Purée (page 195) and grilled or roasted onions.*

What you'll need:

Large cast-iron pan

1.6-pound (700 g) deer loin, or four
6-ounce (175 g) deer steaks (can
substitute filet of beef or, if you're
lucky, moose)

2 teaspoons (6 g) kosher salt

1½ cups (375 mL) hot, nearly
boiling, water

1 sachet English breakfast tea

3 tablespoons (45 mL) grapeseed oil

3 tablespoons (45 g) unsalted
butter, divided

1 sprig rosemary

1 clove garlic (unpeeled), crushed

5 juniper berries, crushed

Kosher salt and freshly cracked
black pepper, to taste

Clean the venison loin of any silver skin; there isn't usually any fat on this lean cut of meat. Season the loin on all sides with the salt and let stand at room temperature for 30 minutes.

Meanwhile, infuse the hot water with the tea for 10 minutes. Remove the tea sachet and discard.

Preheat your oven to 350°F (180°C), with the rack in the centre position.

In a large cast-iron pan on medium-high heat, heat the oil. Sear the venison loin until all sides are nicely caramelized and golden brown, 7 to 8 minutes. Add 2 tablespoons of the butter and the rosemary and garlic. Using a large spoon, baste the venison with the foaming butter for 3 minutes.

Transfer the pan to the oven. Because venison is a lean meat, I prefer a doneness that's between medium-rare and medium; anything more than that would ruin the meat, in my opinion. So the venison should be in the oven for 8 to 10 minutes or until it reaches an internal temperature of 120°F to 125°F (49°C to 52°C).

Transfer the venison to a small tray. Pour the butter from the pan over the loin, cover it loosely with a piece of foil, and let it rest for no less than 15 minutes (see tip).

continued

Meanwhile, return the cast-iron pan (with the rosemary and garlic still in it) to the stove on medium heat. Add the juniper berries and deglaze the pan with the tea. Using a wooden spoon, scrape the bottom of the pan to get all the nice tasty bits, known as the *fond*. Reduce the liquid by half and strain through a tamis into a small saucepan. Put the pan on medium heat and whisk in the remaining butter, along with all the juices from the tray on which the venison has been resting. Season with salt and pepper.

Slice the venison loin, transfer to a serving plate, and pour the hot sauce over top.

TIP *Resting the meat gives the juices enough time to redistribute; otherwise, all that flavour will just flow away when you cut into the meat. Venison is especially juicy—I'd say more than beef—so you'll end up with a bloody mess (pun intended) if you don't rest the meat long enough. It's also important to be aware that the residual heat will continue to cook the meat after you remove it from the pan.*

⚜

Pâté au Saumon

Salmon Pie

Yield: 4 PORTIONS

Preparation time: 1 HOUR +
1 HOUR COOLING

Cooking time: 1 HOUR

What you'll need:

8 by 6-inch (20 by 15 cm) oval pie dish, 3 inches (7 cm) deep

1-pound (450 g) salmon fillet, skinned and deboned

1 tablespoon (10 g) kosher salt, divided

2 Yukon Gold potatoes, peeled and diced into ½-inch (1 cm) cubes

¼ cup (60 mL) grapeseed oil

8 button mushrooms, quartered

2 shallots, thinly sliced

1 bulb fennel, thinly sliced

1 leek (white part only), thinly sliced

4 tablespoons (60 g) unsalted butter

¼ cup (40 g) all-purpose flour

½ cup (125 mL) white wine

2 cups (500 mL) Fish Stock (page 312) or homogenized milk (3.25% milk fat)

2 tablespoons (30 mL) chopped fresh dill

2 eggs, boiled for 10 minutes, peeled and quartered

1 egg yolk + 1 tablespoon (15 mL) homogenized milk (3.25% milk fat), lightly beaten for egg wash

½ batch Pâte Brisée (page 299)

🐟 *Similar to chicken pot pie, or even a variation of the* tourtière, *pâté au saumon is a popular dish in Québec. It's often mixed with leftover pomme purée, but I've always found it too dry when done that way. Instead, I prefer cubing the potatoes and going heavier on the sauce. If you have good-quality canned salmon, or jars of salmon from a fishing trip, this is the perfect recipe for it. Serve with a salad or green vegetables.*

With your chef's knife, cut the salmon fillet into roughly ¾-inch (2 cm) cubes. Season with half of the salt. Transfer the salmon to a medium bowl, cover, and refrigerate until ready to use.

Place the potatoes in a medium pot and add enough cold water to cover. Season heavily with salt. Bring to a boil on medium-high heat, then reduce the heat and simmer until tender, about 5 minutes. Drain and set aside.

Meanwhile, in a large sauté pan on medium-high heat, heat the oil. Sear the mushrooms until golden brown, 4 to 5 minutes. Add the shallots, fennel, and leek, and cook, stirring once in a while, until all the vegetables are tender, about 5 minutes. Add the butter and let melt, then sprinkle in the flour, mix well, and cook for 1 minute. Add the wine, stirring until the sauce has thickened. Stir in the fish stock along with the remaining salt and bring to a simmer. Lower the heat to low and cook gently for 5 minutes. Transfer the sauce to a large bowl and let cool at room temperature for 1 hour or until fully cooled.

Preheat your oven to 425°F (220°C), with the rack in the centre position.

To assemble the pie, take the salmon cubes out of the fridge and pat them dry with a paper towel. Fold the salmon into the sauce, along with the reserved potatoes and the dill. Transfer the mixture to the baking dish and distribute the boiled egg quarters in the mixture.

On a lightly floured work surface, roll out the pastry dough into an 8 by 10-inch (20 by 25 cm) oval, ⅛ inch (3 mm) thick. Brush the rim of the pie dish with the egg wash and lay the pastry dough disc in the dish. Use kitchen scissors to cut off some of the excess dough overhanging the pie dish, then seal the pastry dough to the side rim of the pie dish. Roll out

continued

some of the dough trimmings to decorate your pie whichever way you feel inspired in the moment. Use a sharp knife to cut a small hole in the centre of the pie to create a *cheminée* that lets steam escape. Brush the dough with the egg wash.

Bake the pie for 30 minutes, then lower the heat to 350°F (180°C) and bake for another 30 minutes, until the pastry is nicely golden brown and the salmon mixture is piping hot.

⚜

Tourtière du Lac St-Jean

Rustic Meat Pie

Yield: 8 TO 10 PORTIONS

Preparation time: 2 HOURS + 12 TO 16 HOURS MARINATING

Cooking time: 4¼ HOURS + 2 HOURS COOLING

It has long been debated what the real tourtière *is, especially in the Lac St-Jean region. Should we even call it a* tourtière—*maybe it's a* cipaille *or a* pâté à la viande? *Do you eat a* tourtière *with or without ketchup? These are all, of course, very important questions.* Tourtière *made in the style of Lac St-Jean is different. It has cubes of different meats instead of ground meat, and sometimes incorporates wild meat from hunting season. The pie also contains cubed potatoes and is baked way longer in the oven, in a deep dish. It can even have layers of pastry in between the filling, which is one of the reasons for the longer bake. I always thought the traditional way of cooking it—we're talking 6 to 8 hours in the oven—is, well . . . too long. I prefer to braise the meat for the filling first, then add it to the pastry shell and bake the pie for about 2 hours. Which version of this iconic dish is the best? It's up to you to decide.*

What you'll need:

8-inch (20 cm) round or oval cast-iron casserole dish, 4 inches (10 cm) deep

2.2 pounds (1 kg) pork shoulder, diced into ½-inch (1 cm) cubes

2.2 pounds (1 kg) beef short ribs or shank, deboned and most of the fat removed, diced into ½-inch (1 cm) cubes

5 ounces (150 g) lard or unsmoked bacon, diced into thick lardons

1 cup (250 mL) amber beer from Québec

5 large cloves garlic, finely chopped

2 large sweet onions, thinly sliced

6 to 8 juniper berries, crushed with a mortar and pestle

3 sprigs thyme, leaves only

2 bay leaves

1 tablespoon + 2 teaspoons (16 g) kosher salt

1 teaspoon (3 g) Épices à Tourtière (page 194)

In a large bowl, mix the pork, beef, lard, beer, garlic, onions, juniper berries, thyme, bay leaves, salt, and *épices à tourtière*. Cover and marinate in the fridge for a minimum of 12 hours, and up to 16 hours.

Preheat your oven to 325°F (160°C), with the rack in the centre position.

Add the marinated meat mixture with all the liquid to a large ovenproof pot. Stir gently on medium-high heat until all the liquid is evaporated, about 15 minutes. In a separate pot on high heat, bring the chicken stock to a simmer. Sprinkle the flour on the meat mixture, then add the stock, stirring slowly. Cover tightly and braise in the oven for 1½ hours. Stir in the potatoes and cook for 30 minutes, until the meat and potatoes are fork-tender. Let cool at room temperature for 1 hour. Discard the bay leaves.

Meanwhile, on a lightly floured work surface, roll out two-thirds of the dough into a large rectangle about ¼ inch (5 mm) thick. Lay the dough in the bottom and up the sides of the casserole dish, letting the excess hang over the edges. Roll out the remaining dough to ¼ inch (5 mm) thick, in the shape of your casserole dish, and set aside.

Increase the oven temperature to 425°F (220°C).

continued

4 cups (1 L) Chicken Stock (page 308, or store-bought) or water (approx.)

3 tablespoons (30 g) all-purpose flour

2.2 pounds (1 kg) Yukon Gold potatoes, peeled and diced into ½-inch (1 cm) cubes

1 batch Pâte à Pâté (page 298)

1 pound (450 g/3 legs) Cuisse de Canard Confit (page 47), pulled and roughly chopped

1 egg yolk + 1 tablespoon (15 mL) homogenized milk (3.25% milk fat), lightly beaten for egg wash

Add the duck confit to the meat mixture and mix well. Pour into the casserole dish. Cut off any excess dough from around the edges. Brush the edges lightly with egg wash and cover with the reserved dough. Form a *cheminée* by cutting a small hole in the centre of the top crust to let steam escape while baking. Pinch the edges of the crust to seal, and trim off any excess dough. Decorate the top of your *tourtière* as desired. Brush a thin layer of egg wash over top.

Place the *tourtière* on a baking sheet and bake for 30 minutes. This gives the *tourtière* a crispy inside crust. Lower the oven temperature to 350°F (180°C) and continue baking for 1½ hours. Remove from the oven and let stand for 1 hour before cutting and serving.

TIP *You can cook the* tourtière *the day before; let it cool for a few hours, then put it in the fridge overnight. Warm it up in the oven at 325°F (160°C) for 1 to 2 hours before serving.*

Tarte aux Bleuets

Blueberry Pie

Yield: ONE 9-INCH (23 CM) PIE, 8 PORTIONS

Preparation time: 20 MINUTES

Cooking time: 75 MINUTES + 2 HOURS COOLING

What you'll need:

9-inch (23 cm) pie plate

1 batch Pâte Brisée (page 299)

4 cups (600 g) organic fresh or frozen blueberries

1 cup (220 g) granulated sugar

⅓ cup (45 g) cornstarch

1 egg yolk

1 teaspoon (5 mL) water

1 tablespoon (15 mL) raw turbinado sugar

❧ *Every kid loves to go berry picking. I know I did. Once you've eaten as many berries as you've put in your bucket, it's time to think about making a delicious blueberry pie. Because one thing is for sure: those berries won't last long on your kitchen counter. In Québec, everyone talks about being lucky enough to pick up wild blueberries from Lac St-Jean when the season begins. If you can get your hands on those, you're in for a serious treat. I like making a lattice-top pie crust for blueberry pie—it's a little tricky at first, but you'll quickly get the hang of it and it'll really impress your guests. Maybe for your first kick at the can, you can just lay the dough strips on top of each other in a form of a lattice instead of going under and over each one every time. I say take the challenge and just do it—you'll be pleasantly surprised with the result.*

Preheat your oven to 425°F (220°C), with the rack in the centre position.

Following the method for the *pâte brisée*, you should have two dough discs that are 14 inches (35 cm) in diameter by ⅛ inch (3 mm) thick. Place the first disc of dough into the bottom and up the sides of the pie plate, and leave about 1 inch (2.5 cm) of overhang; use kitchen scissors to trim off any excess dough.

In a large mixing bowl, combine the blueberries, sugar, and cornstarch. Mix together until all the blueberries are fully coated.

In a small bowl, lightly beat the egg yolk with the water to make an egg wash.

To make the lattice crust, cut the second disc of dough into 10 to 12 strips that are 10 inches long by 1 inch wide (25 cm by 2.5 cm). Lay half of the strips horizontally across your pie, spacing them evenly. Start with the longest strips in the middle and work out to the edges. Remember to save some longer strips for the vertical part of your lattice.

Next, fold back alternating strips of dough to just past the centre of the pie. Place your longest remaining strip of dough vertically down the centre of the pie, perpendicular to the horizontal strips. Unfold the folded strips of dough back over this perpendicular vertical strip; you should now have a basket weave.

continued

Now fold back the strips of dough that lie under the vertical strip and repeat these steps by laying a second vertical strip of dough evenly spaced to the right of the centre strip. Unfold the folded strips back over the new vertical strip. Continue to the right until you reach the outer edge, then repeat the process to the left of the centre strip to complete your full lattice crust.

Fold the bottom crust overhang up over the edges of the strips. Pinch the dough together with your fingers and crimp it to get a nice seal. Lightly brush the crust with the egg wash, and sprinkle the top of your pie with the turbinado sugar.

Place the pie on a baking sheet and bake for 15 minutes, then lower the heat to 350°F (180°C) and continue baking for 1 hour. If the top starts to brown too much, place a sheet of foil over the pie. Let the pie cool completely on a wire rack before cutting into it, around 2 hours.

TIP *Don't mix the sugar with the berries until you're ready to fill the pie shell and have the strips for your lattice ready to go. The berries will release their juices once combined with sugar, and you'll end up with a big mess.*

Tarte au Sucre

Sugar Pie

Yield: ONE 9-INCH (23 CM) PIE,
8 PORTIONS

Preparation time: 1 HOUR +
2 HOURS CHILLING

Cooking time: 40 MINUTES +
2 HOURS COOLING

What you'll need:

9-inch (23 cm) round tart pan

2 tablespoons (30 g) unsalted butter

3 tablespoons (25 g) cornstarch

2 tablespoons (20 g) all-purpose flour

1½ cups (375 mL) heavy or whipping cream (35% milk fat), divided

1⅓ cups (300 g) firmly packed brown sugar

Good pinch kosher salt

½ teaspoon (2 mL) vanilla extract

1 batch Pâte Brisée (page 299)

1 egg yolk + 1 tablespoon (15 mL) homogenized milk (3.25% milk fat), lightly beaten for egg wash

In case you didn't know, the traditional French-Canadian diet is rich in calories, fat, and sugar. Tarte au sucre *is a perfect example. Its high fat content from butter and heavy cream was needed to help Québecers survive the harsh elements, while its high sugar content was a necessary counterbalance for the brutal conditions of life—a true taste of sweet* joie de vivre. *Sugar pie was traditionally made with 100% maple sugar, as brown sugar was rare and unavailable. These days, sadly, maple syrup is expensive and brown sugar is everywhere.* Tarte au sucre *is still a dinner staple on every Québécois family table; even now, my grandmother makes the best one I've ever tasted. Mine is an adaptation of her recipe, and it'll still blow your brains out. I like serving the tart with a light crème Chantilly (page 228) to balance the intense sweetness.*

In a medium pot on medium-high heat, melt the butter, then whisk in the cornstarch and flour to create a roux. Cook for 1 minute, whisking constantly, then slowly and gradually whisk in the cream until the roux absorbs the liquid and the mixture thickens to a paste, 3 to 4 minutes. Lower the heat to medium, and whisk in the brown sugar, salt, and vanilla. Continuing to whisk, bring the mixture to a simmer again, about 10 minutes. Turn off the heat, and pass the mixture through a fine tamis into a medium bowl. Let the mixture cool at room temperature.

Meanwhile, on a lightly floured work surface, roll the *pâte brisée* into two discs ⅛-inch (3 mm) thick that fit into the 9-inch (23 cm) round tart pan. Lay the first disc of dough in the bottom and up the sides of the pan. Pour in the brown sugar mixture. Brush the edges of the dough with the egg wash, and lay the second disc on top. Seal the edges by pressing down with your fingers. Trim off the excess dough and press down around the perimeter of the pie with a fork, or flute the edges with your fingers. Make a little round *cheminée* (page 159) in the centre of the top pie crust to allow steam to escape. Brush the top of the pie with the egg wash. Chill the pie in the fridge for 2 hours before baking to make sure the dough and filling are cold.

Preheat your oven to 425°F (220°C), with the rack in the centre position.

Bake the pie for 40 minutes, until the pastry is a nice golden brown. Let cool on a wire rack for 2 hours. Serve at room temperature. (You can keep any leftovers in the fridge for up to 5 days, or freeze them for up to 2 months.)

Tarte au Sirop d'Érable

Maple Syrup Tart

Yield: ONE 9-INCH (23 CM)
TART, 8 PORTIONS

Preparation time: 45 MINUTES +
30 MINUTES COOLING

Cooking time: 70 TO 80 MINUTES
+ 2 HOURS COOLING

What you'll need:

9-inch (23 cm) round tart pan

⅓ cup (80 g) unsalted butter

3 tablespoons (30 g) all-purpose flour

3 tablespoons (25 g) cornstarch

2 cups (500 mL) maple syrup

¾ cup (175 mL) heavy or whipping cream (35% milk fat)

½ batch Pâte Brisée (page 299)

1 large egg + 2 egg yolks

Maldon salt, to finish

❧ *I absolutely love this maple syrup tart. Truth be told, I might even prefer it to the Sugar Pie (page 65). It's slightly less sweet and a lot more refined, especially if you use a quality maple syrup, and the texture is more custardy because of the eggs. Serve at room temperature, with a dollop of crème Chantilly (page 228) or Crème Fraîche (page 296).*

Preheat your oven to 375°F (190°C), with the rack in the centre position.

In a medium pot on medium heat, melt the butter. Stir in the flour and cornstarch, and cook for 2 minutes, whisking constantly (this is called making a roux). Whisk in the maple syrup and cream. Bring to a simmer, and continue simmering until thickened. Lower the heat to low and cook, whisking constantly, for approximately 10 more minutes. Remove from the heat and let the mixture cool completely.

On a lightly floured work surface, roll out the *pâte brisée* into a ⅛-inch (3 mm) thick disc that fits into the 9-inch (23 cm) round tart pan. Lay the disc of dough onto the bottom and up the sides of the pan. Place the tart shell in the fridge for 30 minutes before baking. To blind-bake the tart shell, line it with parchment paper so the surface of the dough is totally covered. Press the parchment paper completely to the sides of the tart dough, then fill the tart pan with enough dried beans as weights to hold down the dough and prevent it from rising.

Bake the tart shell for 30 minutes, then remove the beans and parchment paper and bake for another 10 minutes, until it's a sandy light-golden colour and you don't see any wet spots.

Lower the oven temperature to 325°F (160°C).

Whisk the egg and yolks into the maple syrup mixture and pour it into the tart shell. Bake for 30 to 40 minutes, until the centre of the tart is just set and the outside starts to bubble up. Remove from the oven, sprinkle the top with Maldon salt, and place on a wire rack to cool completely, about 2 hours. Serve at room temperature, or place it in the fridge to eat the next day.

⚜

Pouding Chômeur

Poor Man's Pudding

Yield: 8 TO 10 PORTIONS

Preparation time: 20 MINUTES

Cooking time: 45 MINUTES + 15 MINUTES COOLING

Pouding chômeur *literally translates to "unemployed man's pudding," and it's also known as poor's man pudding. This dessert was created by female factory workers during Québec's early Depression years. Nowadays, it's casually served as a regional dessert, maybe a little bit more popular during maple syrup season* (la saison des sucres) *at the sugar shack, but as you'll see, it isn't specifically made with maple syrup. The syrup can be made with brown sugar, granulated sugar, maple syrup, or a combination of the three, while the cake is a very basic batter. At the depths of the Great Depression, when household finances were at their tightest, stale bread was used instead of cake batter. This staple dessert is, in my opinion, quintessentially Québécois. It's delectably rich and incredibly simple, kind of like a saucy pineapple upside-down cake minus the fruit. Serve it with your favourite vanilla ice cream.*

What you'll need:

10-inch (25 cm) square glass baking dish, 2 inches (5 cm) deep

3 tablespoons (45 g) + ⅓ cup (75 g) room-temperature unsalted butter, divided

¾ cup + 1 tablespoon (165 g) granulated sugar

1⅓ cups (215 g) all-purpose flour

1 tablespoon + 1 teaspoon (15 g) baking powder

1 egg

½ cup + 3 tablespoons (170 g) homogenized milk (3.25% milk fat)

½ teaspoon (2 mL) vanilla extract

2½ cups (400 g) firmly packed dark brown sugar

1 cup (250 mL) heavy or whipping cream (35% milk fat)

1 cup (250 mL) water

Icing sugar, for dusting

Preheat your oven to 350°F (180°C), with the rack in the centre position. Grease the baking dish with 3 tablespoons (45 g) of the butter and place it on a baking sheet.

In a medium bowl, cream the granulated sugar and ⅓ cup (75 g) butter by hand with a wooden spoon. Add the flour and baking powder and continue stirring until fully incorporated. Slowly whisk in the egg, milk, and vanilla, and mix until fully incorporated. Try not to overmix the batter.

In a small pot on medium heat, whisk together the brown sugar, cream, and water. Bring to a boil.

Using a rubber spatula, scrape the batter into the baking dish. You might think that it's not enough batter for the size of the dish, but bear in mind that the batter will expand quite a lot. Gently pour the hot syrup on top. It will look like a big mess—don't worry, that's normal! It will all come together while baking.

Bake for 45 minutes or until golden brown and a toothpick inserted in the centre comes out clean. Let cool on a wire rack at room temperature for 15 minutes, then dust some icing sugar on top.

✦

CLASSIC FRENCH

 I HAVEN'T YET SEEN a Canadian cookbook that significantly features old-school classic French cuisine, save for a few recipes here and there in some Québécois cookbooks, such as *pithivier*, *pâté en croute*, and trout quenelles. Classic French dishes are the first thing every cook learns at culinary school, and they always have a place in your heart. Yet even though these techniques are the foundation for everything we prepare in the kitchen, most chefs move on to other cuisines after culinary school and apprenticeship. I continue to draw inspiration from legendary chefs like the Roux brothers, Raymond Blanc, and Pierre Koffmann when creating dishes like *îles flottantes*, *cailles en sarcophage*, and duck *cassoulet*.

Home cooks are often too intimidated to tackle classic French dishes, but it's really not as difficult as it seems. Cooking old-school French food is no more difficult than making Thai or Italian food. If you can make fresh pasta from scratch, you can probably put together a *pâte brisée* just as easily to make a meat pie—it's no different. The key is focusing on the small steps that make a large task easier and the little rules that help to improve a dish. Remember to put salt in the water when blanching asparagus and carrots. Sear your meat and deglaze the pan afterward to develop fullness of flavour. And always taste your food as you're cooking it to check for seasoning. In short, take your time and pay attention as you go through the process of making a dish. The more you practice, the better you'll get.

Pâté de Faisan

Pheasant Terrine

Yield: 1 TERRINE

Preparation time: 45 MINUTES +
24 HOURS CURING

Cooking time: 80 MINUTES +
1 HOUR RESTING AND 24 TO
48 HOURS CHILLING

What you'll need:

Terrine mould, 10 inches by
3½ inches (25 by 9 cm), with a lid

1.3 pounds (600 g) skinless pheasant
meat (half leg meat and half breast
meat), deboned and diced into
½-inch (1 cm) cubes, divided

12 ounces (350 g) pork shoulder,
deboned and diced into ½-inch
(1 cm) cubes

4 ounces (125 g) chicken livers,
deveined and cleaned

3 tablespoons + 1 teaspoon (50 mL)
Armagnac (or cognac or brandy),
divided

2 tablespoons (18 g) kosher salt,
divided

¼ teaspoon (1 g) curing salt, divided

1 teaspoon (3 g) freshly cracked
black pepper, divided

6 ounces (175 g) pancetta, diced
into ½-inch (1 cm) cubes

4 ounces (125 g) foie gras, diced
into ½-inch (1 cm) cubes

⅔ cup (150 mL) heavy or whipping
cream (35% milk fat)

2 slices white bread, crusts removed,
finely diced

⅓ cup (75 g) dried apricots, diced

3 fresh bay leaves

This was the first terrine I put on the menu when I opened St. Lawrence. Pheasant is such a beautiful bird. Its meat is so flavourful, especially for poultry, and the taste always reminds me of fall and hunting season. The disadvantages are that it's not always readily available and it's on the expensive side, given that pheasants are smaller than chickens and their legs tend to be tough. But that makes pheasant perfect for a terrine, as you can stretch it out to serve many people with just one bird. It's also divine when paired with foie gras, apricots, and Armagnac. If you can't find pheasant, chicken or rabbit will do.

In a medium bowl, combine the pheasant leg meat, pork shoulder and chicken liver. Add about 2 tablespoons (30 mL) Armagnac, half of the kosher salt, half of the curing salt, and half of the pepper. Using your hands, mix well. In a second medium bowl, add the pheasant breast, pancetta, and foie gras. Add the rest of the Armagnac, salts, and pepper. Cover both bowls with plastic wrap and refrigerate for 24 hours.

The next day, preheat your oven to 325°F (160°C), with the rack in the centre position.

Using a meat grinder or food processor, grind the pheasant leg meat, pork shoulder, and chicken livers to a coarse grind. If you don't have a meat grinder, you can hand-chop the meats with a chef's knife into ¼-inch (5 mm) chunks or pulse in a food processor for 20 to 30 seconds, or you can ask your butcher to grind them for you.

In a medium bowl, combine the cream and bread and let stand for 10 minutes. In a large bowl, combine the ground meat, pheasant breast meat, pancetta, foie gras, cream mixture, and apricots, mixing well. Taste for seasoning by cooking a small patty of the pâté in a small sauté pan.

Transfer the meat mixture to the terrine mould, pressing down to make sure there are no air pockets. Arrange the three bay leaves on top of the pâté. Place the mould in a large, deep baking pan and pour in boiling water until it reaches halfway up the mould. (This is called cooking in a *bain-marie.*) Cover the mould with the lid.

Bake for 1 hour, then remove the lid and bake for another 20 minutes or until the internal temperature reaches 150°F to 155°F (66°C to 68°C). Remove the terrine from the oven and let it sit at room temperature for 1 hour.

Line the top of the terrine mould with plastic wrap and put a small weight on top (such as a box of salt or a small can of tomatoes). Refrigerate for a minimum of 24 hours; however, it would taste better after 48 hours, as this allows more time for the flavours to mature.

To serve, dip a paring knife in hot water and slide it against the sides of the terrine to loosen it from the mould. Turn it upside down on a serving plate and carve generous slices.

❖

Artichauts en Barigoule

Braised Artichoke Stew

Yield: 4 PORTIONS
Preparation time: 40 MINUTES
Cooking time: 15 TO 20 MINUTES

My love of artichokes continues with this classic recipe, one of the best ways to eat this interesting, underrated, and strange vegetable. Frozen artichoke hearts are a time-saving substitute, though the flavour and texture of fresh artichokes are, by far, much superior and definitely preferred. Slices of grilled bread and some delicious Aïoli (page 295) are two of my favourite accompaniments for this dish. The aïoli's fatty richness, garlicky flavour, and acidity perfectly complement this vegetable stew that's a traditional springtime staple in Provence.

1 lemon

4 large globe artichokes

5 tablespoons (75 mL) olive oil, divided

3 thick slices smoked bacon (2.5 ounces/75 g), cut into ¼ by ½-inch (6 mm by 1 cm) lardons

8 pearl onions, peeled and halved

2 cloves garlic, thinly sliced

1 stalk celery (1.75 ounces/50 g), cut into small dice

1 medium carrot (2.5 ounces/75 g), peeled and cut into small dice

½ bulb fennel, cut into small dice

2 sprigs thyme

2 bay leaves

½ cup (125 mL) white wine

1 cup (250 mL) Chicken Stock or Vegetable Stock (page 308 or 313, or store-bought) or water

¼ cup (15 g) fresh flat-leaf parsley leaves

1 teaspoon (3 g) kosher salt

Freshly cracked black pepper, to taste

Fill a large bowl with cold water. Using a peeler, peel three strips of lemon zest from the lemon; set aside. Cut the lemon in half and squeeze the juice into the water.

Gently pick off the first layer of the outer leaves from each artichoke. Using a sharp paring knife, cut off the stalks about ¾ inch (2 cm) from the base, and cut ¾ inch (2 cm) off the leaf tips. Turn each artichoke by cutting around the outside of each one to remove any green parts, trimming the leaves a bit at the top and removing any woody parts at the base. Using a melon baller or a small spoon, scoop out each furry choke, found in the centre. Cut the artichoke hearts into quarters and immediately put them in the lemon water to prevent oxidation.

In a medium pot on medium heat, heat 1 tablespoon (15 mL) of the oil. Sauté the bacon lardons, stirring often with a wooden spoon, until nicely caramelized. Add another 3 tablespoons (45 mL) of the oil, and stir in the pearl onions, garlic, celery, carrot, fennel, thyme, and bay leaves. Cook gently for 8 to 10 minutes, until softened but without colouration. Stir in the artichokes and lemon zest. Deglaze the pot with the wine and reduce by half. Add the stock and bring to a simmer. Lower the heat to low, cover, and cook for 10 to 15 minutes or until you can just pierce the artichokes with slight resistance to the tip of your paring knife. Discard the bay leaves. Toss in the parsley leaves, salt, pepper, and the remaining oil. Taste for seasoning.

Serve the artichokes with all the vegetables and broth in a bowl. If you prefer a more intense flavour, use a slotted spoon to transfer the artichokes and vegetables into a bowl and reduce the cooking liquid by half on high heat. Pour the reduced liquid over the artichokes and serve either warm or cooled to room temperature.

Feuilleté d'Asperges au Beurre de Cerfeuil

Asparagus with Chervil Butter Sauce and Puff Pastry

Yield: 4 PORTIONS
Preparation time: 30 MINUTES
Cooking time: 45 MINUTES

Puff Pastry:

6 ounces (175 g) Pâte Feuilleté Rapide (page 300, or store-bought)

1 egg yolk + 1 tablespoon (15 mL) homogenized milk (3.25% milk fat), lightly beaten for egg wash

Asparagus:

3 cups (750 mL) water

1 teaspoon (3 g) kosher salt

1 teaspoon (6 g) granulated sugar

Peel of ½ lemon

16 large stalks green asparagus, trimmed and peeled

2 tablespoons (30 g) unsalted butter

Chervil Butter Sauce:

1 tablespoon (15 mL) grapeseed oil

3 tablespoons (45 mL) finely chopped shallots

1 cup (250 mL) white wine

3 tablespoons (45 mL) white wine vinegar

3 sprigs thyme

1 bay leaf

1 cup (225 g) cold unsalted butter, cubed

¼ cup (60 mL) heavy or whipping cream (35% milk fat)

1 teaspoon (3 g) kosher salt

1 tablespoon (15 mL) fresh lemon juice

3 tablespoons (45 mL) fresh chervil, roughly chopped + extra whole leaves for garnish

If I had to make a list of my top three vegetables, asparagus would be on it, particularly white asparagus as it is very special. White asparagus would be my preference; they are more delicate and sweet, with just a hint of bitterness, while green asparagus is more on the grassy side. But white asparagus are often unavailable and more pricey. I like asparagus prepared simply with a sauce, in this case a beurre blanc, *but it's also exquisite with a Sauce Hollandaise or* mousseline.

FOR THE PUFF PASTRY: Preheat your oven to 425°F (220°C), with the rack in the centre position. Line a small baking sheet with parchment paper.

On a lightly floured work surface, roll out the pastry into an 8 by 4-inch (20 by 10 cm) rectangle, about ¼ inch (5 mm) thick. Using a paring knife, trim the rectangle and cut it into 4 smaller rectangles, each measuring 2 by 4 inches (5 by 10 cm).

Place the pastry rectangles on the prepared baking sheet. Brush the tops with the egg wash, making sure none of it trickles down the sides or it will prevent the pastry from rising properly.

With a paring knife, score a few lines to make a diamond pattern.

Bake for 20 to 25 minutes or until golden brown. Remove from the oven and set aside. Lower the oven temperature to 225°F (110°C).

FOR THE ASPARAGUS: In a large saucepan wide enough to fit the asparagus, bring the water, salt, sugar, and lemon peel to a boil on high heat. Add the asparagus and lower the heat to a simmer. Cook until the asparagus is tender but still firm in the centre, 3 to 4 minutes. Meanwhile, prepare an ice bath. Using tongs, transfer the asparagus to the ice bath to stop the cooking.

Increase the heat to high and reduce the cooking liquid to ¼ cup (60 mL). Remove from the heat and set aside.

FOR THE CHERVIL BUTTER SAUCE: In a small saucepan on medium-high heat, heat the oil. Sauté the shallots until soft and translucent but without colouration. Add the wine, vinegar, thyme, and bay leaf, and reduce until

continued

3 tablespoons (45 mL) of the liquid remains. Strain through a tamis, pressing down with the back of a spoon to extract all the liquid.

Pour the liquid back into the saucepan. Return to a boil on medium-high heat. Move the saucepan off the heat and gradually add the cubes of cold butter while whisking constantly. Continue whisking until all the butter is incorporated, placing the saucepan briefly on the heat and taking it back off again every once in a while to help the butter melt. Whisk in the cream. Do not boil the sauce at this stage or it will split. The sauce should be silky, smooth, and glossy. Turn off the heat and season the sauce with salt and lemon juice. When you're ready to plate, stir in the chervil at the last moment.

TO FINISH: Just before serving, warm your serving plates in a 225°F (110°C) oven.

Return the asparagus to the pan with the reduced cooking liquid and place on medium heat. Add the 2 tablespoons (30 mL) butter and glaze the asparagus until heated through. If the liquid in the pan begins to split because it's over-reduced, add 1 tablespoon (15 mL) water to maintain the emulsion.

Scoop the chervil butter sauce onto the plate. Arrange a few stalks of green asparagus atop the sauce. Garnish with the remaining chervil leaves all around the asparagus. Top with the puff pastry and serve immediately.

⚜

Poireaux à la Flamande

Braised Leeks with Brown Butter and Egg Vinaigrette

Yield: 4 PORTIONS
Preparation time: 35 MINUTES
Cooking time: 30 MINUTES

Leeks are a wonderful vegetable that becomes sweet and tender with the benefit of long cooking. They're part of the same allium family as garlic and onions, but they have a much milder taste than their vegetable cousins. After potatoes, onions, garlic, and asparagus, the tasty leek is among the top vegetables used in French cuisine. Preparing them à la Flamande, as they do in northern France, is perfect; like all the vegetables I just mentioned, leeks love to be combined with eggs and butter. Try this preparation, and you'll never see leeks the same way again.

4 large leeks

1 teaspoon (3 g) kosher salt

Freshly cracked black pepper, to taste

1 shallot, thinly sliced

1 small carrot, peeled and diced into ½-inch (1 cm) cubes

1 stalk celery, diced into ½-inch (1 cm) cubes

1 clove garlic, roughly chopped

2 sprigs thyme

⅓ cup (75 g) unsalted butter, divided

3 large eggs, room temperature

Juice of 1 lemon, divided

1 tablespoon (15 mL) chopped fresh flat-leaf parsley

Olive oil, to garnish

Maldon salt, to finish

Fennel fronds, to garnish (optional)

Preheat your oven to 350°F (180°C), with the rack in the centre position.

Carefully trim the root ends of the leeks, leaving enough so all the layers remain attached. Cut off the thick, woody dark-green top of each leek, where it starts to change from pale to dark green. Slice the leeks lengthwise down the centre from the root to the green part. Wash the leeks vigorously under slow-running cold water, using your fingers to scrape away any remaining dirt and sand.

Place the leeks in a shallow ovenproof baking dish large enough to hold them all in a single layer. Pour in enough water to submerge the leeks halfway. Season with the salt and pepper. Evenly distribute the shallot, carrot, celery, garlic, thyme, and 1 tablespoon (15 g) of the butter over the leeks. Cover the dish with a piece of foil, place on medium heat, and bring to a gentle simmer.

Transfer the baking dish to the oven and bake until the leeks are tender without being mushy. This will take 20 to 30 minutes, depending on the size of the leeks; check them regularly at and after the 20-minute mark. Remove from the oven and let cool at room temperature.

In a small pot, bring 4 cups (1 L) water to a boil. Gently place the eggs in the boiling water, lower the heat to a light simmer, and cook for 9 minutes. Meanwhile, prepare an ice bath. Transfer the eggs to the ice bath for 5 minutes. Peel and roughly chop the eggs. Set aside in a small bowl.

In a small saucepan on medium-high heat, cook the remaining butter a little past the melting point, browning the milk solids in the butter and

continued

creating a wonderfully nutty aroma. Remove from the heat, add half of the lemon juice, and, using a spoon, immediately stir in the chopped eggs. Mix in the parsley and season with salt and pepper.

To serve, lay the leeks on a serving platter (along with any other vegetables you've prepared), and spoon in a little bit of the broth. Squeeze the remaining half of the lemon juice on top of the leeks and drizzle with olive oil. Season the leeks with Maldon salt and top with the warm egg sauce. Garnish with fennel fronds or flat-leaf parsley.

VARIATION *For a different presentation, you can slice the leeks into small chunks and omit the cubed vegetables on the plate.*

⚜

Vol-au-Vent à la Financière

Veal Sweetbreads, Chicken Quenelles, and Shrimp in Puff Pastry Cases

Yield: 6 PORTIONS
Preparation time: 3 HOURS
Cooking time: 1½ HOURS

"What does it mean?" is usually the first thing that comes to mind when someone hears the name of this dish. Translated into English, vol-au-vent *means "lifted by the wind" or "windblown," referring to the light and airy puff pastry case. My mom loved to do chicken and peas in a creamy sauce (think chicken pot pie filling) for her* vol-au-vents, *but you can use seafood, vegetables, or any type of meat you want, really. Legendary chef Antonin Carême invented* vol-au-vent *in the early nineteenth century, and culinary icon Auguste Escoffier included a recipe for it* à la Financière *in his groundbreaking* Larousse Gastronomique. *I rounded out the classic version with the addition of veal sweetbreads and shrimp—call it surf and turf, if you wish.*

6 medium Vol-au-Vent Cases (page 304)

12 ounces (350 g) veal sweetbreads

Chicken Quenelles:

9 ounces (250 g) boneless skinless chicken breasts, cut into 1-inch (2.5 cm) cubes

1 egg white (1.4 ounces/40 g)

¾ cup (180 mL) heavy or whipping cream (35% milk fat) + extra if needed

3 tablespoons (30 g) all-purpose flour

2 teaspoons (7 g) kosher salt

Sauce Blanquette:

4 tablespoons (60 g) unsalted butter, cubed

3 tablespoons (30 g) all-purpose flour

½ cup (125 mL) white wine

2 tablespoons (30 mL) cognac

Approx. 2 cups (500 mL) Chicken Stock (page 308, or store-bought)

Start by making the *vol-au-vent* cases. If you want to save some time, you might be able to find frozen puff pastry cases. Just make sure that the dough is made with 100% butter.

In a large pot on medium-high heat, bring heavily salted water to a boil. Gently transfer the veal sweetbreads to the water. Once the water has returned to a simmer, lower the heat and cook for 10 minutes. Meanwhile, prepare an ice bath. Scoop the sweetbreads out of the water and transfer directly to the ice bath to stop the cooking. Once cool, use a paring knife to remove the membrane and any excess fat. Cut the sweetbreads into small 1-inch (2.5 cm) cubes. Reserve in the fridge until needed.

FOR THE CHICKEN QUENELLES: Place the chicken and egg white in a food processor or a blender and process for 1 minute on medium speed until you have a smooth purée. (Optional: Make your quenelles extra smooth by using a plastic scraper to press the purée through a fine-mesh sieve into a bowl.) Add the cold cream and pulse in the food processor until fully incorporated. Add the flour and salt, and mix for 1 minute until you have a homogeneous paste.

Make yourself a little tester to ensure the seasoning and texture are to your liking. To do that, bring a small pot of water to a boil on high heat. Lower the heat to a simmer and drop 1 teaspoon (5 mL) of the purée into the water. Poach for 4 minutes on one side, then turn the mousse over and poach for 4 minutes on the other side. Remove the mousse and cut it open

continued

1 teaspoon (3 g) kosher salt

½ cup (125 mL) Crème Fraîche (page 296, or store-bought)

2 egg yolks

Juice of ¼ lemon

Finishing:

3 tablespoons (45 mL) grapeseed oil

9 ounces (250 g) morel or button mushrooms, halved

Kosher salt and freshly cracked black pepper, to taste

9 ounces (250 g) side-striped shrimp or white prawns, peeled and deveined

2 tablespoons (30 mL) fresh curly parsley leaves, to garnish

with a small knife. Look at the doneness to get an idea of how long it takes to cook, and taste it for seasoning and to see if the texture is light enough. If the quenelle is too dense for your liking, incorporate a touch of heavy cream into the paste to lighten the mixture.

Once you're happy with the texture, make all the quenelles, forming them with two tablespoons dipped in water after each quenelle. In a large pot on medium-high heat, bring 8 cups (2 litres) of water to a boil, then lower the heat so that the liquid is barely simmering. Line a plate with paper towel and have it at the ready beside the stove. Poach the quenelles in small batches for 5 minutes on each side. Use a slotted spoon to remove carefully and transfer them to the lined plate so the paper towel absorbs any extra moisture. You could also steam the quenelles for 10 minutes.

FOR THE SAUCE BLANQUETTE: In a medium saucepan on medium-high heat, melt the butter until foamy. Whisk in the flour and cook, whisking, for 2 minutes. Add the wine and cognac, whisking until the liquid is fully incorporated and the mixture starts to thicken. Slowly pour in the stock and add the salt, whisking constantly until the mixture is homogeneous. Bring to a simmer, lower the heat to low, and cook for 30 minutes. Stir in more stock or water if the sauce becomes too thick.

In a small container, whisk together the crème fraîche, egg yolks, and lemon juice. Set aside.

TO FINISH: Preheat your oven to 350°F (175°C), with the rack in the centre position.

While the sauce is simmering, heat the oil in a large skillet on medium-high heat. Sauté the mushrooms and veal sweetbread nuggets for 5 minutes and season with salt and pepper. Lower the heat to medium, add the shrimp, and cook to half doneness, about 1 minute. Drain off any excess oil and remove from the heat.

When the sauce is ready, mix in the mushrooms, veal sweetbreads, shrimp, and chicken quenelles. Simmer for 2 minutes, until the shrimp is pink, firm, and opaque and everything is warmed through. Whisk a small ladle of warm sauce into the crème fraîche mixture to temper it, then gently whisk the tempered crème fraîche into the sauce of goodness. Don't boil the sauce again, as the eggs will curdle.

To serve, warm up the vol-au-vent cases in the preheated oven for 2 to 3 minutes, put on a plate, and scoop some sauce over them, along with the sweetbreads, shrimp, mushrooms, and quenelles. Garnish with parsley.

⚜

Homard à la Parisienne

Lobster à la Parisienne

Yield: 2 PORTIONS
Preparation time: 1½ HOURS
Cooking time: 30 MINUTES

What you'll need:

Small piping bag with a star tip

2-pound (900 g) live lobster

½ batch Mayonnaise St. Lawrence (page 296), divided

Kosher salt and freshly cracked black pepper, to taste

6 cherry tomatoes

1 medium potato, peeled and diced into ½-inch (1 cm) cubes

1 large carrot, peeled and diced into ½-inch (1 cm) cubes

1 medium turnip, peeled and diced into ½-inch (1 cm) cubes

8 haricots verts, cut into ½-inch (1 cm) pieces

⅓ cup (60 g) English green peas

3 eggs

6 quail eggs

½ teaspoon (2 mL) Dijon mustard

❧ *When I was ten or eleven years old and my family was living in New Brunswick, we decided to take a summer road trip and camp through the province until we reached Prince Edward Island. One night, my father decided to stop at a restaurant serving all-you-can-eat lobster. I was over-the-moon excited, because we never went to restaurants to begin with, and the fact that there was a mountain of lobster to eat for dinner made me extremely happy. I'm pretty sure that meal took my love for lobster completely over the top. My favourite way to eat it has always been at room temperature with either homemade mayonnaise or warm garlic butter.* Lobster à la Parisienne *is basically a fancied-up version of lobster mayonnaise. The elaborate presentation is stunning and will definitely wow your guests. I serve the lobster with a* salade Macédoine, *another French classic, which provides texture and freshness.*

Bring a large pot of salted water (see tip) to a boil on high heat.

Butcher the lobster humanely (see tip, page 34) and segment the body, claws, knuckles, and tail. (Each of these lobster parts has a different cooking time, and I personally don't enjoy overcooked lobster.) With some butcher twine, tie a teaspoon to the tail so it stays straight while cooking. To keep the head for the presentation, cook it in boiling water for 10 minutes, let cool, and clean it by removing the innards and only keeping the outside shell, using your chef's knife to separate the tip of the head from the body. Discard the body.

Drop all the lobster parts into the boiling water. Prepare an ice bath. After 4 minutes, transfer the tail to the ice bath using tongs; at 6 minutes, transfer the small claw; at 7 minutes, the knuckles; and at 8 minutes, the large claw. Leave in the ice bath for 10 minutes, then transfer the lobster body, tail, and claws to a tray. Take the lobster tail and turn it over with the shell side down. Using a pair of kitchen scissors, cut down the centre towards the end of the tail. Using your thumbs, fold the shell back, opening the incision you've just made. Extract the meat from the shell. With your knife, make a small cut on top of the tail to remove the intestine vein. Rinse under cold water. Reserve the tail tip for presentation. To remove the meat from the claws, crack them open carefully with your chef's knife, extract the meat, and discard the cartilages.

continued

Cocktail Sauce:

2 tablespoons (30 mL) Mayonnaise St. Lawrence (page 296)

½ tablespoon (7 mL) ketchup

¼ teaspoon (1 mL) Sriracha

¼ teaspoon (1 mL) cognac

Garnish:

Fresh chervil leaves

Remove the knuckle meat from the shells. (You can use a rolling pin to remove the meat from the legs, but that's optional.) Chop the knuckle meat into small chunks, place it in a small bowl, and mix in 1 teaspoon (5 mL) of the mayonnaise. Season with salt and pepper.

Cut off the top of each cherry tomato, and cut off a small horizontal slice from the bottom so it will stand upright on the plate. Using a paring knife, carefully remove the seeds and flesh of the tomato. Stuff the tomato with the lobster knuckle mixture and top with the chervil. When all the tomatoes are stuffed, place them on a plate and put them in the fridge.

Bring a medium pot of salted water to a boil on medium-high heat. Prepare an ice bath. Blanch the potato cubes for about 10 minutes, until they are cooked but still have a bite. Using a slotted spoon, transfer them to the ice bath to stop the cooking. Repeat with the carrot and turnip, blanching for about 7 minutes; the haricots verts, blanching for about 3 minutes; and the peas, blanching for no more than 1 minute. Once the vegetables have cooled, transfer them to a medium mixing bowl and mix in 3 to 4 tablespoons of the mayonnaise. Season with salt and pepper.

In a small pot of boiling water on medium-high heat, cook the eggs and quail eggs until hard-boiled: 9 minutes for the chicken eggs and 3 minutes for the quail eggs. Transfer the eggs to ice water to stop the cooking and carefully peel them under the water. Cut little slices from the bottom of each quail egg so it can stand upright, and arrange the eggs on a plate.

Slice off the top third of each chicken egg, remove the yolks, and place them in a small mixing bowl. (You can discard or eat the egg whites.) Add 1 tablespoon (15 mL) of the mayonnaise and the mustard. Mash the yolks with a fork and mix until creamy, then season with salt and pepper. Transfer the mixture to a small piping bag with a star tip and pipe it into the quail eggs. Place the quail eggs on a plate and put them in the fridge.

FOR THE COCKTAIL SAUCE: In a small bowl, mix together the mayonnaise, ketchup, Sriracha, and cognac.

TO ASSEMBLE: Time to plate the dish. Arrange the lobster head and tail tip at opposite outer edges of a large serving plate. In between the head and tail, put the vegetable mixture (the *salade Macédoine*) and spread it into an even layer. Slice the lobster tail into six pieces and arrange them on top of the salad. Put a few dollops of cocktail sauce on top of each tail slice. Place one claw on each side of the *Macédoine* and top with cocktail sauce. Arrange the stuffed tomatoes and devilled quail eggs around the lobster. Garnish with chervil leaves.

TIP *How many times have I seen people's shocked reactions when I put salt in the water for blanching vegetables, cooking potatoes or pasta, or, in this case, boiling lobsters. They look at me in a way that says salt is something that's going to kill them. But what they don't realize is that there's so much water in the pot, a pinch of salt won't make a difference. It doesn't have to be as salty as ocean water, but salt enhances flavour, and the water needs to be properly salted for that to happen. In my experience, 2% is the perfect amount—2 tablespoons (20 g) to 4 cups (1 L) of water is my formula for salted water. You can go as high as 3% for things like potatoes that need more salt to bring out their flavour. It may seem like a lot of salt to many people, but it makes all the difference.*

⚜

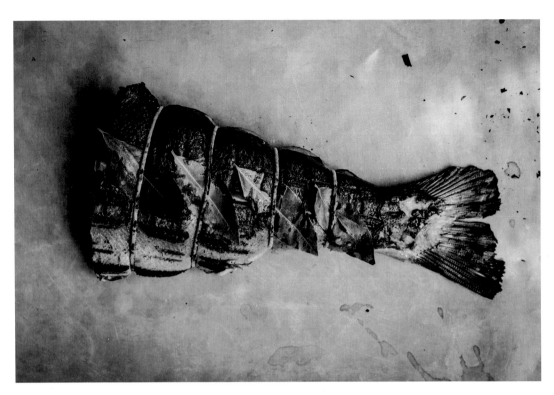

Queue de Saumon Grillé et Sauce à l'Oseille

Grilled Salmon Tail and Sorrel Sauce

Yield: 4 PORTIONS
Preparation time: 20 MINUTES
Cooking time: 30 MINUTES

This recipe was inspired by the iconic dish of the Troisgros brothers, saumon à l'oseille. Jean and Pierre Troisgros took over their parents' restaurant at L'Hôtel Moderne in Roanne, France, and opened La Maison Troisgros, standing the culinary world on its ear as revolutionary pioneers of nouvelle cuisine. Their tiny restaurant earned three Michelin stars in 1968 and was named the best restaurant in the world by Gault & Millau in 1968. Through four generations, the Troisgros family culinary tradition still flourishes today. You could certainly use a straight-up piece of salmon or salmon steak to make this seminal dish, but using the tail makes it special. Ask your fishmonger to cut one for you.

What you'll need:

3 to 4 pieces of butcher's twine, each 12 inches (30 cm) long, soaked in water for several hours

Salmon Tail:

1.5-pound (675 g) salmon tail piece

2 teaspoons (6 g) kosher salt

Freshly cracked black pepper

2 tablespoons (30 mL) grapeseed oil

Bay leaves (optional)

Sorrel Sauce:

3 tablespoons (45 g) unsalted butter

1 shallot, finely chopped

½ cup (125 mL) Noilly Prat vermouth, or dry white wine

2 cups (500 mL) heavy or whipping cream (35% milk fat)

2 cups (100 g) sorrel leaves (stems removed), roughly cut into large pieces

Kosher salt and freshly cracked black pepper, to taste

Juice of ½ lemon

FOR THE SALMON TAIL: Preheat the barbecue grill until one side is red hot, but leave the other side on low heat.

Using a pair of scissors, trim off about one-third of the tail so it doesn't burn on the grill. Starting from the back (dorsal fin) side of the salmon, use a filleting knife to lift the flesh away from the bones, just as if you were going to fillet the fish. But stop ½ inch (1 cm) before the backbone so that the fillet remains attached. Turn the fish over and repeat on the other side. Prepare the belly side of the fish the same way. This will release the four fillets while leaving them attached to the backbone and the tail. Finally, make a shallow incision straight down the middle, along the length of both sides of the salmon, to ensure that it cooks evenly.

Season the fish inside and out with the salt and pepper. Reshape the salmon tail, lay bay leaves along the length of the tail, and tie it (not too tightly) with the soaked butcher's twine in three or four evenly spaced places along the length of the fish. (It's important to soak the twine in water beforehand, or it will burn from the flames of the grill.)

Brush the fish all over and the barbecue grill with the grapeseed oil to prevent the fish from sticking. Place the fish on the grill, taking care to put the thickest part on the hottest spot. Cook for 8 to 10 minutes per side (depending on your desired doneness and the heat of your barbecue). Don't fuss with the tail too much while it's cooking as you don't want to damage it. The flesh should be just warm in the centre of the thickest part

continued

of the tail. Move the fish from the hot side to the low-heat side of the grill and get your sauce going.

FOR THE SORREL SAUCE: In a small saucepan on medium-high heat, melt the butter. Sauté the shallot for 2 minutes or until soft. Deglaze with the vermouth. Bring to a boil and reduce by half. Stir in the cream and reduce by one-third or until the sauce coats the back of a spoon. Remove from the heat, then add the sorrel and stir until wilted. You want to add it at the last minute as it oxidizes quickly and will lose its bright green colour if you stir it in too far in advance. Season with salt, pepper, and the lemon juice.

Place the salmon tail on a large plate and remove the string. Gently remove the skin. Run a knife (or even a fork) close to the bones and gently lift each fillet onto individual plates. The thicker part of the fish should be pink near the bone, while the rest of the tail will be a little more cooked. Spoon the sorrel sauce onto the plate and place the salmon fillet over it—be generous with the sauce. If you have leftover sauce, serve it in a warm sauce boat directly on the table.

⚜

Canard aux Pommettes
Duck with Crabapples

Yield: 2 TO 4 PORTIONS

Preparation time: 40 MINUTES + 24 HOURS DRYING

Cooking time: 40 MINUTES + 20 TO 30 MINUTES RESTING

✒ *Duck has always been a mainstay of French cuisine. It's high in fat, which can be rendered and used as a substitute for butter and oil. And duck can be prepared as confit, an ancient preservation method of cooking and storing duck meat in its own fat to last for months in a cool place. Confit is made across France, but the technique was introduced in Gascony, where they traditionally preserve the whole duck—not just the legs—and incorporate each part of the bird into different dishes. In a more refined way, roasting the breasts on the crown is a great technique, as you get a more uniform doneness and the breasts don't shrink when they hit the pan. Dishes pairing duck with fruits such as oranges, cherries, apples, and even olives are in the finest repertoire of French cuisine. I used crabapples for this recipe because they were in season; that said, I really love the classic pairing of* canard aux cerises, *so if you can find some sweet and juicy cherries, slide them into this dish instead of the crabapples. Just pit the cherries and sauté them in butter, then continue preparing the sauce according to the method. You'll end up with a wonderful cherry sauce to accompany the roast duck.*

What you'll need:

Cast-iron pan

1 young duck, such as Grade A Pekin duck

Kosher salt

6 sprigs thyme

6 whole crabapples

3 tablespoons (45 g) unsalted butter, divided

1 shallot, finely diced

2 tablespoons (30 mL) Grand Marnier or brandy

¼ cup (60 mL) red wine

½ cup (125 mL) duck demi-glace (reduced Duck Stock, page 311)

2 tablespoons (30 mL) red wine vinegar

1 small sprig rosemary

Freshly cracked black pepper, to taste

2 tablespoons (30 mL) honey

Butcher the duck by removing the legs and wings. Reserve these parts to make confit (page 47). Leave the breasts on the bone and, with a sharp paring knife, lightly score the skin. Place a wire rack on a baking sheet, place the duck crown on the rack, and refrigerate it, uncovered, for 24 hours to dry the skin. This step makes a huge difference, resulting in extra-crispy skin when it's cooked.

The next day, preheat your oven to 350°F (180°C), with the rack in the centre position.

Season the duck generously with salt. Heat a cast-iron pan on medium-high heat. (You won't need to add any fat to the pan, as the duck is full of it.) When the pan is hot, sear the duck crown, starting with one breast. Lower the heat to medium; you're looking to render the maximum amount of fat from the breast. After 4 to 5 minutes, when the skin is caramelized to a golden brown, flip the duck to the second breast and sear until golden brown. Using a spoon, baste the inside of the crown with the rendered duck fat. Discard the excess duck fat and transfer the duck crown to a baking sheet. Place the thyme sprigs around the duck and arrange the crabapples

continued

on top. Dab a small knob of butter on each crabapple, using 1 tablespoon (15 g) of the butter in total. Roast for 12 to 15 minutes, until a meat thermometer inserted in the thickest part of a breast registers 130°F (54°C). Transfer the duck back to the cast-iron pan to rest at room temperature for the next 20 to 30 minutes. Continue cooking the crabapples until they are cooked through but still holding their shape, about another 15 minutes.

Meanwhile, prepare the sauce. In a medium saucepan on medium-high heat, melt 1 tablespoon (15 g) of the butter. Add the shallot and cook until soft, about 2 minutes. Add the Grand Marnier, use a long match to light it, and flambé to cook off the alcohol. When the flames die down, stir in the wine and reduce until the pan is almost dry, then incorporate the duck demi-glace, vinegar, and rosemary. Bring to a simmer, then lower the heat to low and cook for 10 minutes. Remove from the heat, discard the rosemary, and whisk in the remaining butter. Season with salt and pepper.

Using a sharp knife, debone the two breasts (or you can present the duck whole to your guests before taking it back to the kitchen for carving). Season the flesh of the duck with salt. If the meat that was close to the bone is too pink for your liking, gently sear that side in a hot cast-iron pan with a little bit of butter for 1 minute. But you definitely want the breast to be a nice rosé colour and not overcooked. Carve the breast at a 45-degree angle into ¼-inch-thick (5 mm) slices and arrange them on a serving plate. Drizzle the crabapples with honey and arrange them around the duck. Sauce generously and serve your leftover sauce on the side in a warm sauce boat.

TIP *If you haven't already tried it, there's nothing like starting your day with eggs and potatoes cooked in duck fat. In that case, keep the rendered duck fat in a small container in the fridge for the next day. Breakfast of champions, to be certain.*

The French word for "flamed" or "flaming," flambé involves adding liquor to a hot pan or pouring it over a food and lighting it on fire. It burns off the harsh alcohol taste while keeping the subtle flavour notes.

⚜

Morue à la Dieppoise

Cod with Mussels and Shrimp in a White Wine Cream Sauce

Yield: 4 PORTIONS

Preparation time: 45 MINUTES + 30 MINUTES TEMPERING

Cooking time: 30 MINUTES

❦ Cod is my favourite fish to cook, and this speciality of France's Normandy region is named after the port city of Dieppe, where lots of cod is traded. I love the technique of combining poaching and baking. The poaching liquid of fumet, white wine, and mussel liquor is full of flavour and keeps getting better as you continue to cook the fish in it, basting as you go. If you want to practice your skills, turn some very fresh button mushrooms for the ultimate throwback touch; the technique is described below. It makes for a stunning presentation, and your guests will think you've studied at Le Cordon Bleu.

1.3 to 1.6-pound (600 to 700 g) skin-on cod fillet, deboned

2 teaspoons (6 g) kosher salt

3 tablespoons (45 g) unsalted butter, divided

5 ounces (150 g) button mushrooms, sliced

2 shallots, thinly sliced

1 pound (450 g) mussels, scrubbed and debearded

½ cup (125 mL) white wine

1 cup (250 mL) Fish Stock (page 312)

5 ounces (150 g) shrimp (such as side-striped), peeled and deveined

5 whole button mushrooms, for presentation (optional)

Juice of ½ lemon, for the mushrooms

3 tablespoons (30 g) all-purpose flour

½ cup (125 mL) Crème Fraîche (page 296, or store-bought)

1 egg yolk

Juice of ¼ lemon, for the sauce

Fresh *fines herbes* (such as tarragon leaves, chopped chives, and chervil leaves), to garnish

Maldon salt, to taste

Season the flesh side of the fish with the salt. Let rest at room temperature for 30 minutes.

Meanwhile, preheat your oven to 300°F (150°C), with the rack in the centre position.

In a large pot on medium-high heat, heat 1 tablespoon (15 g) of the butter until foamy. Stir in the sliced mushrooms and shallots. Lower the heat to medium and gently cook, stirring once in a while, for 5 minutes. Add the mussels, wine, and fish stock, cover tightly, and increase the heat to medium-high. Shake the pot every minute or so until all the mussels have opened, 3 to 5 minutes. Discard any mussels that haven't opened by the 5-minute mark.

Transfer the mussels to a large bowl, remove the meat from the shells, and set aside. Strain the cooking liquor though a tamis into a medium saucepan. Press gently on the mushrooms and shallots with the back of a spoon to extract as much liquid as possible. Discard the mushrooms and shallots. On medium heat, bring the mussel liquor to a gentle simmer, then add the shrimp and poach for 30 seconds. Remove the shrimp from the liquor and reserve with the mussels.

Transfer the hot mussel liquor into an ovenproof pan large enough to fit the cod. Lay the cod in the pan, skin side up. Bake for 10 to 15 minutes, basting the fish with the liquid every 2 to 3 minutes, until you can easily pull the skin from the flesh of the fish and the fish is just warm in the centre when tested with the tip of a paring knife. Let rest in the pan on top of the stove.

continued

Meanwhile, if you're feeling up to a challenge, let's turn those five mushrooms for presentation. "Turning" a mushroom means cutting out strips from the cap in an elegant spiral pattern. I'll be honest, it is a difficult technique to master and may cause you a lot of frustration while you're learning how to do it. Hold the blade of a sharp paring knife loosely in your fingers on a bias, cutting edge out. Place your thumb behind the blade, on top of the mushroom cap. Using your thumb as a pivot, push the blade forward and down, carving strips out of the cap. The rotation should be smooth and regular. If the centre is not perfect, make a star by pushing the point of the knife into the cap. As you finish each mushroom, transfer it to a small bowl of water with the juice of half a lemon to prevent oxidation. Once you've finished all the mushrooms, cook them in boiling salted water for about 2 minutes, then, using a slotted spoon, transfer them to a bowl and set aside.

In a small bowl, using your fingers, incorporate the flour into the remaining butter to make a smooth paste. This is called *beurre manié*.

Transfer the fish to a plate and set aside. On medium heat, bring it back to a simmer. While whisking constantly, add half the *beurre manié*. The sauce will start to thicken within 30 seconds. You want to end up with a smooth sauce that coats the back of a spoon. If it isn't thick enough, whisk in more *beurre manié*, a little at a time, until it's the right consistency. Remove from the heat.

In a small bowl, mix together the crème fraîche and the egg yolk. Gently whisk the crème fraîche mixture into the sauce. (At this point, you don't want to boil the sauce again, or it will split.) Taste and add salt as needed, and add lemon juice for acidity.

Add the cod fillet to the sauce and, on low heat, reheat the fish, gently basting it. Place the mussels, shrimp, and turned mushrooms around the edges of the pan to warm them up and finish cooking the shrimp (they should be pink, firm, and opaque). Be careful not to increase the heat from low; otherwise, you'll split the sauce and overcook everything. With a large spoon, baste the fish, mussels, shrimps, and mushrooms with the sauce.

Transfer the cod to the centre of a large platter (or cut it into four portions and plate each one separately). Arrange the turned mushrooms on top of the fish, and the mussels and shrimp around it. Pour the sauce generously over everything, garnish with the *fines herbes*, and sprinkle the fish with Maldon salt.

VARIATION *If you have any spare puff pastry in the fridge or freezer, why not garnish the dish with some* fleurons *(see tip, page 301)?*

TIP *Translated as "kneaded butter,"* beurre manié *is a mixture of equal amounts in weight of flour and softened butter. This paste is whisked into hot sauces, soups, and stews as a thickening agent. It's particularly effective for creating smooth sauces because it gradually releases the flour as the butter melts, thus preventing lumps from forming.*

⚜

Blanquette de Veau

White Veal Stew

Yield: 6 PORTIONS

Preparation time: 45 MINUTES + 24 HOURS MARINATING

Cooking time: 2½ HOURS

➳ Blanquette de veau *is a ragoût in which the veal hasn't been browned during the cooking process. It was traditionally prepared with meat from a very fatty part of the belly that was kept on the bone, but today it's usually cooked with leaner cuts of meat and without the bone. My version falls between the good old days and modern methods. I like to use veal shank— call it osso buco if you prefer. Meat from the shank is extremely tender and gelatinous, and the bones give more flavour to the sauce. Serving the marrow along with it is a huge bonus. In my opinion, all the ingredients in a* blanquette, *including all the vegetables, should be white: the veal, the pearl onions, the mushrooms, the wine, and the crème fraîche. The carrots used for braising that are often included when serving should not be part of the finished dish.*

Blanquette de veau *is often served with a simple rice pilaf, egg noodles, or potatoes. To soak up all the luscious bone marrow, make sure you serve some grilled slices of sourdough bread rubbed with a clove of garlic.*

Braise:

3 pounds (1.4 kg) veal shank (osso buco), about 4 to 5 large pieces

1 tablespoon (10 g) kosher salt

½ cup (125 mL) dry white wine

8 cups (2 L) Chicken Stock (page 308, or store-bought) or water (approx.)

1 medium carrot, peeled

1 small onion, peeled and studded with two whole cloves

1 leek (white part only), left whole

Bouquet garni of leek greens, thyme, parsley stems, bay leaves, and 1 celery stalk (see tip, page 47)

24 pearl onions, peeled

16 small button mushrooms

Fresh curly parsley leaves, to garnish

FOR THE BRAISE: Cut the veal into 1-inch (2.5 cm) cubes and reserve the marrow bones in the fridge in a bowl of cold water. Season the meat with the salt and place it in a medium bowl. Pour the wine over the meat, stir to coat, cover tightly, and refrigerate for 24 hours.

The next day, preheat your oven to 325°F (160°C), with the rack in the centre position.

Place the meat with the marinade in a large, heavy ovenproof pot or Dutch oven, cover it with the stock, and bring to a gentle simmer on medium heat. Skim any impurities from the surface. After 30 minutes, add the carrot, studded onion, leek, and bouquet garni. Cover with a lid, transfer to the oven, and braise for 1 hour. Add the marrow bones and braise for another 30 minutes or until the meat is fork-tender. Remove the pot from the oven.

Carefully decant 2 cups (500 mL) of the braising liquid into a medium saucepan. Add the pearl onions, cover, and cook on medium-low heat until fork-tender. Add the mushrooms and cook for 10 minutes. Drain the liquid back into the pot with the meat. Transfer the pearl onions and mushrooms to a baking tray.

continued

Sauce:

3 tablespoons (45 g) unsalted butter

3 tablespoons (30 g) all-purpose flour

1½ cups (375 mL) reduced braising liquid

1½ cups (375 mL) heavy or whipping cream (35% milk fat)

3 egg yolks

2 tablespoons (30 mL) Crème Fraîche (page 296, or store-bought)

1 teaspoon (4 g) kosher salt

Freshly ground white pepper, to taste

⅛ teaspoon (0.5 mL) freshly grated nutmeg

Juice of ½ lemon

Using a slotted spoon, transfer the meat and bones to the baking tray with the onions and mushrooms, and cover with foil to keep everything warm while you're finishing the sauce. Discard the vegetables and bouquet garni.

FOR THE SAUCE: Strain the braising liquid through a chinois (see tip) or tamis (page 20) and reduce down to 1½ cups (375 mL). Set aside in a small bowl. In the same pot on medium heat, melt the butter, then whisk in the flour to make a smooth roux. Continue cooking for 3 minutes, whisking constantly, until the roux becomes frothy. While still whisking, slowly pour the braising liquid back into the pot and stir until fully incorporated. Bring to a gentle simmer, whisk in the cream, and return the sauce to a gentle simmer for 5 minutes. Remove from the heat.

In a medium bowl, whisk together the egg yolks, crème fraîche, salt, pepper, and nutmeg. Stir this mixture into the sauce. Taste and adjust the seasoning with salt and pepper. Squeeze the lemon juice directly into the sauce to cut the richness.

Transfer the meat, vegetables, and bone marrow to a large cocotte. Pour any juices from the tray into the sauce and stir to incorporate. Pour the sauce over the meat. Garnish with the parsley and present the cocotte to your guests.

⚜

TIP *A chinois is a cone-shaped strainer made with super-fine metal mesh. It's traditionally used for straining stocks, sauces, and soups that need to be very smooth.*

RICE PILAF

Yield: 4 PORTIONS
Preparation time: 15 MINUTES
Cooking time: 25 MINUTES

1 cup (250 mL) white basmati rice

2 tablespoons (30 g) unsalted butter

2 cloves garlic, finely chopped

1 stalk celery, finely chopped

1 small yellow onion, finely chopped

⅓ cup (75 mL) white wine

1¼ cups (300 mL) Chicken Stock (page 308, or store-bought) or water

1 teaspoon (4 g) kosher salt

1 fresh bay leaf

Preheat your oven to 350°F (180°C), with the rack in the centre position.

Rinse the rice well under cold water and drain.

In a medium ovenproof pot on medium-high heat, heat the butter until foamy. Lower the heat to medium and sweat the garlic, celery, and onion, stirring occasionally, until tender, about 10 minutes. Add the rice, stirring to combine thoroughly. Stir in the wine and simmer until reduced by half. Stir in the stock, salt, and bay leaf, cover with a tight lid, and return to a simmer.

Transfer the pan to the oven and cook for 15 to 18 minutes or until the rice is tender and all of the liquid is absorbed. Take the pot out of the oven, and let rest, covered, for 10 minutes. Discard the bay leaf before serving.

⚜

Lapin à la Moutarde

Braised Rabbit with Mustard Sauce

Yield: 4 PORTIONS

Preparation time: 25 MINUTES + 24 HOURS CURING

Cooking time: 1½ TO 2 HOURS

1 whole rabbit (about 3.3 pounds/ 1.5 kg), cut into 8 pieces, or 4 rabbit legs

1 tablespoon (10 g) kosher salt

⅓ cup (100 g) Dijon mustard

1 tablespoon (15 mL) grapeseed oil

⅓ cup (75 g) unsalted butter

4 small shallots, peeled and halved

4 cloves garlic, crushed

4 tablespoons (40 g) all-purpose flour

½ cup (125 mL) dry white wine

1 tablespoon (15 mL) grainy Dijon mustard

3 bay leaves

2 sprigs thyme

1¾ cups (425 mL) Chicken Stock (page 308, or store-bought) or water

1 cup (250 mL) Crème Fraîche (page 296, or store-bought) or high-fat sour cream

1 tablespoon (15 mL) roughly chopped fresh tarragon

1 tablespoon (15 mL) finely minced fresh chives

Juice of ½ lemon

Maldon salt and freshly cracked black pepper, to finish

⋙ *A few years ago, chef Joël Watanabe of Kissa Tanto and I cooked together at a collaboration dinner event promoting the opening of St. Lawrence. Classic French was the dinner theme, and Joël prepared a rabbit with mustard sauce that he'd learned from his dad. His version was almost a* lapin à la crème, *judging by the amount of crème fraîche in the dish, and it was absolutely delicious. My version of the dish is inspired by Joël's father's recipe. Pomme Purée (page 195) and spinach lightly cooked in butter are perfect accompaniments. Roasted carrots or a simple green salad are also lovely sides—basically, everything rabbits love to eat! And don't forget to have bread on the table to soak up all the extra sauce.*

Season the rabbit with the kosher salt on all sides. Using your hands, generously spread the Dijon mustard on the rabbit and massage it to make sure all the pieces are well coated. Place the rabbit on a baking sheet, cover with plastic wrap, and refrigerate for 24 hours.

The next day, preheat your oven to 425°F (220°C), with the rack in the centre position.

Brush a baking sheet with the oil and lay out the pieces of rabbit on it. Bake for 15 to 20 minutes to caramelize the outside of the rabbit. Remove from the oven and set aside. Lower the oven temperature to 325°F (160°C).

In a large braising pan on medium heat, melt the butter until foamy. Add the shallots and garlic and cook gently, stirring often, until light golden. Add the flour, stirring to coat the shallots and garlic. Deglaze the pan with the wine, stirring with a wooden spoon to make sure the liquid is thick and without lumps of flour. Then add the stock and bring to a simmer. Add the rabbit, grainy Dijon mustard, bay leaves, and thyme. Cover the pan and transfer it to the oven. Braise the rabbit for 75 to 90 minutes or until the meat is almost fall-off-the-bone tender.

Take the pan out of the oven and check the consistency of the sauce: it should be thick enough to coat the back of a wooden spoon. If it's too thin, reduce it gently on medium heat for 8 to 10 minutes. It's okay to keep the rabbit in the sauce as long as the reduction is done at a gentle simmer. Discard the bay leaves.

continued

Place the crème fraîche in a small mixing bowl and slowly whisk in some of the braising liquid. (This process is called tempering and heats up the crème fraîche slowly, so it doesn't split.) Pour the warmed crème fraîche into the pan and stir gently until it's incorporated into the sauce—be careful not to break down the rabbit while you're stirring. Remove from the heat and stir in the tarragon, chives, and lemon juice. Once you've added the lemon juice, don't heat up the sauce any further or it will split. The lemon juice is there to brighten the dish and add some depth while lifting the flavours; without it, the rabbit would be very rich.

Serve one or two pieces of rabbit per person with a generous amount of sauce, finishing the rabbit with a sprinkling of Maldon salt and pepper.

⚜

Navarin Printanier d'Agneau

Lamb Stew with Spring Vegetables

Yield: 4 PORTIONS
Preparation time: 45 MINUTES
Cooking time: 2 TO 2½ HOURS

This comforting lamb dish celebrates the fresh vegetables available at the start of the growing season. Printanier *means spring, while* navarin *refers to the stew's traditional inclusion of turnips, or* navets *in French. This is a welcome break from the heavier stews served in wintertime—it's light and colourful with the baby spring vegetables.*

1.6 pounds (700 g) boneless lamb shoulder, cut into 1-inch (2.5 cm) cubes

2 teaspoons (6 g) kosher salt

3 tablespoons (45 mL) grapeseed oil

1 tablespoon (15 g) unsalted butter

1 large onion, cut into large chunks

1 large carrot, peeled and cut into large chunks

1 tablespoon (15 mL) tomato paste

3 cloves garlic, crushed

3 tablespoons (30 g) all-purpose flour

1 cup (250 mL) white wine

3 cups (750 mL) Chicken Stock (page 308, or store-bought) or water

Bouquet garni of thyme, rosemary, and bay leaf (page 47)

Freshly cracked black pepper

Spring Garnish:

8 small potatoes (9 ounces/250 g)

8 baby carrots (9 ounces/250 g)

8 baby turnips (9 ounces/250 g)

⅔ cup (100 g) fresh fava beans

⅔ cup (100 g) fresh peas

3 tablespoons (45 mL) water (approx.)

3 tablespoons (45 g) unsalted butter

Kosher salt and freshly cracked black pepper, to taste

Fresh flat-leaf parsley leaves, to garnish

Preheat your oven to 325°F (160°C), with the rack in the centre position. Season the lamb with the salt. In a large stovetop-safe casserole pan on high heat, heat the oil. Brown the meat until evenly coloured on all sides.

Lower the heat to medium, and add the butter, onion, and carrot. Sweat the vegetables along with the meat for 7 minutes, stirring often. Add the tomato paste and garlic. Sprinkle the flour over the meat and vegetables, stir until well-coated, and cook for 2 minutes. Stir in the wine, chicken stock, and bouquet garni. Season with pepper. Bring to a simmer, cover, and cook in the oven for 1½ hours or until the tip of a paring knife slides into the meat without resistance (if not, return to the oven for 30 minutes).

Transfer the meat to a plate and strain the sauce through a chinois (see note, page 102) into a bowl. Discard the vegetables. Return the sauce to the pan and reduce the sauce by half on medium-high heat. Return the meat to the pan and spoon the strained, reduced sauce over it. Set aside, covered, on the stove.

FOR THE SPRING GARNISH: Bring a large pot of salted water to a boil. Cook the vegetables separately until they are tender but retain a little resistance in the middle. Start with the potatoes, then the carrots, turnips, favas, and peas. Meanwhile, prepare an ice bath. Using a slotted spoon, transfer the vegetables to the ice bath to stop the cooking.

In a large saucepan on medium heat, heat the water and butter. When the butter has melted, add the vegetables and glaze gently until heated through. If the glazing liquid splits and becomes greasy, add a few more tablespoons of water.

Place the lamb on a large serving plate and cover with the sauce. Arrange the vegetables around and on top of the meat. Garnish with the parsley just before you bring it to the table.

Pot-au-Feu

Braised Beef with Stewed Vegetables

Yield: 6 PORTIONS

Preparation time: 30 MINUTES +
24 HOURS CURING

Cooking time: 2½ HOURS

❧ *Though beef shin is cut from one of a cow's harder-working muscles, the trick to its magical transformation is a long, slow braise. The high collagen content of its connective tissues melts into gelatin over time, making the meat moist and tender as it cooks and adding richness to your stew. When buying deboned beef shin, ask your butcher to cut the shin bones in half and give them to you. They're a wonderful addition to the broth that imparts loads of flavour.*

3.3-pound (1.5 kg) beef shin, deboned, rolled, and tied

1 tablespoon + 1 teaspoon (15 g) kosher salt

Freshly cracked black pepper

Beef marrow bones from the shin

Bouquet garni of leek greens, bay leaf, thyme, and parsley (see tip, page 47)

9-ounce (250 g) piece salted pork belly or pancetta

2 medium onions, peeled and studded with 2 whole cloves each

8 medium carrots, peeled and cut into chunks

8 small potatoes

4 cloves garlic, peeled

2 small leeks (white and light green parts only), cut into chunks

2 stalks celery, cut into chunks

2 medium turnips, cut into wedges

1 small rutabaga, cut into chunks

½ head savoy cabbage (or 1 small head), cut into wedges

4 pieces bone marrow

Fresh flat-leaf parsley leaves, to garnish

Cornichons, Dijon mustard, and Maldon salt, for serving

Place the beef shin on a baking sheet. Season it with the kosher salt and season generously with pepper. Place the marrow bones in a large bowl and cover with cold water. Refrigerate both, covered, for 24 hours.

The next day, place the meat and marrow bones in a large, deep pot. Add the bouquet garni, pork belly, and studded onions. Cover with cold water and bring to a gentle simmer on high heat, skimming the surface occasionally to remove any scum or impurities. Partially cover, leaving the lid ajar, lower the heat to low, and simmer for 1¼ hours. Add the carrots, potatoes, garlic, leeks, celery, turnips, rutabaga, and cabbage, and add more water if needed. Simmer gently, partially covered, for 45 minutes. Add the bone marrow and simmer gently, partially covered, for 30 minutes or until all ingredients are tender when pierced with a skewer or the tip of a paring knife.

Taste the broth and season generously with salt, just as you would season a soup.

Carefully remove the beef shin from the pot and transfer to a tray to cool for 30 minutes. When cool enough to handle, snip the butcher's twine with a pair of kitchen scissors and discard. Using a sharp knife, slice the meat into 6 portions and transfer it, along with the marrow bones and all the vegetables, to a large serving plate with some broth or directly into individual bowls. Make sure that everyone has one of everything. Garnish with the parsley and serve with cornichons, mustard, and flaked salt.

✤

Poulet à la Crème

Braised Chicken in Cream Sauce

Yield: 4 TO 6 PORTIONS

Preparation time: 30 MINUTES +
24 HOURS CURING + 1 HOUR
TEMPERING

Cooking time: 45 MINUTES

➤ Poulet à la crème *is shockingly easy to make, and its extreme richness makes it very comforting, especially when the weather is cold. It definitely ranks among chefs as a favourite home-cooking recipe. One of my mentors, Rob Feenie, absolutely loves it; every time we see each other, we have some sort of discussion about this iconic dish, whether it's about the time he first had it in France, the fact that he could eat it every day for the rest of his life, or versions of the recipe from some of the best French chefs in the world. When it comes to making* poulet à la crème, *Rob and I agree it should be rustic and simple, and the chicken should be cooked on the bone. You can add wild mushrooms to the sauce if you wish, as Georges Blanc does, or opt to keep it simple. Serve with Crêpes Vonnassiennes "Mère Blanc" (recipe follows) and a leafy green salad with a classic vinaigrette.*

4.5-pound (2 kg) whole chicken

2 tablespoons (20 g) kosher salt
(see tip)

Freshly cracked black pepper

½ cup (115 g) unsalted butter,
divided

1 medium onion, peeled and cut into
4 wedges

4 tablespoons (40 g) all-purpose
flour

½ cup (125 mL) white wine (use one
you like to drink)

1⅔ cups (400 mL) Chicken Stock
(page 308, or store-bought) or water

Bouquet garni of bay leaf, thyme,
and parsley stems (see tip, page 47)

½ cup (125 mL) Crème Fraîche
(page 296, or store-bought)

2 egg yolks

Pinch freshly grated nutmeg

TIP *When salting chicken, the perfect amount of salt is 1% of the bird's weight in grams. So, for a 4.5-pound (2 kg) bird, I use 2 tablespoons (20 g) of kosher salt.*

Cut the chicken into 8 pieces. (If you don't know how to do this, ask your butcher to perform the task.) Make sure you're aware of the weight of the bird, so you can figure out the perfect amount of salt. Place the chicken pieces on a baking sheet and generously season on all sides with salt and pepper. Place the chicken in the fridge uncovered to dry the skin, and let it cure for 24 hours.

Take the chicken out of the fridge 1 hour before cooking and let stand at room temperature.

In a large braising pan on medium-high heat, melt half the butter. Add the chicken pieces, skin side down, and lightly brown them. (You might have to do this in two batches so you don't overcrowd the pan.) Transfer the chicken pieces to a plate.

Add the onion to the pan, along with the remaining butter. Lower the heat to medium and cook gently for 3 minutes, stirring occasionally, until the onion starts to take on some colour, making sure the butter doesn't burn. Add the chicken pieces back in. Sprinkle the flour evenly over the onion and chicken. Add the wine, stirring gently, and simmer until the sauce thickens. Add the stock and bouquet garni, stirring well. Lower the heat

continued

to low, cover, and simmer gently for 15 minutes or until a meat thermometer inserted in the thickest part of a breast registers 155°F (68°C). Using tongs, transfer the chicken breasts to a plate.

Continue cooking the legs and thighs, covered, for 15 to 20 minutes or until a meat thermometer inserted in the thickest part of a leg registers 155°F (68°C). Using tongs, transfer the legs and thighs to the plate with the breasts. Discard the bouquet garni and onions (although personally, I like to keep the onions, as they're delicious). Check the consistency of the sauce. It should lightly coat the back of a spoon; if it's too thin, reduce the liquid further.

In a medium bowl, mix the crème fraîche with the egg yolks and season with nutmeg. While whisking constantly, gradually add a ladleful of the hot sauce to the crème fraîche mixture to temper it. Whisk the tempered crème fraîche mixture into the sauce. You should have a beautiful light sauce. Return all the chicken pieces and any accumulated juices to the sauce, gently stirring to incorporate. Taste for seasoning and spoon into a large dish.

CRÊPES VONNASSIENNES "MÈRE BLANC"

Potato Pancakes

Yield: ABOUT 12 SMALL PANCAKES

Preparation time: 20 MINUTES

Cooking time: 45 MINUTES

9 ounces (250 g) russet potatoes, peeled and cut in quarters

3 tablespoons (30 g) all-purpose flour

1 egg

2 egg whites

⅓ cup (90 mL) heavy or whipping cream (35% milk fat)

½ teaspoon (3 g) kosher salt

¾ cup (175 mL) Beurre Clarifié (see tip, page 125)

In a medium pot, add the potatoes, cover with cold water, season with salt, and bring to a boil. Lower the heat and simmer until tender. Purée the potatoes with a ricer and let cool in a bowl for 10 minutes to let the steam escape.

Using a wooden spatula, work the flour into the potatoes, then gradually mix in the whole egg, then the egg whites, gently, without whipping them. Stir in the cream and salt, being careful not to overwork the batter. The batter should be smooth and creamy. If it's lumpy, pass it through a tamis.

In a large non-stick frying pan on high heat, heat one-quarter of the clarified butter. Ladle in three 4-inch (10 cm) rounds of batter, or whatever fits nicely in the pan. Be careful—the pancakes cook quickly, so be ready with an offset spatula to flip them and then transfer them to a serving dish. Repeat with the remaining batter, adding more *beurre clarifié* between each batch.

TIP *You can make the batter ahead of time if you wish; that way, the cooking process will be less stressful come dinnertime.*

✢

Coq au Vin

Chicken in Red Wine Sauce

Yield: 4 PORTIONS

Preparation time: 1 HOUR + 24 HOURS MARINATING

Cooking time: 1 HOUR

4.5-pound (2 kg) whole chicken, cut into 8 pieces

2 tablespoons (20 g) + 1 teaspoon (4 g) kosher salt, divided

Freshly cracked black pepper

1 cup (250 mL) strong red wine (such as Côtes du Rhône)

1 cup (250 mL) water

Bouquet garni of parsley, thyme, and bay leaf (see tip, page 47)

6 cloves garlic, crushed

1 large onion, cut into wedges

1 large carrot, peeled and cut into thick slices

5 tablespoons (50 g) all-purpose flour

⅓ cup (75 mL) grapeseed oil

3 tablespoons (45 mL) brandy or cognac

2 cups (500 mL) Chicken Stock (page 308, or store-bought) or water

18 pearl onions, peeled

⅓ cup (75 g) unsalted butter, divided

1½ cups (250 g) button mushrooms, halved

7 ounces (200 g) smoked bacon, cut into large lardons

2 slices white bread, cut into triangles and crusts removed

Kosher salt and freshly cracked black pepper, to taste

Juice of ½ lemon

2 tablespoons (30 mL) finely chopped fresh flat-leaf parsley, for garnish

The precise origins of coq au vin *are unknown because people have been braising chicken in wine since ancient times. Various legends trace it as far back as the days of Julius Caesar. But it's widely known that the dish was used to tenderize tough, sinewy rooster—hence the name "rooster in wine"— by marinating the meat and then braising it low and slow for a long time. The traditional version calls for a robust red wine from Burgundy, but that would put the dish on the reasonably spendy side. In my opinion, a cheap and cheerful full-bodied red table wine will do just fine. Boiled potatoes, fresh egg noodles, or Rice Pilaf (page 102) are the perfect comfort food accompaniments for this dish. When they're in season, substitute morels or chanterelles for the button mushrooms; they add a wonderful earthiness.*

THE NIGHT BEFORE   Season the chicken pieces with 2 tablespoons (20 g) of the salt and a generous amount of pepper. Set aside in a large bowl and put in the fridge.

In a medium pot, bring the wine to a boil on medium-high heat. Lower the heat and let it simmer for 2 minutes to remove the harsh alcohol taste, then remove it from the heat to cool completely (if you wish, cool it faster in a medium bowl on ice).

Add the cooled wine to the chicken, along with the water, bouquet garni, garlic, onion, and carrot. Mix to combine, cover, and let marinate in the refrigerator for 24 hours.

THE DAY OF   Remove the bowl from the fridge and strain the marinade through a chinois (page 102) into a separate bowl, reserving the bouquet garni and vegetables. Pat the chicken dry with a paper towel.

In a large shallow bowl, mix the flour with the remaining 1 teaspoon (4 g) of the salt. Roll the chicken pieces in the flour until thoroughly coated.

In a large sauté pan on medium-high heat, heat the oil. Sear the chicken pieces, skin side down, for about 5 minutes or until the skin is a nice golden brown. (You might have to do this in two batches so you don't overcrowd the pan.) Transfer the chicken pieces to a plate.

continued

Lower the heat to medium and add the garlic, onion wedges, and carrot to the pan. Cook until soft, about 5 minutes. Add the brandy, use a long match to light it, and flambé to cook off the alcohol. When the flames die down, return the chicken and any accumulated juices to the pan, along with the marinade, bouquet garni, and chicken stock. Bring to a simmer. Cover with a lid, lower the heat, and simmer gently for 15 minutes, or until a meat thermometer inserted in the thickest part of a breast registers 155°F (68°C). Using tongs, transfer the breast pieces to a plate. Reserve.

Continue cooking the legs and thighs gently, uncovered, for 15 minutes until the juices of the chicken run clear when pierced with a knife, or a meat thermometer inserted in the thickest part of a leg registers 155°F (68°C).

Meanwhile, place the pearl onions in a small sauté pan with one-third (25 g) of the butter and pour in enough water to cover the onions. Bring to a boil on medium heat and boil until the water has evaporated and the onions look glazed and shiny. Season with a small pinch of salt, remove from the heat, and set aside.

In a medium sauté pan on medium-high heat, heat the remaining butter until foamy. Fry the mushrooms until golden brown, 5 to 6 minutes, and season with salt. Using a slotted spoon, transfer the mushrooms to a bowl.

Wipe the pan clean and fry the bacon lardons on medium-high heat until golden brown.

When the chicken legs and thighs are cooked, add them to the plate with the breasts. Strain the braising liquid through a tamis into a large pot, discarding the solids, and reduce on medium heat until the sauce coats the back of a wooden spoon. Add the pearl onions, mushrooms, and lardons and gently reheat them.

Meanwhile, set your oven to broil and toast the bread under the broiler.

Return all the chicken and any accumulated juices to the sauce and gently return to a simmer to reheat them. Taste for seasoning and stir in the lemon juice.

Transfer the *coq au vin* to a serving dish, sprinkle with the parsley, and garnish with the toast triangles.

VARIATION *You can use a dry Riesling instead of red wine to make* coq au Riesling—*an excellent substitution that gives you a lighter dish, more suitable for warmer days. Since Riesling is a lighter wine, you won't have to boil it, and you can go for a full 2 cups (500 mL) in the marinade.*

⚜

Cailles Confites aux Choux

Quail Confit with Cabbage

Yield: 6 PORTIONS

Preparation time: 30 MINUTES +
24 HOURS CURING

Cooking time: 2 HOURS

Quails:

6 whole jumbo quails

Kosher salt (see tip)

6 juniper berries

6 bay leaves

6 sprigs thyme

Freshly cracked black pepper

3.3 pounds (1.5 kg) duck fat

Cabbage:

1 small head savoy cabbage

⅓ cup (75 g) unsalted butter, divided

5 ounces (150 g) smoked bacon, cut
into large lardons

3 cloves garlic, roughly chopped

2 carrots, peeled and cut into batons
2 inches (5 cm) long and ¼ inch
(5 mm) wide and thick

1 large shallot, sliced

1 teaspoon (3 g) kosher salt

1 cup (250 mL) Chicken Stock
(page 308, or store-bought)

Freshly cracked black pepper

Sauce:

¾ cup (175 mL) chicken jus
(reduced Chicken Stock, page 308)

1 tablespoon (15 g) unsalted butter

≫ *The confit technique was invented to preserve ingredients for a long period of time. It was common to confit whole birds, not just the legs. Confit of whole quails in duck fat with lots of thyme and bay leaves is an easy and very satisfying preparation—your kitchen will smell divine. The trick is to cook them very gently, as you don't want the duck fat to boil at all. Keep it below simmering so the breasts don't become dry. The cabbage, bacon, and carrots will complement this rustic dish perfectly.*

TIP *The perfect amount of salt is 1% of the combined weight of the quails in grams.*

FOR THE QUAILS: Rinse the quails inside and out under cold running water. Use paper towels to pat them dry. Weigh the birds to determine the amount of salt you'll need (see tip), then season them both outside and inside the cavity. Place a wire rack atop a baking sheet, transfer the salted quails to the rack, and cure in the fridge for 24 hours.

The next day, preheat your oven to 300°F (150°C), with the rack in the centre position.

In a mortar and pestle, or with the bottom of a pot, crush the juniper berries. Season the inside of each quail with the crushed juniper berries, then add 1 bay leaf, 1 sprig thyme, and pepper to the cavity of each bird.

In a large ovenproof pot on medium-high heat, melt the duck fat until it's warm to the touch. Place the quails in the pot, close to each other and standing cavity side up. Heat the fat to 185°F (85°C). Cover the pot with a lid or foil and transfer the pot to the oven. Roast for 1½ hours or until you feel no resistance when you pull the legs gently away from the body of a quail without detaching them. Uncover and let cool at room temperature for 30 minutes. Using a slotted spoon, carefully transfer the quails to a baking sheet.

FOR THE CABBAGE: While the quails are cooling, bring a large pot of salted water to a boil on high heat. Remove and discard the outer leaves from the cabbage. Cut the cabbage into ½-inch (1 cm) strips. Add the cabbage to the boiling water and blanch for 1 minute. Drain and transfer to an ice bath to stop the cooking; once cool, squeeze out the excess water and reserve.

continued

In a medium pot on medium-high heat, melt half the butter. Sauté the bacon lardons, garlic, carrots, and shallot for 4 minutes, stirring often. Add the cabbage and cook, stirring occasionally, for 4 minutes. Season with the salt and pour in the stock. Cover, lower the heat to medium-low, and cook for 12 minutes. Uncover and cook for 3 to 4 minutes or until no liquid remains. Remove from the heat, stir in the remaining butter, and season with pepper. Taste for seasoning.

Set the oven to broil, maintaining the rack at the centre position. Broil the quail for 3 to 4 minutes or until the skin is caramelized.

FOR THE SAUCE: Meanwhile, in a small saucepan on medium-high heat, bring the chicken jus to a simmer, then whisk in the butter.

On a serving platter, arrange the quail on top of the cabbage and spoon some sauce around it to finish.

Poisson en Croûte de Sel

Fish Baked in a Salt Crust

Yield: 4 PORTIONS
Preparation time: 45 MINUTES
Cooking time: 30 MINUTES

🌿 *Baking fish in a salt crust creates a seal that locks in the juices and gives you moist, tender fish that isn't overly salty at all. As a bonus, there's the wow factor of presenting the whole baked fish and cracking into the crust in front of your guests at the dinner table—a definite showstopper.*

Sauce Vierge:

3 whole tomatoes

2 cloves garlic, crushed

1 small shallot, finely chopped

12 coriander seeds, crushed

1 cup (250 mL) olive oil

2 tablespoons (30 mL) fresh flat-leaf parsley, chopped

2 tablespoons (30 mL) fresh basil, chopped

1 tablespoon (30 mL) fresh tarragon, chopped

Grated zest and juice of 1 lemon

Kosher salt and freshly cracked black pepper, to taste

Fish:

4.5-pound (2 kg) whole fish (such as sea bass, branzino, snapper, or salmon), scaled, gutted, and fins and gills removed (ask your fishmonger to prepare it for you)

1 lemon, sliced into ¼-inch (5 mm) thick rounds

½ bunch dill

2 tablespoons (30 mL) olive oil

4.5 pounds (2 kg) coarse salt

½ cup (70 g) all-purpose flour

2 tablespoons (30 mL) fennel seeds

2 sprigs thyme, leaves stripped and chopped

2 sprigs rosemary, leaves stripped and chopped

4 egg whites

FOR THE SAUCE VIERGE: Bring a medium saucepan of water to a boil on medium-high heat. Prepare an ice bath.

Using a paring knife, remove the stalks from the tomatoes and make a small cross-shaped incision at the bottom. (This makes them easier to peel.) Plunge the tomatoes into the boiling water for 20 seconds, then immediately transfer to the ice bath to stop the cooking. Using a paring knife, peel the skin off the tomatoes. Cut them in half, squeeze out all the excess seeds and moisture, then dice them into ¼-inch (5 mm) cubes.

In a small saucepan, combine the diced tomatoes, garlic, shallot, coriander seeds, and oil. Warm gently on low heat until the sauce is just warm when touched with your finger. Turn down the heat as low as it will go. The sauce needs time to ripen and mature its flavour; it should be perfect after 30 minutes. Stir in the parsley, basil, tarragon, lemon zest and juice, a healthy pinch of kosher salt, and pepper. Taste for seasoning.

FOR THE FISH: Preheat your oven to 425°F (220°C), with the rack in the centre position. Line a baking sheet with foil.

Rinse off the fish and pat dry with paper towels. Lay out the lemon slices in a row, one overlapping the other, then place them in the fish cavity, along with the dill. Brush the outside of the fish with the olive oil; this will help to remove the salt crust after baking.

In a large mixing bowl, whisk together the coarse salt, flour, fennel seeds, thyme, rosemary, and egg whites. The mixture should be the texture of wet sand. Pack one-third of the salt mixture in an even layer on the lined baking sheet. Place the fish on the bed of salt and cover it with a ½-inch-thick (1 cm) layer of the mixture so that it's enveloped from head to tail. Pack it down firmly, making sure there aren't any gaps.

continued

Bake the fish for 25 to 30 minutes (about 1½ minutes per ¼ pound/100 g of fish), or until a meat thermometer inserted in the thickest part of the fish registers 125°F (52°C) and the tip of a paring knife inserted behind the fish head feels warm when you touch it to your lip. The salt crust should be lightly coloured. Let rest at room temperature for 10 minutes.

Working gently, use a sharp serrated knife to cut around the outside edge of the salt crust, carefully avoiding cutting into the fish. Reveal the fish by lifting off the crust—it should come off in one piece. You might want to do this at the table, in front of your guests, for the added drama.

Remove the fish skin. Cut around the head and down the spine. Use the blade of the knife or a spoon to lift the top fillet (on the dorsal fin side), then trim the fillet on the belly side. Transfer the fillets to a serving plate. Remove the lemon slices and dill. Lift the spine, starting from the tail, and remove it. Separate the remaining fillets and transfer them to the serving plate.

Finish the dish with the warm *sauce vierge* and serve immediately.

⚜

Côte de Veau à la Normande

Veal Chops with Apples and Calvados

Yield: 4 PORTIONS
Preparation time: 20 MINUTES
Cooking time: 30 MINUTES

➤ *The flavours from France's Normandy region have always intrigued me, likely because it's where my ancestors originated. Normandy and Québec share a number of similarities: the countryside is abundant in apple trees, the weather will surprise you with sudden capricious showers and cloudbursts, and the people are profoundly original, with strong personalities. Just like the Québécois, the Normans are fiercely independent and have never completely mixed into the national melting pot. Or maybe I'm captivated by Normandy because no other region can boast such a variety of cheeses, and because a great number of their dishes are drowned in cream and butter, washed down by outstanding cider. Whatever the reason, this classic dish of apples, veal, cream, and Calvados is simply sublime. I like to serve it with gnocchi à la Parisienne (recipe follows).*

4 bone-in veal chops, about 1 inch (2.5 cm) thick

Juice of 1 lemon

2 Granny Smith apples

½ cup + 1 tablespoon (125 g) unsalted butter, divided

2 shallots, thinly sliced

¼ cup (60 mL) Calvados

1 cup (250 mL) dry apple cider

1 cup (250 mL) Chicken Stock (page 308, or store-bought)

½ cup (125 mL) heavy or whipping cream (35% milk fat)

Kosher salt and freshly cracked black pepper

¼ cup (60 mL) grapeseed oil

4 sprigs thyme

4 cloves garlic (unpeeled), crushed

2 cups (250 g) chanterelle mushrooms (or any mushrooms of your liking)

Beurre Manié:

1 tablespoon (10 g) all-purpose flour

2 teaspoons (10 g) unsalted butter

Preheat your oven to 350°F (180°C), with the rack in the centre position.

Remove the veal chops from the fridge and let stand at room temperature for at least 1 hour before cooking.

Meanwhile, squeeze the lemon juice into a medium bowl. Peel and core the apples, reserving the skins and cores for the sauce. Cut each apple into 8 wedges and put them in the lemon juice, tossing to coat (this will prevent them from oxidizing and turning brown). In a medium saucepan on medium heat, melt 2 tablespoons (30 g) of the butter. Add the apples and cook for 5 minutes, stirring often, until golden brown. They should be cooked but still have a slight crunch. Season with salt and a generous amount of pepper. Remove from the heat and set aside.

To make the sauce, in a small saucepan on medium heat, melt 2 tablespoons (30 g) of butter. Sweat the shallots for 2 minutes, stirring often. Add the apple skins and cores, and sweat for 3 minutes. Pour in the Calvados, use a long match to light it, and flambé to cook off the alcohol. When the flames die down, add the apple cider and reduce until there is almost no liquid left. Add the stock and cook for 5 minutes. Stir in the cream and lower the heat to simmer gently for 5 minutes. Strain the sauce through a fine tamis and discard the shallots and apple skins and cores.

In a small bowl, mixing by hand, incorporate the flour into the butter to make a smooth paste. This is called *beurre manié*.

continued

Return the sauce to the small saucepan and bring to a simmer on medium heat. Whisk in the *beurre manié*; the sauce will start to thicken. Simmer gently for 3 minutes. Season with salt and pepper. Remove from the heat, cover, and keep warm.

In a large ovenproof frying pan on high heat, heat the oil. Season the veal chops generously with salt and pepper and pan-fry on one side for 3 to 4 minutes or until seared with a nice golden-brown crust. Turn off the heat, flip the chops over, and add the thyme and garlic.

Transfer the pan to the oven and roast for 5 minutes or until a meat thermometer inserted in the thickest part of a veal chop registers 130°F (54°C). Transfer the chops, thyme, and garlic to a large plate. Put 1 teaspoon (5 g) butter on each veal chop, cover the dish with foil, and let rest at room temperature for 10 to 15 minutes while you finish the sauce. (Leave the oven on in case you need to warm up the chops later.)

In the same frying pan on medium-high heat, melt the remaining butter. Sauté the mushrooms for 4 to 5 minutes, until they start to brown and there is no more mushroom liquid in the pan. Season with salt and pepper. Add the apples to warm them up. Drain off any excess fat.

Add the mushrooms and apples to the cream sauce. Warm the sauce on low heat, then stir in the cooking juices that have accumulated under the veal chops, mixing well.

The chops should still be warm; if not, reheat them in the oven for a few minutes. Transfer the veal chops to individual plates and spoon the mushrooms, apples, and sauce over top.

⚜

GNOCCHI À LA PARISIENNE

Parisian Gnocchi

Yield: 4 PORTIONS
Preparation time: 20 MINUTES
Cooking time: 20 MINUTES

Made from choux pastry, this is a different type of gnocchi than the typical potato recipe most people are familiar with. It can be prepared ahead of time, ready to sear à la minute *in a hot pan with clarified butter. Add a handful of parsley leaves and some freshly grated Parmesan cheese at the end, and you have yourself a lovely side dish.*

What you'll need:

Stand mixer fitted with the paddle attachment (optional)

Piping bag with a large round tip

1 cup (250 g) homogenized milk (3.25% milk fat)

¼ cup (50 g) unsalted butter, cubed

1 teaspoon (3 g) kosher salt

½ teaspoon (1 g) freshly cracked black pepper

1 cup (150 g) all-purpose flour, sifted

3 eggs (5 ounces/150 g)

⅔ cup (60 g) freshly grated Parmesan cheese

1 teaspoon (5 mL) Dijon mustard

Olive oil, for greasing

¼ cup (60 mL) Beurre Clarifié (see tip) or duck fat

½ bunch fresh flat-leaf parsley, leaves only

Lemon juice

Kosher salt and freshly cracked black pepper, to taste

In a medium pot on medium heat, combine the milk, butter, salt, and pepper. Bring to a simmer, making sure all the butter is melted. Add the flour, all at once, and stir vigorously with a wooden spoon. Lower the heat to medium-low; the mixture will start to ball up and pull away from the sides of the pot. Cook, stirring constantly, for 2 minutes to cook the starch in the flour.

Transfer the warm flour mixture to a medium bowl. While stirring with a wooden spoon, add the eggs one at a time until fully incorporated into the dough. Add the Parmesan and mustard, and continue stirring until homogeneous. Transfer the dough to a piping bag with a large round tip.

Bring a large pot of water to a boil on medium-high heat. Lightly grease a baking sheet with olive oil. Working in batches, pipe the gnocchi directly into the water, cutting them into ¾-inch (2 cm) lengths with a paring knife. When the gnocchi float to the top of the water, start a timer for 4 minutes. When the time is up, use a slotted spoon to transfer the gnocchi to the oiled pan. Let cool completely at room temperature, then transfer to the fridge until needed.

When ready to serve, in a non-stick frying pan on medium-high heat, heat the clarified butter until very hot. Add the gnocchi in a single layer and cook for about 45 seconds without touching them. When they turn golden brown, lower the heat to medium-low, stir the gnocchi, and cook for 3 to 4 minutes or until they're warm in the centre. Stir in the parsley and a squeeze of lemon juice. Season with salt and pepper.

TIP *To make ¾ cup (175 mL) clarified butter, start with 1 cup (225 g) unsalted butter, cubed. In a small saucepan on medium-high heat, melt the butter. Lower the heat to medium-low and cook gently until most of the foam disappears. Strain the butter through a coffee filter to remove any dregs that have settled at the bottom. Transfer the clarified butter to an airtight container and store in the fridge until needed.*

Paris-Brest aux Noisettes

Hazelnut Paris-Brest

Yield: ONE 9-INCH (23 CM) PARIS-BREST, 8 PORTIONS

Preparation time: 1 HOUR + 24 HOURS CHILLING

Cooking time: 55 MINUTES + 30 MINUTES COOLING + 30 MINUTES CHILLING

What you'll need:

Two piping bags, one with a large round tip (#808) and one with a French star tip (#867)

Stand mixer fitted with the balloon whisk attachment

Croquant:

⅓ cup + 1 tablespoon (80 g) firmly packed brown sugar

⅓ cup (65 g) softened unsalted butter

½ cup (80 g) all-purpose flour

Paris-Brest:

1 batch Pâte à Choux (page 297)

Icing sugar, for dusting

Hazelnut Cream:

3 sheets gelatin

¾ cup (180 g) + 1⅔ cup (400 g) heavy or whipping cream (35% milk fat), divided

1 cup (250 g) hazelnut praline (store-bought)

Caramelized Hazelnuts:

3 tablespoons (45 g) granulated sugar

1 teaspoon (5 mL) water

48 whole hazelnuts, skinned and roasted

⮞ *My friend Lisa Yu, who's the pastry chef at Monarque in Montréal, introduced me to the* croquant, *which gives a better texture to the choux pastry. She also taught me to use this particular variant with hazelnut cream, which is much lighter and more enjoyable than the traditional combo of pastry cream and butter.*

Day 1

FOR THE CROQUANT: In a medium bowl, using a silicone spatula, mix the brown sugar with the butter until fully incorporated, then mix in the flour. Place the mixture on a large sheet of parchment paper and top with another sheet of parchment paper. Using a rolling pin, roll out the croquant into a 10-inch (25 cm) circle that's ¹⁄₁₆ inch (2 mm) thick. Place the croquant (still inside the parchment) on a baking sheet and put in the freezer.

FOR THE PARIS-BREST: Place the pâte à choux in a piping bag with tip #808. Reserve in the fridge.

FOR THE HAZELNUT CREAM: In a small bowl, soak the gelatin in cold water for 10 minutes.

Meanwhile, in a small pot on medium heat, heat up ¾ cup (180 g) of the cream. Squeeze the excess water from the soaked gelatin and whisk the gelatin into the warm cream.

In a mixing bowl, whisk together the hazelnut praline, warm cream, and 1⅔ cup (400 g) cold cream until fully incorporated. Transfer to an airtight container and refrigerate for 24 hours.

Day 2

Preheat your oven to 425°F (220°C), with the rack in the centre position.

Remove the hazelnut cream from the fridge and transfer to the bowl of a stand mixer fitted with the balloon whisk. Whisk on medium speed until medium peaks form, about 5 minutes. Transfer the hazelnut-cream mixture to a piping bag with tip #867.

continued

Remove the croquant from the freezer and peel off the top layer of parchment paper. Using a plate for a template and a paring knife, cut a circle 9 inches (23 cm) in diameter and remove the excess croquant mixture. Now cut a 7-inch (17 cm) circle centred inside the 9-inch (23 cm) circle. It doesn't have to be perfect, so don't panic. Remove the croquant from the centre—you should be left with a ring, like a big doughnut. Place the croquant ring in the freezer, and discard the rest or use for future puffs or éclairs.

Line a baking sheet with parchment paper. Using a pencil, draw a circle 9 inches (23 cm) in diameter on the paper. Flip the paper over; you should still be able to see the circle through it. Pipe a ring of choux pastry dough around the circle, ensuring that the pencil line is at the centre of your piped dough. Pipe a second ring inside the first one, making sure the rings are touching each other. These two pastry circles will be your base. Pipe a third ring on top of the two rings, using the centre seam between them as your guide. You now have a circular pyramid. Place the croquant ring directly on top of the choux ring.

Bake for 10 minutes, then lower the heat to 375°F (190°C) and leave the oven door slightly ajar by wedging it open with the handle of a wooden spoon. This allows steam to escape and prevents the choux pastry from collapsing. Bake for 45 minutes. Turn off the oven and let the Paris-Brest sit for 15 minutes with the oven door still ajar. Then, remove the Paris-Brest from the oven and let cool on a wire rack at room temperature for at least 30 minutes.

FOR THE CARAMELIZED HAZELNUTS: Meanwhile, in a small pot on medium-high heat, heat the granulated sugar and water, stirring until the sugar is dissolved. Add the hazelnuts and cook, stirring, until the nuts are well coated in a light golden-brown caramel, about 5 minutes. Pour out onto on a silicone baking mat or parchment paper and let cool. Separate the hazelnuts.

TO ASSEMBLE: Using a serrated knife, carefully slice horizontally through the cooled Paris-Brest, one-third of the way from the top. The top third of the pastry ring is the top, and the lower two-thirds is the base. Pipe the hazelnut cream onto the base, moving the tip from side to side to create a beautiful pattern. There are no rules here. Distribute the caramelized hazelnuts evenly over the cream, and cover with the top of the pastry ring. Chill in the fridge for 30 minutes.

Dust the Paris-Brest with icing sugar. Using the same serrated knife, slice it into eight portions.

❖

Îles Flottantes et Crème Anglaise

Poached Meringues and Crème Anglaise

Yield: 4 PORTIONS
Preparation time: 45 MINUTES
Cooking time: 25 MINUTES

By the time I was about fifteen years into my cooking career, I had only ever made this dish once. Îles flottantes, *also known as* oeufs à la neige, *is a classic French dessert that most young cooks tackle in culinary school before shelving it forever. No restaurant really serves it these days; perhaps it's too old school or uncool. Yet serendipitously, it was the catalyst for me discovering the direction I wanted to take my restaurant when I first opened St. Lawrence. Friends came over to my place for dinner one night, and I needed to come up with a gluten-free dessert for them.* Îles flottantes *popped into my head, and I figured I could wing it. When I dropped the meringue quenelles into the hot milk, I suddenly got so excited that I literally had goosebumps. This is what I needed to do: immerse myself in the classics and honour those traditions by bringing them back to life with new energy and soul. My path, and the concept for St. Lawrence, became crystal clear.*

What you'll need:
Stand mixer fitted with the balloon whisk attachment

Crème Anglaise:
1 cup (250 mL) homogenized milk (3.25% milk fat)
1 cup (250 mL) heavy or whipping cream (35% milk fat)
1 vanilla bean, split and scraped
6 egg yolks
⅓ cup (75 g) granulated sugar
Pinch kosher salt

Meringue:
6 egg whites
A few drops of lemon juice
1 cup (300 g) granulated sugar, divided
8 cups (2 L) water

Caramel:
1 cup (200 g) granulated sugar
⅓ cup (75 mL) water
A few drops of lemon juice

FOR THE CRÈME ANGLAISE: In a medium saucepan on medium heat, bring the milk, cream, and vanilla bean to a boil. Remove from the heat, cover, and let infuse for 10 minutes. Discard the vanilla bean.

In a medium bowl, beat the egg yolks, sugar, and salt until creamy. While whisking constantly, slowly pour in the hot milk mixture. Pour the mixture back into the saucepan and cook on low heat until it reaches 185°F (85°C) or coats the back of a spoon. Strain through a sieve, let cool completely, and transfer to the fridge until fully cold.

FOR THE MERINGUES: Using a stand mixer fitted with the balloon whisk, beat the egg whites and lemon juice on high speed until soft peaks form. While continuing to whisk on high speed, gradually add ½ cup (100 g) of the sugar, whisking until the meringue is firm, shiny, and smooth.

In a large saucepan on medium-high heat, bring the water and the remaining sugar to a simmer. Place a clean dishtowel on a baking tray and keep on the counter near your stove. Using a big kitchen spoon dipped in cold water, scoop out a big quenelle of meringue and plunge the spoon into the simmering water. The meringue should detach from the spoon and float. After 3 minutes, flip the meringue over and cook for another 3 minutes. Remove the "island" and let it cool on the towel. Repeat with the remaining meringues. You should be able to cook three quenelles at a time, for a total of six.

continued

FOR THE CARAMEL: In a small saucepan on medium heat, stir together the sugar, water, and lemon juice. Bring to a simmer, about 5 minutes. Prepare a medium bowl filled halfway with ice to stop the caramel from getting too dark. Increase the heat to medium-high and cook, without stirring, until light golden brown, 4 to 5 minutes. Remove from the heat, put the pot directly on the ice to stop the cooking, and let cool for 2 to 3 minutes.

To serve, place the cold crème anglaise in a serving bowl. Place the "islands" on top—they will float. Using a large spoon, drizzle the hot caramel all over the meringues. If the caramel is hard at the bottom of the pot because of the ice, just reheat it on medium heat. At the table, scoop out an island with the crème anglaise into individual bowls in front of your guests.

VARIATION *Garnish with roasted sliced almonds.*

⚜

Crème Caramel
Caramel Custard

Yield: 8 PORTIONS

Preparation time: 30 MINUTES +
30 MINUTES CHILLING

Cooking time: 45 MINUTES +
3 HOURS OR OVERNIGHT
COOLING

I love making one big crème caramel for a feast. Everyone's always so wowed when it's brought to the table. But you could also bake the custard in small ramekins for individual servings. In the past, I was never really a big crème caramel fan because I felt it tasted too eggy, maybe because it's often overcooked. So I started adding more yolks to replace the whole eggs, somewhat like a crème brûlée custard. My version is a bit richer and less eggy—maybe less traditional, but more pleasing to my palate. It's a matter of opinion, for sure, but this recipe is bang on for me.

What you'll need:

One 10-inch (25 cm) round baking dish, or six ¾-cup (175 mL) ramekins

Caramel:

¾ cup (150 g) granulated sugar

3 tablespoons (45 mL) water

Juice of ¼ lemon

½ teaspoon (2 g) kosher salt

Custard:

1⅓ cups (325 mL) homogenized milk (3.25% milk fat)

1⅓ cups (325 mL) heavy or whipping cream (35% milk fat)

1 teaspoon (5 mL) vanilla extract (or, better yet, 1 vanilla bean, split and scraped)

3 eggs

3 egg yolks

½ cup + 2 tablespoons (130 g) granulated sugar

FOR THE CARAMEL: In a small saucepan on medium heat, mix together the sugar, water, and lemon juice, and cook, without stirring, until it forms a light-golden-brown caramel. Stir in the salt. Pour the caramel into the baking dish (or divide equally among the ramekins). Chill in the fridge for about 30 minutes or until fully set.

FOR THE CUSTARD: Preheat your oven to 325°F (160°C), with the rack in the centre position.

In a medium pot on medium heat, combine the milk, cream, and vanilla, and heat to 185°F (85°C).

In a medium bowl, beat the eggs, egg yolks, and sugar. While whisking constantly, gradually pour in the hot milk mixture. Strain the liquid through a sieve into a pitcher to make it easier to pour into the mould. It will most likely have a layer of foam on top of the liquid—remove it with a large spoon. Remove the baking dish from the fridge and pour in the custard mixture; it should be very full (or divide the custard mixture evenly among the ramekins).

Prepare a *bain-marie* by laying a towel in the bottom of a large baking pan. In a large pot on medium-high heat, bring 8 cups (2 L) water to a simmer. Place the baking dish (or ramekins) on the towel and pour the simmering water into the pan until the water is halfway up the dish.

Bake for 45 to 60 minutes, until the custard is just set (ramekins will be faster, about 40 minutes). Start checking on the custard early, as the baking time will depend on the thickness of your baking dish. If you shake the dish gently, the custard should still be jiggly in the centre and not totally

set. It will almost feel like it isn't ready, but remember that it will continue to cook and set as it rests. Wearing oven mitts, carefully remove some water from the *bain-marie* with a small ladle, then lift the baking dish (or ramekins) from the water bath and let cool at room temperature for 1 hour.

Refrigerate the cooled custard for at least 3 hours or, better yet, until the next day. Run a knife around the inside edge of the dish (or ramekins) to loosen the custard. Invert onto a plate, and serve very cold.

⚜

Tarte Tatin

Apple Tart "Tatin"

Yield: ONE 9-INCH (23 CM) TART, 8 PORTIONS

Preparation time: 45 MINUTES

Cooking time: 1 HOUR + 1 HOUR COOLING

What you'll need:

9-inch (23 cm) round baking dish, 2 inches (5 cm) deep

11 ounces (300 g) Pâte Brisée (page 299) or Pâte Feuilleté Rapide (page 300)

¾ cup (165 g) + 2 tablespoons (30 g) granulated sugar, divided

3 tablespoons (45 mL) water

2 tablespoons (30 g) cold unsalted butter, cut into small cubes

6 Granny Smith apples (about 1.75 lb/800 g), peeled, halved, and cored

Vanilla ice cream or Crème Fraîche (page 296, or store-bought), for serving

➤ Tarte Tatin *was created accidentally at the Hôtel Tatin, which was run by two sisters of the same name. One of the sisters was overworked one day and started to make a traditional apple pie but left the apples cooking in butter and sugar for too long. Smelling them burning, she tried to rescue the dish by putting the pastry base on top of the pan of apples and quickly finishing the cooking by putting the whole pan in the oven. After turning out the upside-down tart, she was surprised to find how much the hotel guests appreciated the dessert. Strictly speaking, puff pastry is the traditional dough used to make* tarte Tatin. *But I find that if you don't eat it right away, the pastry quickly becomes soggy and loses its crispiness. Pâte brisée is much more texturally forgiving if you aren't going to town on the whole tart all at once.*

Start by preparing the *pâte brisée*. On a lightly floured work surface, roll out the pastry to ¼ inch (5 mm) thick and cut a 10-inch (24 cm) circle. Lightly prick all over with a fork, wrap in plastic wrap, and put in the fridge.

Preheat your oven to 425°F (220°C), with the rack in the centre position.

To make the caramel, in a small saucepan on medium-high heat, stir together the ¾ cup (165 g) sugar and the water until the mixture becomes a light-golden caramel (it will darken more as it bakes). Turn off the heat and gradually add the butter, whisking constantly until fully incorporated. Transfer the caramel to the baking dish.

Arrange one apple half, cut side down, in the centre of the baking dish. Cut the remaining apples into quarters (wedges) and arrange them in concentric circles to fill all the empty spaces. Pack in as many apple wedges as possible, very tightly together, ensuring that there aren't any empty spaces left between them. This makes the tart nice and dense and gives you perfect slices. You'll probably have to cut some of the apples into smaller pieces to fill in the gaps. Sprinkle the 2 tablespoons (30 g) sugar evenly on top.

Place the disc of *pâte brisée* on top of the apples. Using the back side of a paring knife or offset spatula, tuck the edges of the pastry inside the baking dish and prick a few holes in the pastry to let steam escape.

Bake the tart for 20 minutes. Lower the oven temperature to 375°F (190°C) and bake for 40 minutes, until the pastry is golden brown and crispy. Let cool for at least 1 hour (it will still be warm when you serve it).

To unmould the tart, run a sharp knife around the edges of the dish. Place a large serving plate over the tart. Firmly holding the plate and the baking dish together, turn the dish upside down. Shake the dish gently to release the tart and its juices onto the plate. Serve with your favourite vanilla ice cream, or simply with some crème fraîche.

❧

ADDITIONAL IMAGE ON PAGE 136

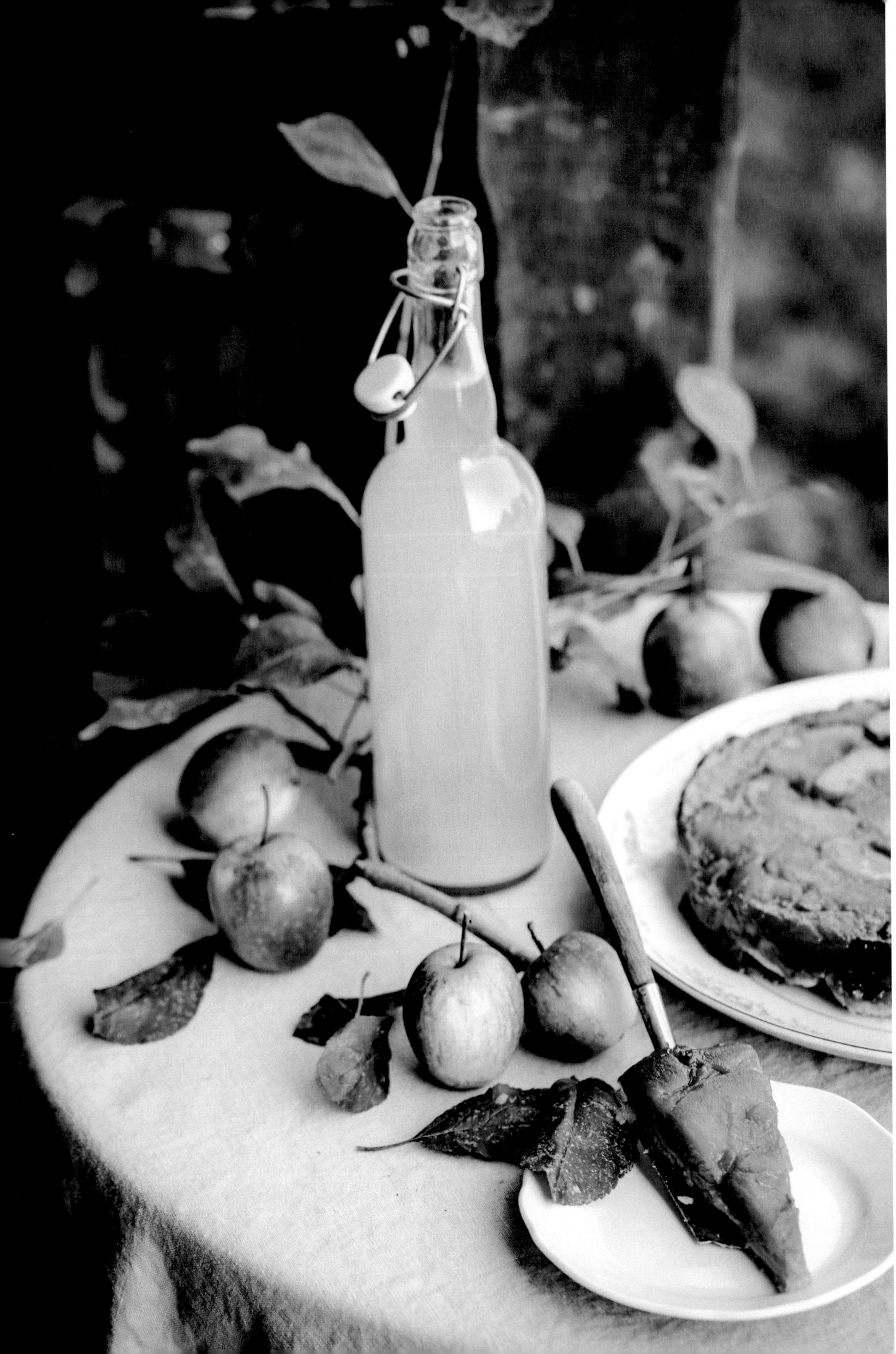

LEFT: TARTE TATIN, PAGE 134 RIGHT: GALETTE DES ROIS, PAGE 138

Galette des Rois

Almond Pithivier

Yield: 8 TO 10 PORTIONS

Preparation time: 45 MINUTES + 1¼ HOURS CHILLING

Cooking time: 55 MINUTES + 15 MINUTES COOLING

↘ *The* galette des rois *was invented to celebrate the day the three kings visited an infant named Jesus, and it's baked throughout January in France. Some people say this tradition is, rather, to celebrate the winter solstice. Either way, the practice is to hide a bean (such as dry fava bean) or a porcelain figurine inside the pithivier; this dates back to the Roman Empire. The* fève *(bean) represents the king, and the person who discovers the* fève *in their serving is declared the king or queen of the night. If you have kids, have them craft a golden paper crown for the winner to wear. You'll be surprised by how enthusiastic both kids and adults are about winning the crown.*

What you'll need:

Piping bag with large plain tip

Almond Cream:

½ cup (120 g) unsalted butter, softened

⅓ cup + 1 teaspoon (110 g) icing sugar

1½ cups (150 g) ground almonds

1 egg

1 egg yolk

2 tablespoons (25 g) all-purpose flour

1 tablespoon (15 mL) cognac or rum

Pithivier:

1.3 pounds (600 g) Pâte Feuilleté Rapide (page 300, or store-bought)

1 egg yolk + 1 tablespoon (30 mL) homogenized milk (3.25% milk fat), lightly beaten for egg wash

1 tablespoon (15 mL) water

½ batch Crème Pâtissière (page 282)

Icing sugar, for dusting

FOR THE ALMOND CREAM: In a large bowl, using a plastic spatula, work in the butter with the icing sugar until fully incorporated. Gradually mix in the ground almonds, then the egg, egg yolk, flour, and cognac, one after another. Mix until smooth. Cover with plastic wrap and refrigerate for 15 minutes while you prepare the *pâte feuilleté rapide* and *crème pâtissière*.

FOR THE PITHIVIER: Cut the pastry dough into two pieces, one slightly bigger than the other (9 ounces and 12 ounces/250 g and 350 g). On a lightly floured work surface, roll out the smaller piece into a 10-inch (25 cm) circle that's ⅛ inch (3 mm) thick. This will be your base. Roll out the larger piece into a 12-inch (30 cm) circle that's ⅛ inch (3 mm) thick. Place both circles side by side on a baking sheet and cover the pan with plastic wrap. Refrigerate for 30 minutes.

In a small bowl, lightly beat the egg yolk with the water to make an egg wash.

Remove the pastry dough from the fridge. In a large bowl, using a plastic spatula, fold together the almond cream and pastry cream until mixed and homogeneous. Transfer the mixture to a piping bag with a large plain tip. Pipe the cream over the base in an even circle, leaving a 1½-inch (3 cm) border around the edge. Brush a little bit of the egg wash around the edge and carefully drape the other pastry dough circle on top, pressing down on the edges to seal. Chill in the fridge for 30 minutes, uncovered.

Preheat your oven to 425°F (220°C), with the rack in the centre position.

Remove the *pithivier* from the fridge and glaze it with the egg wash. Using the tip of a paring knife, mark some lines radiating out from the centre, in the shape of a rosette.

Bake the *pithivier* for 15 minutes. Lower the oven temperature to 350°F (175°C) and bake for 20 minutes. Lower the temperature to 300°F (150°C) and bake for 20 minutes. Let cool on a wire rack for 15 minutes. Dust with icing sugar, and serve warm, with nothing else.

TIP *While still on the baking sheet, slide the* pithivier *into the freezer for one hour so the dough can be handled without damaging it. After an hour, wrap it in plastic wrap, or transfer it to a plastic freezer bag; it will keep in the freezer for up to 1 month. When you're ready to bake the pithivier, let it stand at room temperature for 1 hour, then glaze it and mark the top. Allow an extra 10 minutes of baking time at 325°F (160°C).*

❧

ADDITIONAL IMAGE ON PAGE 137

OCTOBER 2016 . . . it was our first time in Bordeaux, and I remember it like it was yesterday. Dara and I loved the atmosphere and the aesthetic—kind of like a little Paris without the attitude. And the food followed suit.

We were staying in a gorgeous apartment overlooking a beautiful open-air plaza. It was ringed with charming shops and about two dozen café tables at the centre, totally alive with people eating and drinking and laughing. Drawn in by the vibe, Dara and I claimed a table for ourselves and flagged down a server. It soon became clear that they didn't have a menu, so we told him we were looking for a snack. He replied plainly,

"You can have a baguette and camembert and dry-cured sausage." We looked at each other with a bit of a raised eyebrow and a silent "okay . . ." that is, until our order arrived. Our server dropped our food on the table without ceremony, and we were floored. He had brought us a full baguette on a cutting board, a whole wheel of camembert, and a whole *saucisson sec*. Not plated. Not sliced. All rustic and—boom—a big knife so that we could cut it up ourselves. And I haven't even mentioned the wine—a dirt-cheap bottle for less than 10 Euros, and it was seriously fantastic.

Good cheese, good sausage, good bread, good wine. They'd never be brought to your table whole like that in North America where, instead, they'd slice it small and serve it with delicate little portions of nuts and fruit. I loved it. It wasn't a polished restaurant experience, but enjoying food doesn't have to be precious or fancy to be memorable. We were drawn to the fun of it all.

In that same plaza, there was another place making *jambon beurre* sandwiches. Every time we stopped by, they weren't open, and it was really hard to see when they were doing business. But we finally realized that mornings were the way to go. What a pleasure it was to get up early and bring back two *jambon beurre* for our breakfast. Just three components—amazing French butter and *jambon Paris* on a fresh baguette—and it was perfect.

And the eggs, too . . . God. For dinners, we'd buy fresh eggs, taken from the chicken coop that same day, and some freshly foraged wild mushrooms. Along with more of that amazing French butter, and we'd have *une omelette aux champignons*.

Honestly, those were some of our favourite things to eat on that trip. Super simple with no pretensions. And it was just as much about being in the moment as what was on our plate. French food doesn't have to be complicated to be utterly delicious.

Crêpes Suzette

Crêpes with Orange and Grand Marnier Sauce

Yield: 6 PORTIONS

Preparation time: 20 MINUTES +
2 HOURS RESTING

Cooking time: 25 MINUTES

☙ *This beautiful dessert provides a hell of a show for your guests because you flambé it tableside. It's a great classic from the 1950s and 1960s, when it was very popular in luxury hotels and even three-star Michelin restaurants across France. Sadly, because the preparation usually takes place in the dining room and is performed by a trained server, it has disappeared. I've never had the chance myself to experience it in a restaurant, but you and I can make it at home!*

What you'll need:

9-inch (23 cm) crêpe pan or non-stick skillet

Crêpe Batter:

2 eggs

2 tablespoons (20 g) granulated sugar

Good pinch kosher salt

2 cups (500 mL) homogenized milk (3.25% milk fat), divided

¼ cup (55 g) melted unsalted butter + extra for cooking

1¾ cups (250 g) all-purpose flour, sifted

Grated zest of 1 orange

Grated zest of 1 lemon

Orange and Butter Sauce:

1⅔ cups (400 mL) orange juice

½ cup (100 g) granulated sugar

½ cup + 2 tablespoons (150 g) cold unsalted butter, cubed

3 tablespoons (45 mL) Grand Marnier, if you decide not to flambé (see note)

Julienned zest and segments of 2 oranges

¼ cup (60 mL) Grand Marnier for the flambé, if you're going for it

FOR THE CRÊPE BATTER: In a large mixing bowl, whisk the eggs with the sugar and a healthy pinch of salt. Mix in ½ cup (125 mL) of the milk and the melted butter. Place the flour in a second bowl and make a well in the centre. Whisk in the liquid until fully incorporated with no lumps. Gradually whisk in the remaining milk until you have a thin crêpe batter, then mix in the orange and lemon zest. Cover with plastic wrap and refrigerate for 2 hours.

FOR THE ORANGE AND BUTTER SAUCE: In a medium saucepan on medium-high heat, bring the orange juice and sugar to a simmer. Lower the heat to low and reduce by half, about 10 minutes. Remove from the heat and whisk in the cold butter, one cube at a time, to emulsify the sauce. Whisk in the orange zest. Cover with a lid and keep warm.

TO COOK THE CRÊPES: Heat the crêpe pan on medium-high heat and add a little butter. Ladle a small portion of batter into the pan until it thinly covers the bottom; return any extra batter to the bowl. Cook until the edges of the crêpe start to brown and curl up, about 45 seconds. Flip and cook for 15 seconds, then transfer the crêpe to a plate and keep warm by covering it with a dish towel. Repeat until you have two to three crêpes per person, adding a little butter to the pan between each crêpe.

TO SERVE: Preheat your broiler, with the rack in the top position.

Warm up the sauce on medium heat until hot, but don't bring it to a simmer—you don't want it to split.

Fold each crêpe in half and then in half again, and place along the middle of a baking sheet in a single row. Broil for 30 to 60 seconds or until the crêpes start to crisp up and are warm. Transfer to serving plates, garnish with orange segments, and generously spoon sauce onto the crêpes.

continued

If you decide to flambé the crêpes tableside, in a small saucepan on high heat, bring the Grand Marnier to a boil. Using a long match, set the liquor on fire. Spoon some of the flaming Grand Marnier onto the crêpes in front of your guests.

VARIATION *If you don't want to flambé tableside but still want the Grand Marnier flavour, whisk 3 tablespoons (45 mL) Grand Marnier into the sauce with the orange zest.*

⚜

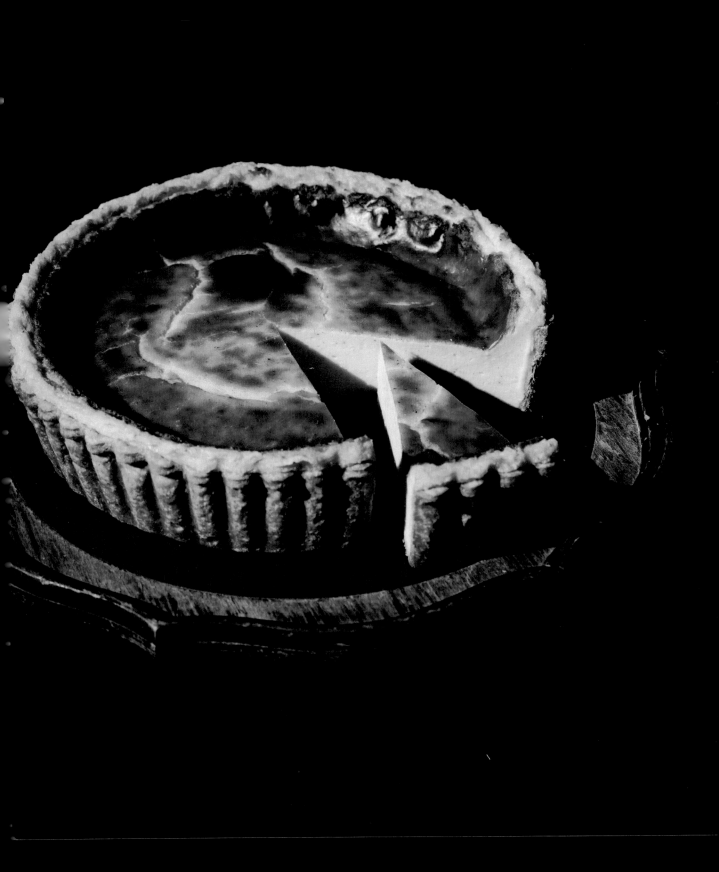

Flan Parisien
Parisian Custard Tart

Yield: 12 PORTIONS

Preparation time: 45 MINUTES +
1 HOUR CHILLING

Cooking time: 1¼ HOURS +
5 HOURS OR OVERNIGHT
COOLING

What you'll need:

9-inch (23 cm) round tart mould
with removable bottom, 2 inches
(5 cm) deep

1 batch Pâte Brisée (page 299)

4 cups (1 L) homogenized milk
(3.25% milk fat)

1 cup (250 mL) heavy or whipping
cream (35% milk fat)

1 vanilla bean, split and scraped

14 egg yolks (7.5 ounces/210 g)

1⅓ cups (195 g) icing sugar

½ cup + 1 tablespoon (75 g)
cornstarch

¾ cup (100 g) cold unsalted butter,
cubed

꙳ *A flan is typically a custard. Its origin can be traced all the way back to the Roman Empire, and it holds a place in many cultures today: French, Italian, Portuguese, Mexican, and Filipino, among many others. Flan was made as a savoury dish, usually with meat or fish. The well-known Quiche Lorraine (page 245) is basically a flan. In this recipe, the vanilla custard's simple flavour makes it very easy to pair the tart with any seasonal fruits of your choice.*

When you're ready to roll out the *pâte brisée*, remove the dough from the fridge and let it soften slightly so that it's malleable but still cold. Unwrap the dough and press the edges of the disc so that there aren't any cracks. On a lightly floured work surface, roll out the pastry to ⅛ inch (3 mm) thick. Line the tart mould with the pastry and make sure there is a border that stands about ¼ inch (5 mm) above the ring. Place the tart mould in the freezer while you prepare the custard.

In a large saucepan on medium heat, bring the milk, cream, and vanilla bean to a simmer. Remove from the heat, cover, and let rest for 10 minutes, then remove the vanilla bean.

Meanwhile, in a medium bowl, whisk together the egg yolks, icing sugar, and cornstarch. While whisking constantly, slowly pour in the hot milk. Pour the egg mixture back into the pan and heat on high heat until the custard thickens, whisking constantly so it doesn't stick or burn on the bottom of the pot. Transfer the custard to a bowl and let cool for 5 minutes. Whisk the cold butter into the custard. Take the tart shell out of the freezer and pour the custard into the centre, filling to the top edges. Refrigerate until cold, about 1 hour.

Preheat your oven to 350°F (180°C), with the rack in the centre position.

Bake the tart for 1¼ hours. You're looking for a nice caramelization on the top, and the custard should be set but still jiggly. It should also look puffy, like a soufflé. Don't panic—this is normal, and the custard will gradually deflate as it cools.

Let the tart rest for 1 hour at room temperature, then refrigerate it for at least 4 hours before unmoulding and slicing the portions. I'd personally wait until the next day to serve it.

⚜

ST. LAWRENCE

WHAT DEFINES A GREAT RESTAURANT? People pay too much attention to awards and ratings. Then they look at the food and only the food, with the idea in mind that it has to be a certain way to be dubbed a great restaurant. Just a thought here, but perhaps restaurants are less about the food than we think, and our relationship to them is more emotional and social than gustatory. One of the most important aspects of a restaurant is ambience—the feel of the place, and the way it makes you feel. Your meal will never be great if you don't feel good being in the space.

I like to watch people at the tables at St. Lawrence, talking, plotting, flirting, celebrating. There are elderly people, solo diners, tourist families, couples on a date. The tables are side by side, so you rub elbows with your neighbours, swap menu advice, get chatting. I realized that this is the true fun and flow of the French restaurant experience. The waiter brings another glass of wine, conversations are sparked, one table sings "Happy Birthday," another table is laughing loudly. The French, after all, are master purveyors of *joie de vivre*. My goal from the beginning was to transport customers to a different place than Vancouver the moment they enter the restaurant. Ambience still is and will always remain a top priority and a major ingredient to our recipe for success. We're providing an experience more than just the meal itself.

Our *éclair à la mousse de foie de canard* is, perhaps, the quintessential St. Lawrence indulgence. We take a classic French choux pastry dessert and turn the concept on its head to make it a savoury dish. Instead of piping in praline-flavoured cream, we fill it with foie gras mousse, top it with maple icing, stud it with crispy chicken skin, and serve it with a cherry and red wine reduction. If that doesn't scream, "Holy crap, yes, please," I don't know what does.

Oreilles de Crisses

Fried Pork Rinds with Maple Syrup and Montréal Steak Spice

Yield: 50 TO 75 PIECES
Preparation time: 30 MINUTES
Cooking time: 1½ HOURS + 12
TO 16 HOURS DEHYDRATING

2 pounds (900 g) pig skin (ask your butcher for this)
Vegetable or canola oil, for frying
MTL Steak Spice (recipe follows)
Maple syrup, to finish

Once upon a time, in a lumber camp in Québec, a tough brawler named Chris had ears that swelled up like cauliflower after one too many fights. Because of the similarity between his cauliflower ears and fried pork rinds, the bullies made fun of him, saying, "Qui veut des oreilles du grand Chris?" which means, "Who wants the ears of big Chris?" This sweet and salty snack is among the Québécois favourites at the sugar shack. It's traditionally made with deep-fried salted fatback, but I prefer to use the skin. It's lighter, fluffier, and far less greasy. In the kitchen, we call these Québec chicharrones. *Sprinkled with our steak spice and drizzled with a good maple syrup, they are salty and sweet, and incredibly addictive. I challenge you to stop eating them once you start.*

Place the pig skin in a large stockpot and add enough cold water to cover. Bring to a simmer on medium-high heat. Lower the heat to maintain a gentle simmer and cook for about 1½ hours or until the skin tears when pulled.

Line two baking sheets with parchment paper. Using a large strainer, remove the skin from the water and layer each piece of skin flat in between sheets of parchment paper. Do this while the pig skin is still warm, or the pieces will stick together because of their natural gelatin. Let cool at room temperature before putting in the fridge.

Preheat your oven to 170°F (77°C), or lower if you can, with the rack in the centre position.

Using a metal or plastic bench scraper, scrape any excess fat off the pig skin. Using a chef's knife, julienne the skin into 2 by ⅛-inch (5 cm by 3 mm) strips.

Line a baking sheet with parchment paper, arrange the strips evenly on it, and dehydrate in the oven for 12 to 16 hours. The skins look like glass and feel hard when they're fully dehydrated, but you should still be able to bend them a little.

In a deep fryer or a large pot, heat a few inches of oil to 375°F (190°C). Working in small batches, fry the skins until they puff into crunchy little pork-rind clouds. It's easy to tell when they're done, as they'll quadruple in size in about 20 seconds. Immediately transfer them to a mixing bowl.

continued

To finish, toss the rinds with a generous pinch of MTL steak spice and drizzle with maple syrup. Serve immediately.

TIP *Traditionally the* oreilles de crisses *are made from deep-fried salted fatback with the skin still attached. It's extremely good but very rich and fatty. I think that just the skin without the fat attached, along with the sweet and salty seasoning, is lighter and much more enjoyable—meaning you can crush a giant pile of them without the snacking guilt!*

⚜

ÉPICES À STEAK MONTRÉALAISE
MTL Steak Spice

THIS WILL MAKE MORE THAN YOU NEED, BUT YOU'LL HAVE SOME SEASONING IN YOUR PANTRY FOR SUMMER BBQ SEASON.

6 tablespoons (60 g) kosher salt

3 tablespoons (30 g) turbinado sugar

4½ tablespoons (30 g) black peppercorns, ground in a mortar and pestle

4½ tablespoons (25 g) coriander seeds, ground in a mortar and pestle

5 teaspoons (15 g) garlic powder

5 teaspoons (15 g) onion flakes

3½ teaspoons (6 g) mustard powder

¾ teaspoon (3 g) dry dill

¾ teaspoon (3 g) chili flakes

Make the MTL Steak Spices by mixing all the ingredients in a small container. Reserve.

TIP *How to use the MTL spices on a steak—or any other protein for that matter: In a small bowl, mix 1 full tablespoon of the MTL spice with 4 tablespoons of olive oil. Spread the paste on both sides of your steak. The size of your steak for that amount of spices should be around 14 to 18 ounces (400 to 500 g). Let marinate at room temperature for 1 hour before grilling the steak.*

⚜

Pâté en Croûte au Canard et Noisettes

Pâté in Pastry with Duck and Hazelnuts

Yield: 20 TO 24 SLICES

Preparation time: 4 TO 5 HOURS SPREAD OVER 3 DAYS

Cooking time: 1½ HOURS

➤ *I knew deep in my heart that I wanted to have a rotating* pâté du jour *as a permanent menu item at St. Lawrence. But I wanted it to be different, unique. A pâté isn't hard to make for a professional chef, but a* pâté en croûte, *now that's a challenge. Because it isn't the easiest recipe to tackle, not a lot of chefs still make it. It falls into the category of recipes you see in the* Larousse Gastronomique *that immediately evokes nostalgia. Right from the restaurant's opening day, I was hands-on in the kitchen, and I was fully committed to taking on this task even though I knew it wasn't really sustainable long term. We'd only been in business for two weeks when a guy named Colin Johnson, a highly experienced English-trained chef, knocked on the kitchen door looking for a job. I was suddenly blessed by the stars. Colin has a deep passion for making pâté and pies of all sorts— even stronger than mine. His dedication to precision and to the refinement of the process made him the perfect person to take charge of the pâté pro- gram in our kitchen. Over the past four years, Colin has made hundreds of* pâtés en croûte *at the restaurant. It has become one of St. Lawrence's iconic signature dishes with a bit of a cult following, and it will never leave the menu.*

A wee note from Colin: Clear the decks, and clear some space in your fridge and freezer too—you're going to need it. This is going to be a long-weekend project, and a significant degree of commitment is required. Sure, it's a big task, but it can be broken down into four elements. Days one and two will be busy, but it'll be more than worth it when all your mates come 'round and see and taste what you've made as a centrepiece. High fives aplenty.

continued

What you'll need:

Meat grinder

Non-stick terrine mould 3 inches (7.5 cm) deep

Instant-read digital temperature probe

Digital scale that measures accurately and in fractions of grams

Small metal offset spatula

Cheesecloth

Scissors

Rolling pin

Latex kitchen gloves

Dough:

1 batch Pâte à Pâté (page 298)

1 tablespoon (15 g) soft unsalted butter or vegetable oil spray

Farce Mixture (6 cups/1.25 kg):

1.1 pounds (500 g) lean pork shoulder, trimmed of any fat, sinew, and silver skin

12 ounces (350 g) pork back fat

12 ounces (350 g) lean boneless duck leg meat

2 tablespoons (24 g) kosher salt

½ teaspoon (2 g) curing salt (also called Prague Powder #1 and Insta Cure #1)

½ teaspoon (2 g) Épices à Pâté (page 294)

½ teaspoon (2 g) freshly cracked black pepper

A good pinch (1 g) granulated sugar

1 tablespoon (15 mL) cognac or brandy

Cured Mixture:

14 ounces (400 g) boneless duck breast, diced into ½-inch (1 cm) cubes

5 ounces (150 g) pork belly, diced into ½-inch (1 cm) cubes

2½ teaspoons (8 g) kosher salt

Pinch Épices à Pâté (page 294)

Pinch freshly cracked black pepper

Finely grated zest of ½ orange

1 tablespoon (15 mL) cognac or brandy

Filling Mixture:

¾ cup (75 g) unsweetened dried cranberries

2 tablespoons (30 mL) cognac or brandy

Ice cubes

3.5 ounces (100 g) smoked bacon, diced into ½-inch (1 cm) cubes

½ cup (75 g) whole hazelnuts, skinned and lightly roasted

¼ cup (15 g) chopped fresh flat-leaf parsley leaves

3 tablespoons (12 g) chopped celery leaves from the centre of the stalk

2 tablespoons (10 g) fine breadcrumbs

2 tablespoons (5 g) chopped fresh sage leaves

½ cup (125 mL) heavy or whipping cream (35% milk fat)

2 teaspoons (10 mL) Grand Marnier

1 egg

Pâté Reduction:

4 shallots, diced

3 cloves garlic, minced

2 cups (500 mL) white wine

2 tablespoons (30 mL) cognac or brandy

Bouquet garni of 1 bay leaf, 1 sprig thyme, and a few strips of lemon peel, tied up in cheesecloth (see tip, page 47)

Assembly:

2 egg yolks

1 tablespoon (15 mL) heavy or whipping cream (35% milk fat)

Gelée:

6 sheets gelatin

Ice-cold water

2 cups (500 mL) clear Chicken Stock (page 308, or store-bought) or Duck Stock (page 311)

Kosher salt, cognac, and maple syrup to taste

Ice cubes

continued

Day 1

FOR THE DOUGH: Make the *pâte à pâté*, wrap it in plastic wrap, and reserve in the fridge.

FOR THE FARCE MIXTURE: Dice the pork shoulder, pork back fat, and duck leg meat into cubes a little smaller than the inside of your meat grinder's feeder, about ½ inch (1 cm). Place all the diced meat in a medium bowl.

In a small bowl, mix the salt, curing salt, *épices à pâté*, pepper, and sugar. Sprinkle over the diced meats and pour in the cognac. Working quickly with gloved hands, mix the cure into the meats, making sure it's all evenly and thoroughly distributed.

Press the meat down into the bowl and lay a piece of plastic wrap in the bowl, patting it down so that it rests directly on top of the meat. Refrigerate overnight.

FOR THE CURED MIXTURE: In another medium bowl, mix the duck breast meat and pork belly with the salt, *épices à pâté*, pepper, orange zest, and cognac until evenly and thoroughly combined. Cover with plastic wrap, patting it down so that it rests directly on top of the meat. Refrigerate overnight.

FOR THE FILLING MIXTURE: In a small bowl, combine the cranberries and cognac. Cover and soak overnight (the longer, the better).

FOR THE PÂTÉ REDUCTION: In a small pan on medium heat, stir together the shallots, garlic, wine, cognac, and bouquet garni. Reduce until sticky, with almost all of the liquid evaporated. Remove from the heat and let cool. Transfer to a small bowl, cover, and refrigerate.

Day 2

FOR THE DOUGH: Take the *pâte à pâté* out of the fridge and let stand for 30 minutes to warm up.

On a lightly floured work surface, roll out the dough to a 16 by 20-inch (40 by 50 cm) rectangle that's about ¼ inch (5 mm) thick. Place on a parchment-lined baking sheet and return to the fridge for about 30 minutes (this will help to relax the gluten and firm up the dough again).

Take the dough out of the fridge and, on a lightly floured work surface, roll it out to a 20 by 24-inch (50 by 60 cm) rectangle that's about ⅛ inch (3 mm) thick. Work quickly so that the dough stays cold and relatively firm. Place the terrine mould in the centre of the rectangle and press down ever so slightly to leave an indentation that marks the base. Keeping the mould in the exact same position, gently tip it over to one side and press down gently to leave an indentation. Repeat for all four sides of the mould, then lift it off the dough; the lines you pressed will serve as a template for the bottom and sides of your pâté crust. Flip the mould over and gently press the top into an adjacent spot on the dough to create a template for the pâté lid.

Place the terrine mould in the freezer for 20 minutes.

Meanwhile, using a paring knife, cut ½ inch (1 cm) around the outside of your templates for the mould and the lid. The cut-out will look like a collapsed terrine mould: a large rectangle with two smaller flaps of dough on each shorter end. Save the extra dough trimmings to make decorations. Place the lid and the extra dough back on the baking sheet and return to the fridge.

Remove the terrine mould from the freezer and spray the inside lightly with an even coating of vegetable oil. (From experience, I find that greasing the mould helps the dough adhere to the sides better.)

Using a firm but gentle hand, to avoid poking your fingertips through the dough, carefully fold the

continued

 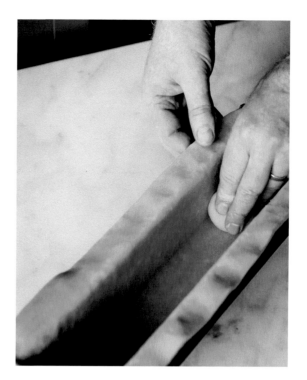

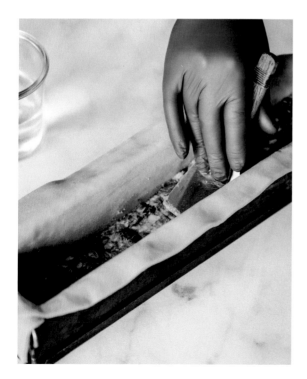 

1) CUT-OUT TEMPLATE FOR MOULD AND LID
2) PRESSING DOUGH INTO SIDES AND CORNERS WITH DOUGH BALL   3) FIRMLY SMOOTHING
FIRST LAYER OF FORCEMEAT   4) PINCHING OVERHANGING DOUGH "WINGS"

dough sides and ends inward onto the base. Gently lay the dough in the greased mould and carefully unfold it to line the mould. Be careful not to compress the dough with your fingers; it should overhang the sides. Lightly press the dough into the base and sides of the mould. Carry on as gently and carefully as you can—this bears repeating. Roll a bit of the extra dough into a ¾-inch (2 cm) ball, dip it lightly in flour, and use it to press the dough snugly onto the sides and into the corners of the terrine mould. Make sure the dough is a uniform thickness so the terrine will bake and brown evenly, and ensure that the corners are joined securely so that fat and juices don't seep out through the seams while the *pâté en croûte* is cooking and, later on, the *gelée* doesn't leak out as you pour it in. You also want to ensure that the dough is pressed directly against the mould all the way around. If it isn't, air pockets will form and create steam, meaning the heat that touches the metal won't touch the dough in the same way, and you'll end up with a lighter-coloured and softer finished product.

Once you've lined the terrine mould, place it in the freezer for 20 to 30 minutes, until it's thoroughly chilled, firm, and well rested, so that the gluten relaxes and doesn't give any spring-back. The firmer the dough is, the easier it is to fill with the forcemeat without damaging or ripping the dough. (All that being said, if you're challenged for freezer space, you can put the terrine mould in the fridge for 1 hour, bearing in mind that the dough will get firm, but it won't get freezer firm.)

FOR THE FARCE MIXTURE: Line another baking sheet with parchment paper. Remove the farce mixture from the fridge and spread it evenly on the parchment paper. Place the baking sheet in the freezer for 20 to 30 minutes, until the edges of the farce mixture become slightly frozen on the outside. (Getting the mixture very cold and working quickly when

you remove it from the freezer will help prevent the fats from separating and smearing into the meat, which would produce a dry, grainy texture in the finished pâté.)

In the meantime, assemble the meat grinder and have a medium bowl at the ready. Take note that you should undertake this next sequence of steps consecutively and distraction-free until you've assembled the *pâté en croûte* and put it back in the freezer (or fridge).

Remove the farce mixture from the freezer and coarsely grind it into the bowl, working quickly to keep it as cold as possible.

FOR THE FILLING MIXTURE: Fill a very large bowl with ice cubes. Rest a slightly smaller bowl on the ice and add the soaked cranberries, all the remaining filling mixture ingredients, the ground farce mixture, and the cured mixture. Remove the bouquet garni from the pâté reduction and spoon the reduction into the bowl. (Combining all the pâté filling over ice helps the ingredients stay as cold as possible and gives the finished pâté a great texture.)

SERIOUS PRO TIP: *For the next step, put on latex kitchen gloves to help slow any heat transfer from your hands to the pâté filling. Working as quickly as possible to keep everything cold, mix everything together by hand until the pâté forcemeat is thoroughly combined. Fair warning: it will be messy and sticky!*

TO ASSEMBLE THE PÂTÉ EN CROÛTE: Have a small wide offset spatula resting in a bowl of cold water close at hand. Take the terrine mould out of the freezer and place about one-eighth of the forcemeat into it, roughly ½ pound (225 g), which is enough to cover the base of the mould with a layer of filling about ½ inch (1 cm) thick. Using the offset spatula, smooth the forcemeat into an even layer along the bottom of the mould and gently but firmly press it right into the corners to ensure there are no air pockets. Once again, be firm but careful to avoid poking any holes in the dough. Dip the spatula in the cold water between uses to prevent it from getting too sticky.

Add another quarter of the forcemeat to the mould, roughly 1⅓ pounds (600 g), and use the offset spatula to gently press and smooth it into an even layer, making sure to get into the corners. Continue layering the forcemeat into the mould, little by little, until you've used it all up and the mould is generously overfull.

Dip the offset spatula in cold water and smooth out the top of the forcemeat, shaping it into a neat and uniform dome just above the top of the terrine mould. This will help the *pâté en croûte* stand tall during and after cooking and gives it a beautiful shape.

If you've worked quickly enough that the dough is still cold, let the terrine mould stand for 5 to 10 minutes at room temperature to warm up a bit, as the dough needs to be soft enough that you can pinch it to make it thinner.

In a small bowl, lightly beat the egg yolks with the cream to make an egg wash.

Pinch the dough "wings" that hang over the sides of the mould between your first two fingers and thumb until they're about half the original thickness, roughly ¹⁄₁₆-inch (2 mm) uniform thickness (you don't want it to be twice as thick where the lid joins the main part). Once all the wings are the correct thickness, use scissors to trim the edges of the dough to a ½-inch (1 cm) overhang.

Lift up the overhanging dough and fold it up over the domed forcemeat. Gently press down on the dough to secure it against the filling. Using the tips of your scissors, snip off the thick "knots" where the corners join (this prevents double-thick chunks of cooked dough on the corners of the finished product), but ensure that the sides are still well sealed. Delicately brush the

dough with egg wash. Don't load up your brush too much or you'll make the dough gloppy. (If the dough is overly moist, it will become soggy and the lid might not adhere properly, causing weak points in the casing. You want a strong seal that securely adheres the lid to the rest of the crust.)

Take the dough lid out of the fridge, centre it above the terrine mould, and lay it down on top of the filling, letting it hang about ½ to ¾ inch (1 to 2 cm) over the edges. Gently but firmly press the lid onto the pâté, especially the egg-washed dough. Using the same pinching technique you used for the sides, pinch the lid overhang to half thickness (this will give the finished product a more seamless and consistent amount of pastry where the lid and sides join). Using scissors, trim the overhang back to ½ to ¾ inch (1 to 2 cm).

From here, you're going to tuck the dough lid down the sides of the tin. Lightly flour a small butter knife and have it at the ready. Starting with one of the longer sides, fold the overhang back up onto the lid. Using the back of the butter knife, gently and carefully tuck the overhang down between the dough and the terrine mould. Lightly flour the butter knife again and repeat the process with the second long side.

Using scissors, trim both ends of the shorter sides diagonally at a 45-degree angle, then use the same technique to push them down the sides of the mould until the dough lid is fully tucked in, nice and neatly.

Lightly brush the surface of the pastry lid lengthwise with egg wash, and brush down into the edges a bit so it doesn't stick to the sides of the mould. Pop the terrine mould back into the freezer for 20 to 30 minutes (or the fridge for 30 to 40 minutes).

TO DECORATE THE PÂTÉ EN CROÛTE: Meanwhile, take the extra dough out of the fridge to make decorations for the top of your *pâté en croûte*. We like to add little *fleurs-de-lys* to ours, but you're the artist—the design is up to you. It's important to ensure that your decorations aren't too thick; if they stand up too high off the

continued

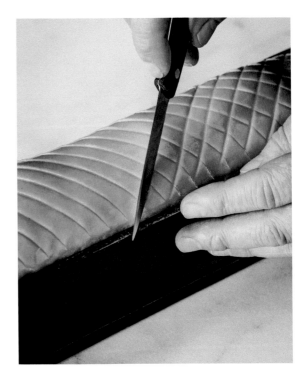

1) TUCKING DOUGH LID DOWN THE SIDE OF THE TERRINE MOULD
2) CROSS-HATCHED SCORING THE EGG-WASHED LID   3) APPLYING DECORATIONS WITH
THE EGG WASH   4) POURING *GELÉE* INTO THE BAKED, COOLED *PÂTÉ EN CROÛTE*

crust, they could easily be unevenly baked, with raw spots, and will end up looking clunky. So, on a lightly floured work surface, roll out the dough to ¹⁄₁₆ inch (2 mm) thickness. Cut out shapes, either freehand with a paring knife or with cutters—be creative. Fluted rings look especially good surrounding the *cheminées* (see below). Make lots of decorations in case some of them don't look quite right or end up breaking. Place your decorations back on the lined baking sheet and slide them back into the fridge for 10 minutes to firm up again. (They are very thin and delicate, so having them really damn cold and firm is the key to success.)

Take the *pâté en croûte* out of the freezer. The first coat of egg wash should be smooth and just slightly tacky to the touch. Lightly load up your pastry brush with egg wash—less is more—and apply a second coat, brushing lengthwise.

Now we're going to use the back of a small paring knife to score a decorative pattern in the top of the dough, making enough of an indentation to establish a visible line without cutting all the way through. With medium pressure, start scoring diagonal lines at a 45-degree angle across the width of the pâté. As you progress, use the previous line as a guide for the next. Once you've scored the entire length, turn the pâté 90 degrees and repeat the process perpendicular to the first set of lines, creating a cross-hatched diamond pattern. (This is how we often score the lid at the restaurant, but definitely feel free to use artistic licence here.)

NEXT UP: Create three equally spaced openings, called *cheminées*, in the dough lid to allow the steam to escape during baking. Use a round pastry cutter of ½ inch (1 cm) or a small paring knife to cut the three holes in the lid only—don't cut down into the filling.

Take the decorations out of the fridge. Pick up the first of three fluted rings that will surround the *cheminées* and lay it in your palm. Lightly load up your pastry brush with egg wash and gently brush the ring on both sides. Lay it down gently on top of the pâté, encircling one of the *cheminées*, and press it down lightly to adhere it to the crust. Repeat with the other two rings. Arrange your other decorations on the lid, brushing them lightly with egg wash on both sides and pressing them gently onto the lid. One last time, return the *pâté en croûte* to the freezer for 25 to 30 minutes (or 30 to 40 minutes in the fridge) prior to baking.

TO BAKE THE PÂTÉ EN CROÛTE: Meanwhile, preheat your oven to 425°F (220°C), with the rack in the centre position. (You'll be baking the *pâté en croûte* in two stages at two different temperatures: the first stage is at a high temperature to bake, colour, and set the pastry; the second stage is at a low temperature to gently set the pâté without the fats separating and ruining the final texture.)

Place the decorated *pâté en croûte* on a baking sheet and bake for 10 minutes. Turn the pan 180 degrees and bake for another 10 minutes, until the pastry is golden brown. Transfer the pan to a wire rack and lower the oven temperature to 250°F (120°C).

While the oven is cooling, roll three pieces of double-thick foil into three tubes and place them in the *cheminées* (these help protect the pastry from any juices that might run out of the pâté and spoil the lovely crisp crust).

Once the oven has cooled to 250°F (120°C), return the *pâté en croûte*, still on the baking sheet, to the oven and bake for about 1 hour, until the internal temperature in the centre of the pâté reaches 140°F (60°C). Turn the pan 180 degrees every 20 to 25 minutes to achieve a lovely even bake. Transfer the *pâté en croûte*,

continued

still on the baking sheet, to a wire rack and let cool for 1 hour at room temperature.

Place the *pâté en croûte*, still on the baking sheet, in the fridge and chill overnight. No matter how tempting it might be, don't remove the mould or cut into the pâté yet—patience!

Day 3

FOR THE GELÉE: In a medium bowl, soak the gelatin sheets in ice-cold water for at least 15 minutes, until softened.

Meanwhile, in a small saucepan on medium heat, warm up the chicken stock. Squeeze the water out of the gelatin sheets and stir them into the warm stock until fully dissolved. Season to taste with salt and, if you wish, a little cognac and perhaps a splash of maple syrup.

Place a medium bowl over ice cubes and pour in the liquid *gelée*. Stir the mixture slowly until it has cooled to about 82°F (28°C); it should be liquid enough to pour into the pâté and find all the nooks and crannies between the forcemeat and the pastry, but cold enough to set quickly once in place. Immediately transfer it to a small pitcher.

With the mould still on the baking sheet, either in your fridge (preferably) or on the counter, carefully pour the *gelée* through a funnel into the *cheminées* until the terrine is filled up. Refrigerate for at least 3 hours, allowing the *gelée* to set completely. It will keep in the fridge for 5 to 7 days.

Take the *pâté en croûte* out of the fridge and remove the terrine mould. Slice the pâté with a serrated knife and arrange the slices on a platter. Serve it with gherkins, vegetable pickles, mustard, and beer.

TIP *At the restaurant, we have access to myriad stocks and by-products left over from other dishes that we put to good use; two good examples are the bones from pig's trotters and the set juice from the bottom of the pan when you make confit duck. We use these to make a gelatin-rich stock that, once clarified to a crystal-clear consommé, makes an excellent base for the* gelée. *If you don't have ready access to these things, a tasty, very clear stock works just as well.*

✤

Terrine Chaude de Homard

Warm Lobster Terrine

Yield: 6 PORTIONS

Preparation time: 1½ HOURS +
OVERNIGHT RESTING

Cooking time: 1½ HOURS

Dinner transforms to a rather sophisticated affair with this beautiful lobster terrine, an amazing preparation that continues my love affair with lobster. It gives us the opportunity to use every part of the lobster and to serve as many as six people with just one large lobster. If we consider the fact that lobster is on the expensive side, it's not a bad food cost per guest for a precious ingredient. The scallop mousse filling's smooth richness makes the terrine extra special. This dish is simply elegant and is, for me, a true St. Lawrence classic.

What you'll need:

6 by 4-inch (15 by 10 cm) terrine mould, 4 inches (10 cm) deep, preferably with a lid

Scallop Mousse:

13 ounces (375 g) scallops, cleaned and diced

2 egg whites

½ tablespoon (5 g) kosher salt

1 cup (250 mL) very cold heavy or whipping cream (35% milk fat)

Terrine:

1 bunch (about 1 pound) green Swiss chard, stems removed

1.8-pound (800 to 900 g) live lobster

FOR THE SCALLOP MOUSSE: Place the bowl and blade of your food processor in the freezer for 20 minutes.

Add the scallops, egg whites, and salt to the food processor and process until puréed. With the motor running, through the feed tube, slowly pour in the cream and process until emulsified. (It's important that all the ingredients are ice cold, or the emulsification could split.) Transfer the mousse to a small bowl, cover with a plastic wrap and refrigerate until ready to use.

FOR THE TERRINE: Bring a medium pot of salted water to a boil on high heat. Prepare an ice bath. Blanch the Swiss chard for 20 seconds, then immediately transfer it to the ice bath to stop the cooking. Pat the Swiss chard dry on a dishtowel to remove any excess water. Set aside.

Dispatch the lobster humanely (see tip, page 34). Twist the tail to remove it from the body, and remove the claws and knuckles. Put the body aside in a bowl on your counter until you're ready to make the sauce. Using butcher's twine, tie the tail to a fork or butter knife to prevent it from curling up when it cooks. (You want it to be straight, as it will be in the centre of the terrine.)

In a small pot on high heat, bring 4 cups (1 L) water and 2 tablespoons (20 g) kosher salt to a boil. Prepare an ice bath. Plunge the claws and knuckles into the boiling water, start your timer and cook for 4 minutes. Transfer to the ice bath. Add the tail to the boiling water and cook for 1½ minutes. Immediately transfer the lobster tail to the ice bath and let cool for 15 minutes.

continued

Lobster Sauce:

4 tablespoons (60 g) unsalted butter

2 cloves garlic, thinly sliced

1 shallot, thinly sliced

1 small leek (white part only), thinly sliced

1 tablespoon (10 g) all-purpose flour

1 teaspoon (5 mL) tomato paste

3 tablespoons (45 mL) cognac

1 cup (250 mL) white wine

1 cup (250 mL) Fish Stock (page 312) or water

½ cup (125 mL) heavy or whipping cream (35% milk fat)

¼ sheet kombu (optional)

2 sprigs tarragon

1 bay leaf

Serving:

Olive oil, for brushing

1 tablespoon (10 g) unsalted butter

Juice of ¼ lemon

Fresh chervil leaves, to garnish

Remove the lobster meat from the shells, making sure to remove the cartilage from the claws and the vein running through the centre of the tail. Discard the shells. Set the tail aside and dice the meat from the claws and knuckles into ½-inch (1 cm) cubes. Using a rubber or silicone spatula, gently mix the cubed lobster meat into the scallop mousse.

Preheat your oven to 325°F (160°C), with the rack in the centre position.

Time to build the terrine. On a flat surface, spread out two layers of plastic wrap, one on top of the other. Place the Swiss chard leaves on the plastic wrap in an even layer that's long and wide enough to line the inside of the terrine mould. Brush the inside of the mould with water and gently transfer the plastic wrap of Swiss chard into it. Press the Swiss chard into the corners so it lines the mould evenly, and let the excess hang over the sides.

Transfer half of the scallop mousse into the mould, spread it out evenly using an offset spatula or a spoon dipped in hot water, and press down on it with a rubber spatula to eliminate any air bubbles. Next, split the lobster tail right down the middle with a sharp knife. You'll end up with two pieces of tail. Flip the two pieces together so you have an even rectangle going down the middle of the terrine. Lay the lobster tail pieces down the centre. Spread the remaining scallop mousse evenly on top. Press down on the mousse to make sure the terrine is compact. Fold the overhanging Swiss chard over the top of the terrine and cover with the plastic wrap, then the lid of the terrine mould; if you don't have a lid, cover with a piece of foil.

Place the terrine mould in a shallow baking pan and pour in enough boiling water to reach halfway up the sides of the mould (this is a *bain-marie*).

Place the *bain-marie* in the oven and bake, rotating the pan every 10 to 15 minutes for more even cooking, for 45 to 60 minutes, or until the temperature in the centre of the terrine reaches 125°F (52°C). Take the temperature often with the help of a probe thermometer—make sure to take it from the centre, not the sides—as it's very important that you don't overcook the terrine. Remove the mould from the *bain-marie*, uncover, and let cool for 1 hour. Recover the terrine with the plastic wrap and refrigerate overnight.

FOR THE LOBSTER SAUCE: Open up the sides of the lobster head, remove the gills, and discard them (they would give the sauce a bitter, fishy taste). Chop the lobster head into small pieces.

continued

In a medium saucepan on medium-high heat, heat the butter until foamy. Add the lobster pieces and cook, stirring, for 4 minutes, until they turn bright red. Mix in the garlic, shallot, and leek, and sauté for 4 minutes, stirring often. Stir in the flour and tomato paste, and cook for 2 minutes. Deglaze the pan with the cognac. You can flambé the cognac if you like the show, or just reduce it to 1 teaspoon (5 mL). Stir in the wine and reduce the liquid by half. Stir in the stock, cream, kombu, tarragon, and bay leaf. Bring to a boil, then lower the heat to medium-low and simmer gently for 30 minutes.

Strain the sauce through a fine chinois (page 102), pressing with the back of a spoon to extract as much sauce as possible. Return the sauce to the pan, place on medium-high heat, and reduce to 1 cup (250 mL). Remove from the heat and set aside.

TO SERVE: Preheat your oven to 325°F (160°C), with the rack in the centre position. Line a baking sheet with parchment paper.

Unmould the lobster terrine, unwrap it, and pat it dry with a paper towel. Using a very sharp knife, cut the terrine into six even slices. Place the slices on the lined pan, brush with a bit of olive oil to prevent drying out, and cover the pan with plastic wrap. Warm the terrine in the oven for 10 to 12 minutes, until it's just warm in the centre. Pop six serving plates into the oven for the last 2 minutes to warm them up.

Return the saucepan to medium-low heat and reheat the lobster sauce, then whisk in the butter and lemon juice. Taste for seasoning. Spoon the sauce onto the warmed plates, place a slice of lobster terrine atop the sauce on each plate, and garnish simply with chervil leaves.

⚜

Steak Tartare et Chips de Pomme de Terre

Beef Tartare and Potato Chips

Yield: 4 PORTIONS

Preparation time: 1 HOUR

Cooking time: 10 MINUTES

What you'll need:

Gaufrette (or Japanese) mandoline

Gaufrette Potato Chips:

2 russet or Kennebec potatoes (unpeeled)

4 cups (1 L) water

1 tablespoon + 2 teaspoons (16 g) kosher salt

Canola oil, for frying

Dressing:

1 tablespoon (15 mL) olive oil

1 tablespoon (15 mL) Dijon mustard

1 tablespoon (15 mL) Worcestershire sauce

½ tablespoon (7 mL) ketchup

Tartare:

10.5 ounces (300 g) beef, trimmed of sinew and fat

2 ounces (55 g) Chèvre Noir or Comté cheese, shaved thinly

1 shallot, finely chopped and rinsed in cold water

2 tablespoons (30 g) finely chopped cornichons

1 tablespoon (15 g) small capers, chopped

2 teaspoons (10 mL) extra-virgin olive oil

1 teaspoon (5 mL) fresh lemon juice

½ teaspoon (2 g) kosher salt

A splash of Tabasco

❧ *Steak tartare is a mainstay at brasseries and bistros. It usually ranks among the favourite menu items, especially for people who love sushi and who ask for their steak* saignant, *as the French would say, meaning rare, or "bloody." My preference is to use eye of round, flank, or sirloin for tartare instead of tenderloin. Tenderloin is almost too tender, and I like my tartare to have a bit of a chew to it. That being said, don't hesitate to use tenderloin if it's your preferred cut. The most important thing is taking the time to source the best-quality beef—not frozen—from a top-notch butcher. Adding cheese to tartare definitely isn't traditional, and our restaurant guests are always surprised by it, asking me, "Why?" I always reply by asking them whether they enjoy the taste of shaved Parmesan on their beef carpaccio. That usually brings the conversation to a swift and logical end. Serve the tartare with the gaufrette potato chips or your favourite plain store-bought potato chips and a small salad. Nothing else will do. Well . . . maybe french fries.*

FOR THE GAUFRETTE POTATO CHIPS: Using a *gaufrette* or Japanese mandoline (see tip), cut the potatoes into thin slices, about ¹⁄₁₆ inch (2 mm) thick. Rinse the potato slices in cold water until the water runs clear. Set aside in a bowl.

In a small pot on medium-high heat, bring the water and salt to a simmer, then pour over the potato slices. Let cool, then spread the potato slices on a dishtowel and pat dry.

In a medium pot on medium-high heat, heat 4 inches (10 cm) of oil to 325°F (160°C), and have a baking sheet lined with paper towels at the ready. Fry the potato slices in 2 to 3 small batches for about 5 minutes each, or until the chips are golden brown—make sure you don't crowd them in the pot or they won't crisp up properly. Blot the chips on the paper towels and set aside.

FOR THE DRESSING: In a small bowl, whisk together all the ingredients. Set aside.

continued

FOR THE TARTARE: Set a medium bowl over ice. Using a chef's knife, chop the beef into very small pieces and place it in the bowl to keep cool until serving. You can chop the meat ahead of time, but no more than 2 hours before plating.

When ready to serve, add all of the remaining tartare ingredients to the bowl, along with the dressing. Mix until well combined and taste for seasoning. Serve with the chips.

TIP   *A mandoline slicer is a super-handy kitchen tool that makes short work of uniformly slicing or julienning large quantities of vegetables. Gaufrettes are sliced with a special wavy blade, and there's also one that makes perfect pommes frites.*

⚜

Éclairs à la Mousse de Foie de Canard

Duck Liver Mousse Eclairs

Yield: 10 ÉCLAIRS, 1 PER PERSON

Preparation time: 2 HOURS + OVERNIGHT CHILLING

Cooking time: 2 HOURS

What you'll need:

6 by 4-inch (15 by 10 cm) terrine mould or bread pan, 4 inches (10 cm) deep

Stand mixer fitted with the whisk attachment (optional)

Piping bag with a star tip

Chicken Skin:

4 ounces (125 g) chicken skin (ask your butcher)

Duck Liver Mousse:

2 small shallots, finely chopped

1 clove garlic, finely chopped

½ cup (125 mL) Madeira or Port

½ cup (125 mL) red wine

2 tablespoons (30 mL) brandy or cognac

7 ounces (200 g) duck foie gras

7 ounces (200 g) duck liver or chicken liver

1 teaspoon (4 g) curing salt (Prague Powder #1 or Insta Cure #1)

1 teaspoon (3 g) kosher salt

½ teaspoon (1 g) freshly cracked black pepper

3 whole large eggs + 1 yolk

½ cup (125 g) brown butter (see tip), at room temperature

✎ *When creating the first St. Lawrence menu, I wanted to come up with festive, over-the-top indulgent items to give Vancouverites something different from their day-to-day kale juice diet. People usually think of éclairs as sweet, not savoury, so to meet in the middle and create éclairs that are both salty and sweet at the same time seemed like a good idea. Our guests' reactions when they tasted the éclairs confirmed that it was. The visual confusion that comes with this dish also makes it a success, as people often think it's a dessert and are pleasantly surprised by their first bite.*

TIP *You'll need a total of ¾ cup (185 mL) brown butter for this recipe: ½ cup (125 mL) for the mousse and ¼ cup (60 mL) for the glaze. To make it, place 1 cup (220 g) unsalted butter in a small pot on high heat and cook a little past the melting point, browning the milk solids in the butter and creating a wonderfully nutty aroma. Let cool completely.*

Day 1

FOR THE CHICKEN SKIN: Preheat your oven to 350°F (175°C), with the rack in the centre position.

On a baking sheet lined with a silicone mat or parchment paper, lay the chicken skin down flat. Top the entire pan with another piece of parchment paper and place another baking sheet of the same size on top.

Bake for 35 to 40 minutes, removing the excess fat every 10 minutes or so, until the skin is golden brown and crispy. Be careful not to burn yourself, as the fat will be extremely hot. (You can keep the chicken fat in your fridge to use in future cooking.) Let cool completely at room temperature, then transfer to an airtight container to the fridge overnight.

FOR THE DUCK LIVER MOUSSE: Preheat your oven to 325°F (160°C), with the rack in the centre position.

In a small saucepan, combine the shallots, garlic, Madeira, red wine, and brandy. Bring to a simmer and reduce by two-thirds, until you have about ⅓ cup (100 mL). Let cool completely.

In a small bowl, mix together the foie gras, duck liver, curing salt, regular salt, and pepper. Let stand for 15 minutes.

Red Wine Reduction:

1⅔ cups (400 mL) red wine

1⅔ cups (400 mL) water

¾ cup (150 g) granulated sugar

5 black peppercorns

2 whole cloves

1 star anise pod

½ cinnamon stick

Maple Glaze:

¼ cup (60 mL) melted brown butter (see tip)

1 tablespoon (15 mL) maple syrup

Pinch kosher salt

Finishing:

½ batch Pâte à Choux (page 297)

1 small jar preserved Guinette cherries from Périgord or any good cherry preserves

Using a blender, blitz the liver mixture with the shallot reduction and the eggs, then emulsify with the brown butter with the blender still running. Strain through a fine tamis.

Transfer the mixture to the terrine mould that you've fully lined with plastic wrap and cover with the lid or a piece of foil. Place the mould in a shallow baking pan and pour in enough boiling water to reach halfway up the sides of the mould (this is a *bain-marie*).

Place the *bain-marie* in the oven and bake until the internal temperature reaches 140°F (60°C), about 35 to 45 minutes. The mousse should be just set, like a flan or crème brûlée. Remove the terrine from the oven and let cool at room temperature for 1 hour, then refrigerate overnight.

FOR THE RED WINE REDUCTION: In a medium saucepan on medium-high heat, combine all the ingredients and bring to a simmer. Reduce to ¾ cup (175 mL). Strain through a tamis into a small container, cover, and refrigerate.

FOR THE MAPLE GLAZE: Place the brown butter in a small aluminum bowl on ice. Whisk in the maple syrup and salt until just set. Cover and let stand at room temperature until needed.

Day 2

TO FINISH: Use the *pâte à choux* to bake 10 éclairs as directed on page 297. Set aside.

Take the duck liver mousse out of the fridge. Using a hot spoon kept in a bowl of hot water, remove and discard the oxidized surface of the mousse. Transfer the mousse to the bowl of a stand mixer fitted with the whisk, and whip on medium speed for 2 minutes or until light and fluffy (you could also do this step by hand, with a whisk). If the mousse is still too firm after 2 minutes, drizzle in 1 to 2 tablespoons of warm water to achieve the right consistency. Transfer the mousse to a piping bag with a star tip and set aside.

Using a chef's knife, finely chop the chicken skin, but don't over-chop it. You want small, crispy bits of skin, not a paste.

Transfer 40 cherries to the red wine reduction.

You're now ready to assemble and plate. Preheat your oven to 350°F (180°C), with the rack in the centre position.

continued

Warm the éclairs for 4 to 5 minutes, until they're crispy on the outside and warm on the inside. Using a serrated knife, cut horizontally through the éclairs, leaving one-third as the top and two-thirds as the base. Pipe the mousse onto the base pieces, using about 2 tablespoons (50 g) per éclair. Brush the top pieces with the maple glaze, sprinkle some chicken skin over top, and place the tops over the mousse. Transfer each éclair to a plate and place four cherries next to it, along with a few spoonfuls of red wine reduction.

TIP *Because we add a fair amount of sugar and reduce the wine to a syrup, don't go crazy and spend too much money on the wine. You can easily find a full-bodied red, like a Cabernet Sauvignon, for $20 or less.*

⚜

Escargots au Beurre à l'Ail

Snails in Garlic Butter

Yield: 4 TO 6 PORTIONS

Preparation time: 1½ HOURS

Cooking time: 45 MINUTES + 30 MINUTES FOR PUFF PASTRY CASES

🐌 *Back in the good old days, like most teenagers, I was perpetually hungry. Somehow, in Mom's kitchen pantry there was always a three-pack of canned escargots. I don't know why they were there, as none of my family members were eating them. The price probably appealed to my mom—around $1.29 a can, from what I remember. I was always craving a snack after school, and one day I decided to open a can, sautéed the escargots with a garlicky butter, and toasted myself a piece of bread to go along with it. The snails reminded me of mushrooms in a way, and I had no problem with mushrooms—I always loved them. After three days, all the cans were gone. I had to wait until the next week before another three-pack appeared in the pantry. This went on for years, and my mom never asked who was eating the snails on a regular basis. They just kept coming back. That's why I needed to have a version of* escargots à l'ail *on the St. Lawrence menu.*

Escargot Butter:

3 cloves garlic, grated on a microplane

½ cup (30 g) fresh flat-leaf parsley leaves, very finely chopped

1 teaspoon (3 g) kosher salt

½ teaspoon (1 g) freshly cracked black pepper

½ cup (120 g) softened unsalted butter

Chlorophyll (optional but recommended):

A big handful of wild ramp leaves or spinach (about 1 cup/250 mL)

2 cups (500 mL) water

FOR THE ESCARGOT BUTTER: In a large mixing bowl, using a rubber spatula, vigorously mix the garlic, parsley, salt, pepper, and butter until the garlic and parsley are incorporated evenly into the butter. Spoon the mixture onto a piece of plastic wrap and roll tightly into a cylinder. Tie the ends securely and refrigerate until needed.

FOR THE CHLOROPHYLL: Wash and dry the ramp leaves. Place the leaves and water in a blender and process for a few minutes, until you have a bright green liquid.

Pour the liquid into a small saucepan. Cook on low heat, stirring constantly, until green particles rise to the surface. (It's important to do this slowly.) Pour the liquid into a container, along with a handful of ice, and refrigerate until cold.

Line a chinois with a coffee filter (see tip, page 102). Drain the cold ramp liquid through the lined chinois. Don't push it through—take your time and let gravity do its job. Once drained, discard the liquid. Scrape as much as possible of the green paste that remains on the coffee filter into an airtight container; you should have about 2 tablespoons (30 mL) chlorophyll. Refrigerate for up to 3 days.

Make the puff pastry cases according to the method on page 304.

continued

Escargot Ragoût:

1 large shallot

1 stalk celery

1 small carrot, peeled

2 tablespoons (30 g) unsalted butter

48 good-quality large Burgundy escargots (see tip)

¼ cup (60 mL) white wine, one you like to drink

½ cup (125 mL) Chicken Stock or Vegetable Stock (page 308 or 313, or store-bought)

½ teaspoon (2 g) kosher salt

Assembly:

12 small Puff Pastry Cases (see variation on page 304)

¾ cup (175 mL) Chicken Stock or Vegetable Stock (page 308 or 313, or store-bought)

Juice of ½ lemon

FOR THE ESCARGOT RAGOÛT: Cut the shallot, celery, and carrot into ⅛-inch (3 mm) cubes (called *brunoise*). You should have about ¼ cup (60 mL) of each.

In a medium pot on medium heat, heat the butter until foamy. Stir in the shallot, celery, and carrot and sweat, stirring often, for 8 to 10 minutes, until tender but without colouration. Stir in the escargots and cook for 2 minutes. Deglaze the pot with the wine. Lower the heat to medium-low and reduce the liquid to almost nothing. Pour in the stock, bring to a gentle simmer, and cook gently for 20 to 25 minutes, until the escargots are tender. Season with salt, remove from the heat, and set aside.

TO ASSEMBLE: Preheat your oven to 350°F (180°C), with the rack in the centre position.

Place the puff pastry cases on a baking sheet and reheat in the oven for 3 to 4 minutes.

Meanwhile, in a medium pan on medium-high heat, bring the stock to a boil. Remove from the heat and gradually whisk in the escargot butter to create an emulsion and give the sauce a rich, shiny gloss (this is called *monter au beurre*). Stir in 1 tablespoon (15 mL) chlorophyll and the lemon juice. Taste and adjust the seasoning. Add the escargot ragoût and reheat for 2 to 3 minutes on low heat.

Transfer the puff pastry cases to a serving plate or platter. Spoon the escargot ragoût into the cases and onto the plate. Sauce generously.

TIP *You can track down cans of good-quality Burgundy escargots in specialty grocery stores or online.*

⚜

Torchon de Foie Gras

Foie Gras Torchon

Yield: 8 TO 10 PORTIONS

Preparation time: 45 MINUTES +
2 TO 3 DAYS CURING

Cooking time: 10 MINUTES

✒ *As far as foie gras preparations go, this old-school method is probably my favourite because it gives a fantastic yield and doesn't lose much fat along the way. Considering the cost of foie gras, it's a wise skill to get under your belt. Serve the duck liver simply with bread and your favourite jam, or try it with our maple gelée and dinner rolls (recipes follow). It keeps very well too, a full week in the fridge or up to three months in the freezer. When frozen, I like to shave or grate the foie gras torchon on top of other dishes to give them a special treatment. I've grated some over oysters, an omelette, a steak, a soup, a salad . . . the list goes on forever and the options are endless.*

1.1 pounds (500 g) good-quality foie gras

1½ teaspoons (5 g) kosher salt

¾ teaspoon (1 g) freshly cracked black pepper

½ teaspoon (2 g) granulated sugar

¼ teaspoon (1 g) curing pink salt (Prague Powder #1 or Insta Cure #1)

2 tablespoons (30 mL) cognac or Armagnac

Day 1

Temper the foie gras at room temperature for about 2 hours, until it is very soft. Pull apart the lobes and remove as many veins as possible. Remove any sinew or membranes from the outside. Working from the bottom of the lobes, use a chef's knife to butterfly them horizontally. Locate the primary vein in the centre of each lobe and slice through the lobe to the vein, following its path and pulling the liver apart to see the vein clearly. Don't worry if it looks like you are destroying the lobe—it will come back together just like butter. The most important thing is to get rid of those veins.

In a small bowl, combine the kosher salt, pepper, sugar, and curing salt. Sprinkle all over the foie gras. Place the liver in a plastic container or on a plate and sprinkle it with the cognac. Press a piece of plastic wrap directly against the liver to minimize air contact, and refrigerate overnight.

Day 2

Remove the foie gras from the container and let it rest for an hour at room temperature (it will be easier to work with). Place the liver on a large piece of plastic wrap and shape it into a loaf about 6 inches (15 cm) long by 3 inches (7.5 cm) wide. Roll the foie gras tightly into a log, twisting and squeezing the ends of the plastic to help compact it. Tie off both ends securely using butcher's twine. Put it in the freezer for 15 minutes to set.

continued

Choose a pot large enough to accommodate the width of the foie gras torchon. Pour in enough water to submerge the torchon and bring to 115°F (45°C) on medium heat. Cook the torchon in the warm water for 10 minutes. Meanwhile, prepare an ice bath. Immediately transfer the torchon to the ice bath and let cool for 10 minutes.

The foie gras will be loose in the plastic wrap. Poke a few holes into the plastic wrap with the tip of a paring knife and make it compact again by rolling it as tightly as possible. Some of the melted foie fat will escape; you can keep or discard it. Twist the ends of the plastic wrap and tie them in a knot or with butcher's twine. Transfer the torchon to a small tray, and refrigerate overnight, or better yet, for 2 days.

Unwrap the torchon and, using a ring mould for perfect edges, slice it into rounds. Serve it with chopped maple aspic and warm maple dinner rolls.

✤

ASPIC AU SIROP D'ÉRABLE
Maple Aspic

Yield: 1 CUP (250 G)
Preparation time: 10 MINUTES
Cooking time: 5 MINUTES + 2 HOURS REFRIGERATION

3 sheets gelatin
½ cup (125 mL) maple syrup
½ cup (125 mL) water

In a small bowl, soak the gelatin sheets in cold water for 10 minutes.

Meanwhile, in a small saucepan on medium heat, heat up the maple syrup and water. Squeeze all the water out of the gelatin and add it to the warm syrup mixture, stirring until fully dissolved. Pour the liquid into a small container and refrigerate until set, about 2 hours. Unmould the maple aspic and dice or chop it.

✤

PETIT PAIN DE LAIT À L'ÉRABLE

Maple Dinner Rolls

Yield: 15 ROLLS, EACH ABOUT
1½ OUNCES (45 G)

Preparation time: 20 MINUTES +
2 HOURS RISING

Cooking time: 30 MINUTES

What you'll need:
Stand mixer, fitted with the dough
hook attachment

1 cup (250 mL) homogenized milk
(3.25% milk fat)

⅓ cup (75 g) unsalted butter

3 tablespoons (45 mL) maple syrup

1 large egg (55 g)

2½ teaspoons (7 g) active dry yeast

2¾ cups (450 g) bread flour or all-
purpose flour

2 teaspoons (8 g) kosher salt

1 egg yolk + 1 tablespoon (15 mL)
homogenized milk (3.25% milk fat),
lightly beaten for egg wash

In a small saucepan, heat the milk, butter, and maple syrup until the butter is melted. Stir, remove from the heat, and let cool completely.

Transfer the milk mixture to the bowl of a stand mixer fitted with the dough hook. Stir in 1 egg and the yeast, and let stand for 10 minutes. Add the flour and salt, and mix on low speed for 5 minutes.

Lightly oil a medium bowl, transfer the dough into it, and cover the bowl with a damp dishtowel. Let rise at room temperature for 1 hour.

On a lightly floured work surface, cut the dough into 15 equal portions. Using your hands, shape each portion into a ball. Lightly spray a baking pan with oil and place the dough balls in it, ensuring that they're barely touching each other. Cover with a damp towel and proof for 1 hour.

Preheat your oven to 350°F (180°C), with the rack in the centre position.

Gently brush the rolls with a thin layer of egg wash. Cover the pan with a deep lid (the same height as the baking pan, to create some steam).

Bake the rolls for 20 minutes. Uncover and bake until the rolls are golden brown, about 10 more minutes. Take out of the oven, unmould the buns, and cool on a baking rack for 15 minutes. Serve warm.

⚜

IMAGE ON PAGE 178

LEFT: FOIE GRAS TORCHON, PAGE 175   RIGHT: COQUILLES ST-JACQUES À LA PARISIENNE , PAGE 180

Coquilles St-Jacques à la Parisienne

Scallops and Potato Gratin

Yield: 8 PORTIONS

Preparation time: 1 HOUR + 45 MINUTES BRINING

Cooking time: 1½ HOURS

What you'll need:

Piping bag with a star tip

Scallops:

4 cups (1 L) water, divided

¼ cup (50 g) granulated sugar

5 tablespoons (50 g) kosher salt

1.5 pounds (675 g) scallops, side muscles removed

Mussels:

2 tablespoons (30 g) unsalted butter

1 shallot, sliced

1 clove garlic, sliced

¼ cup (60 mL) white wine

1 bay leaf

1 pound (450 g) mussels, scrubbed and debearded (see Cod Quenelles, page 183)

2 cups (500 mL) Sauce Mornay (page 306)

🍂 *Although* coquilles St-Jacques *is French in origin, we Québécois have adopted the dish as our own, and it has become a classic Christmas Eve appetizer. It was definitely love at first bite for me, and I wondered where it had been all my life. You should use large scallops (U-10) for this dish. Choosing fresh and local is obviously best, but I acknowledge that it isn't possible for everyone. If available, buy scallops in the shell so you can use the bottom shells for baking. But your local fishmonger will have quality frozen scallops, and you can track down scallop shells or dishes at gourmet grocery or kitchenware stores.*

FOR THE SCALLOPS: Place 3 cups (750 mL) of the water in a large bowl. In a small saucepan on medium-high heat, bring the remaining water to a boil. Stir in the sugar and salt until dissolved. Pour into the bowl. Refrigerate until cold. Add the scallops to the cold brine and refrigerate for 15 minutes.

Preheat the barbecue grill to high, or heat a cast-iron grill pan on high heat until piping hot.

Remove the scallops from the brine and pat them dry. Sear the scallops on one side only—all you want are some grill marks, about 2 minutes. The sear is mainly to impart a smoky background flavour. Cut each scallop into quarters, place them in a small bowl, and refrigerate until ready to use.

FOR THE MUSSELS: In a medium pot on medium-high heat, heat the butter until foamy. Lower the heat to medium and sweat the shallot and garlic for 4 minutes, stirring often to make sure they don't take on any colouration. Add the wine and bay leaf, and cook for 30 seconds to remove the alcohol taste. Add the mussels, cover tightly, and cook until all the mussels are open, about 5 minutes.

Using a slotted spoon, remove the mussels from the pot. Discard any unopened mussels. Strain the cooking liquid through a fine-mesh sieve, pour it back into the pot, and reduce on medium heat to about 3 tablespoons (45 mL). Meanwhile, remove the mussels from their shells, place the meat in a bowl, and refrigerate until ready to use.

Prepare the Sauce Mornay and stir in the reduced mussel liquid. Set aside.

Mushroom Duxelles:

3 tablespoons (45 g) unsalted butter

1 large shallot, finely chopped

1 clove garlic, chopped

9 ounces (250 g) button mushrooms, finely diced

Kosher salt and freshly cracked black pepper, to taste

3 tablespoons (45 mL) white wine

Pommes Duchesse:

1 pound (450 g) russet potatoes

3 tablespoons (45 g) unsalted butter, melted

2 egg yolks

Freshly cracked black pepper, grated nutmeg, and kosher salt, to taste

Assembly:

2 cups (500 mL) coarse rock salt

8 scallop shells

¾ cup (80 g) grated Parmesan cheese

¾ cup (80 g) panko or breadcrumbs, toasted

FOR THE MUSHROOM DUXELLES: In a medium sauté pan on medium-high heat, heat the butter until foamy. Lower the heat to medium, add the shallot and garlic, and cook gently for 3 minutes. Add the mushrooms, season well with salt and pepper, and cook, stirring frequently to be sure the mushrooms don't stick, for 5 minutes. Stir in the wine and cook until all the liquid has evaporated, about 5 minutes. Remove from the heat and let cool.

FOR THE POMMES DUCHESSE: In a medium pot of salted boiling water, cook the potatoes until tender. Drain off the water and let the potatoes cool for a while. When they're cool enough to handle, peel them and pass them through a sieve or a ricer onto a tray or a piece of parchment paper. Spread them out to make sure most of the steam is released.

Transfer the potatoes to a large mixing bowl and, using a wooden spatula, stir in the butter, egg yolks, pepper, nutmeg, and (if needed) some salt. Transfer the potatoes to a piping bag with a star tip.

TO ASSEMBLE: Preheat your oven to 350°F (175°C), with the rack in the centre position.

On a baking sheet, make 8 little piles of coarse rock salt. Nestle the scallop shells into the salt so that they'll be stable. Spoon 1 tablespoon (15 mL) mushroom duxelles into each shell. Pipe small rosettes of *pommes Duchesse* in a ring around the edge of each shell.

Reheat the sauce Mornay on medium-low heat until warm to the touch, then stir in the scallop pieces and mussels. Reheat gently, stirring often; you just want the mixture to be slightly warm, as that will speed up the baking process.

Divide the scallop mixture evenly among the shells, spooning it in over the duxelles in the centre of the *pommes Duchesse* ring. Sprinkle 1 tablespoon (7 g) of grated Parmesan cheese and 1 tablespoon of breadcrumbs (7 g) atop each *coquille* to finish.

Bake the *coquilles St-Jacques* for 12 minutes. Switch the oven to broil and caramelize until the cheese and potatoes are golden, about 2 minutes. Transfer to a plate and serve piping hot.

⚜

IMAGE ON PAGE 179

Quenelles de Morue, Moules, et Sauce Normande

Cod Quenelles with Mussels and Normande Sauce

Yield: 4 PORTIONS

Preparation time: 1¼ HOURS + OVERNIGHT BRINING

Cooking time: 40 MINUTES + 1 HOUR FOR THE SAUCE

In culinary terms, a quenelle is a football-shaped dumpling. The most famous quenelle is a classic Lyonnaise dish made with a lake fish called brochet, *or pike, and served with crayfish sauce. But you can make quenelles with lots of different proteins, such as scallops, shrimp, lobster, chicken, liver, and veal. I was admittedly obsessed with them during my first visit to Lyon, and I ate more than my fair share of* quenelles de brochet sauce Nantua *because I wanted to try as many versions as possible. My wife had to stop me with the power word: "Enough! Can we just have mussels and frites with a green salad?" Quenelles are a wonderful way to use fish trimmings from another dish, thus minimizing food waste, and it's a dish we serve often at the restaurant. Classic French recipes always call for a* panade *(a mixture of flour and milk) and butter in the preparation, but I find that ends up producing an inconsistent and heavy finished product, depending on the fish. My version is what we call a* mousseline, *gently poached and then glazed with the sauce. It's like biting into a cloud.*

Brined Cod:

2 cups (500 mL) water, divided

5 tablespoons (50 g) kosher salt

9 ounces (250 g) ling cod fillet, skinned and deboned

Day 1

FOR THE BRINED COD: In a small saucepan on medium heat, bring ½ cup (125 mL) of the water to a boil. Whisk in the salt until fully dissolved. Remove from the heat and add the remaining water. Transfer to a container and refrigerate until cold.

Fully submerge the cod in the cold brine and let stand for 30 minutes at room temperature.

Take the fish out of the brine, pat it dry, and put it on a plate. Refrigerate, uncovered, overnight. (The overnight brining process does a few things: it seasons the fish properly, kills any bacteria on the surface, and facilitates evaporation of some of the fish's moisture content, resulting in a firmer and meatier texture.)

continued

Mussels:

20 mussels

½ cup (125 mL) dry white wine

1 shallot, peeled and sliced thinly

1 bay leaf

1 sprig of thyme

Quenelles:

1 egg white (1.5 ounces/40 g)

½ cup (125 mL) heavy or whipping cream (35% milk fat)

1 tablespoon (15 g) all-purpose flour, sifted

Serving:

1⅓ cups (325 mL) Sauce Normande (recipe below)

4 puff pastry *fleurons* (see tip, page 301)

Day 2

FOR THE MUSSELS: Give the mussels a scrub under cold running water. Grab their beards (the hairy stuff on the bottom side of the shell) and remove them. In a medium pot on medium-high heat, add white wine, shallot, bay leaf, and thyme. Bring to a simmer then add the mussels. Cover with a lid and cook for 4 minutes. Remove from the heat and transfer the mussels to a bowl to cool down. Strain the mussel stock through a tamis; you can use that mussel stock for the Sauce Normande (recipe opposite). Once the mussels are cool enough to handle, remove the meat from the shells. Discard the shells and keep the mussels in a small bowl, covered, in the fridge.

Make the Sauce Normande (recipe opposite) and set aside.

FOR THE QUENELLES: Place the bowl and blade of your food processor in the freezer for 20 minutes, and make sure all your ingredients are very cold.

Cube the cod and add it to the food processor, along with the egg white. Process for 3 minutes, to a fine paste. With the motor running, through the feed tube, slowly pour in the cream to emulsify the mixture—this is your *mousseline*.

Have a medium mixing bowl at the ready. Spoon one-third of the *mousseline* into a sieve and use a pastry scraper to push the mixture through the sieve into the bowl. (This step is optional but will give your quenelles a significantly smoother texture.) Repeat with two more batches of *mousseline*. Using a spatula, fold the sifted flour into the *mousseline* until fully incorporated.

Fill a large pot two-thirds full of water and bring to 185°F (85°C) on medium-high heat. At this point, it's a good idea to cook a small quenelle to make sure the *mousseline* is seasoned properly and adjusting to taste. Poach it in the water for 5 minutes and taste to check for seasoning; add salt if needed.

Meanwhile, using scissors, cut four 4-inch (10 cm) squares of parchment paper. Spray the squares with oil. Portion the fish *mousseline* into four equal scoops, placing one scoop on each parchment square.

Have a medium bowl of hot water at the ready. Dip two large serving spoons in the hot water, then use them to shape the *mousseline* into four football-shaped quenelles, cleaning the spoons in the hot water after each one. Place each finished quenelle back on its parchment square.

Bring a medium pot of water to a simmer on medium-high heat and set up a steamer on top. Place the quenelles, with the parchment paper, inside the steamer and cook for 10 minutes. To check for doneness, insert a meat thermometer into the centre of a quenelle; it should read 125°F (52°C). Continue cooking for a few more minutes if not ready.

TO SERVE: Meanwhile, in a medium saucepan on low heat, reheat the sauce Normande. Using a slotted spoon, transfer the quenelles to the sauce, along with the mussel meat. Spoon some sauce over the quenelles, cover, and keep warm until the mussels are warmed through and the quenelles are nicely coated with sauce.

Transfer the quenelles to a serving plate, ladle on the mussels and sauce, and garnish with the puff pastry *fleurons* (see page 301). Serve immediately.

VARIATION *I like to serve one large quenelle per person, but if you want to reduce the cooking time, you can use tablespoons (8 minutes cooking time) or teaspoons (6 minutes cooking time) to make smaller quenelles.*

⚜

SAUCE NORMANDE
Normande Sauce

Yield: 2 CUPS (500 ML)
Preparation time: 15 MINUTES
Cooking time: 1 HOUR

2 large shallots, thinly sliced

1½ cups (350 mL) apple cider

1 cup (250 mL) Mussel Stock (see above)

2 cups (500 mL) Fish Stock (page 312)

1 cup (250 mL) heavy or whipping cream (35% milkfat)

¼ cup (60 g) cold unsalted butter, cubed

Juice of ¼ lemon

Kosher salt, to taste

In a medium saucepan on medium-high heat, stir the shallots and the apple cider together, and reduce the liquid by three-quarters. Stir in the mussel stock and fish stock, and reduce by half. Lower the heat to low, stir in the cream, and cook for 10 minutes or until the sauce coats the back of a spoon.

Pass the sauce through a fine tamis and whisk in the butter and the lemon juice. Adjust the seasoning to taste. You should be left with 2 cups (500 mL) of sauce.

If the sauce isn't thick enough to coat the back of a spoon or is too thin for your liking, you can thicken it with a little beurre manié *(page 99), or even a small amount of cornstarch slurry.*

⚜

Gravlax de Saumon au Gin du Québec

Marinated Salmon with Québec Gin

Yield: 12 PORTIONS

Preparation time: 25 MINUTES + 24 HOURS CURING + 12 HOURS CHILLING

Sockeye is my salmon of choice for this recipe. I've never enjoyed eating cooked sockeye—it becomes too dry and sad—but sockeye's texture and fat content make it ideal for both sushi and gravlax. Québec has started to produce interesting gin over the past few years, so it's logical to source a gin from La Belle Province *for this recipe. You can calculate the salt and sugar you need by percentage if your salmon fillet is a different size than the one suggested. For salt, use 10% of the fish's weight in grams; for sugar, use 8%.*

1 teaspoon (5 mL) coriander seeds

1 teaspoon (5 mL) fennel seeds

1 teaspoon (5 mL) juniper berries

1 teaspoon (5 mL) black peppercorns

Finely grated zest of 2 lemons

Finely grated zest of 1 orange

1 cup (130 g) kosher salt

½ cup (100 g) firmly packed brown sugar

One 3-pound (1.3 kg) skin-on salmon fillet (preferably sockeye), deboned

⅓ cup (75 mL) gin; I use gin St. Laurent from Québec

1 teaspoon (5 mL) Dijon mustard

½ bunch fresh dill, chopped

Lemon wedges

Crème Fraîche (page 296, or store-bought), to garnish

Crêpes au Sarrasin (recipe follows)

In a small skillet on medium heat, toast the coriander seeds, fennel seeds, juniper berries, and peppercorns gently to release some of their oils, then crush them with a mortar and pestle.

In a small bowl, combine the ground spices, lemon zest, orange zest, salt, and brown sugar. Place a sheet of parchment paper on a baking sheet and spoon one-third of the cure lengthwise down the centre of the parchment.

Using a sharp knife, make a small incision lengthwise in the middle of the salmon on the skin side. There is a natural line on the skin that will show you the way. (This will allow the salt to penetrate the skin and cure the middle of the fillet a bit better.) Make sure you only cut the skin and not the flesh.

Place the salmon skin side down on top of the cure. Pour the gin over top. Spoon the remaining cure onto the flesh side of the fish, placing a little more where the fillet is thicker and a little less on the tail. Fold the parchment paper over the salmon and wrap tightly with plastic wrap. Place another baking sheet on top of the fish and set a heavy weight on the baking sheet (a cast-iron skillet will do the trick). Refrigerate for 24 hours. (If you're using a thicker salmon, like spring or Atlantic, cure it for 36 hours.)

On a baking sheet, lay a piece of plastic wrap that's large enough to wrap up the salmon fillet. Unpack the salmon, wipe off the cure, and rinse the fish under cold water to remove all the cure. Pat it dry with a paper towel and lay it skin side down on the plastic wrap. Brush the mustard all over the flesh side. Sprinkle the dill onto the flesh side and press gently so the dill sticks to the salmon. Wrap the fish tightly with the plastic wrap and refrigerate for 12 hours.

continued

Unpack the salmon and slice it thinly with a long, sharp knife, wiping down the blade often with a clean towel. Slice the fish at a 45-degree angle, and turn your knife flat when you get to the skin. You should get beautiful wide ribbons that you can arrange on a platter. Try to slice the fish as thinly as possible; thick slices will be overpowered by the Dijon and dill. Serve with lemon wedges, some crème fraîche, and buckwheat crêpes.

TIP *Enjoy leftover gravlax with crème fraîche on a toasted bagel in the morning or for lunch.*

⚜

CRÊPES AU SARRASIN
Buckwheat Crêpes

Yield: 12 CRÊPES

Preparation time: 10 MINUTES + OVERNIGHT CHILLING

Cooking time: 15 MINUTES

1½ cups (250 g) buckwheat flour

½ teaspoon (2 mL) baking soda

1 egg

1 cup (250 mL) homogenized milk (3.25% milk fat)

3 tablespoons (45 g) unsalted butter, melted

1 tablespoon (20 g) honey

1 teaspoon (4 g) kosher salt

1 cup (250 mL) water

Unsalted butter, for cooking

In a medium mixing bowl, combine the flour and baking soda. In a small bowl, whisk together the egg, milk, melted butter, honey, and salt. Whisk the egg mixture into the flour mixture until homogeneous; the batter will be on the thicker side. Wrap the bowl with plastic wrap and chill overnight in the fridge.

Remove the batter from the fridge and whisk in the water, thinning it out into a nice smooth texture.

Heat a non-stick skillet on medium-high heat. Lightly grease the pan with butter, then pour in enough batter to thinly coat the bottom of the pan, swirling the pan as you pour in the batter to help ensure an even coating. Cook the crêpe for 1 to 2 minutes on the first side, until it's golden brown and lifts from the pan easily. Flip it over and cook for 1 minute on the other side. As you finish cooking each crêpe, transfer it to a plate, stacking them on top of one another and keeping them warm by draping a dishtowel over them. Repeat to make twelve crêpes, adding a small knob of butter to the pan between each one.

⚜

Salade d'Endives, Pacanes, Pommes, et Bleu Élizabeth

Endive Salad with Pecans, Apples, and Blue Elizabeth Cheese

Yield: 4 PORTIONS

Preparation time: 45 MINUTES + OVERNIGHT PICKLING

Cooking time: 15 MINUTES

Apple Pickles:

2 Granny Smith apples (unpeeled)

½ cup (125 mL) cold Basic White Pickling Liquid (page 294)

Dressing:

1½ cups (375 mL) organic apple juice

½ cup (125 mL) Crème Fraîche (page 296, or store-bought)

4 teaspoons (20 mL) apple cider vinegar

½ teaspoon (2 g) kosher salt

Candied Pecans:

⅓ cup (65 g) granulated sugar

1 tablespoon (15 mL) water

1 cup (100 g) pecans

Pinch kosher salt

Breadcrumbs:

2 big slices of a nice white sourdough bread, crust removed

2 tablespoons (30 mL) olive oil

Kosher salt and freshly cracked black pepper

Salad:

3 white Belgian endives

3 red endives

3.5 ounces (100 g) Bleu Élizabeth or a blue cheese of your choice

Chopped fresh chives and celery leaves, to garnish

In the winter, salade d'endives is the first salad that comes to my mind. The endives' slight bitterness is a great pairing for the sweet and tangy apple crème fraîche dressing, the sharp blue cheese, and the candied nuts. Endive salad might be considered a bit of a French stereotype, but there's a big reason why people love it: it's simply delicious and it's a great winter salad when no decent greens are available. Even though some might find it boring, I had no doubt that it would have a place on the St. Lawrence menu. After all, I swore to myself when we first opened our doors that I would cook for the people and not to feed my ego.

FOR THE APPLE PICKLES: Halve and core the apples and thinly slice them on a Japanese mandoline. Place the apple slices in a bowl and pour in the cold pickling liquid. Refrigerate for a minimum of 2 hours, or, even better, overnight.

FOR THE DRESSING: Pour the apple juice into a small saucepan on medium-high heat. Bring to a simmer, lower the heat to medium, and cook until the apple juice is reduced to ¼ cup (60 mL).

Transfer the reduced apple juice to a small bowl and whisk in the crème fraîche, cider vinegar, and salt until fully combined. Set aside.

FOR THE CANDIED PECANS: Preheat your oven to 350°F (175°C), with the rack in the centre position.

Spread out the pecans evenly on a small baking sheet and toast in the oven for 7 minutes. Take out of the oven to cool down on the countertop.

In a small pot on medium-high heat, heat the sugar and water, stirring until the sugar is dissolved. Add the pecans and cook, stirring, until they are well coated in a light-golden-brown caramel. Pour out onto a silicone baking mat or parchment paper, season with the salt, and let cool. Separate the pecans.

FOR THE BREADCRUMBS: Preheat your oven to 400°F (200°C), with the rack in the centre position.

continued

Cut the bread slices into ½-inch (1 cm) cubes and toss them in the olive oil. Season with a good pinch of salt and a few twists of pepper. Spread out the bread cubes in a single layer on a baking sheet lined with parchment paper.

Bake for 10 to 12 minutes, until the croutons are fully dry and golden brown. Let cool, then smash the croutons with a mortar and pestle to make breadcrumbs.

FOR THE SALAD: Now it's finally time to dress the salad. Once you've halved and cored the white and red endives, separate all the leaves and place them in a big bowl. Add the apple pickles, candied pecans, and half of the dressing. Toss well to incorporate the dressing. Taste and add more dressing as desired.

Transfer the salad to a serving plate and shave or crumble the blue cheese on top. Sprinkle the breadcrumbs over the salad and garnish with the chives and celery leaves.

Tourtière au Cerf

Venison Meat Pie

Yield: ONE 9-INCH (23 CM) PIE,
8 PORTIONS
Preparation time: 30 MINUTES
Cooking time: 1¼ HOURS

Tourtière is, for me, the dish that best represents Québec. It can be traced back to the 1600s, and there's no master recipe; every family has their own twist. The style of this traditional meat pie changes from region to region as well. Originally, it was made with game birds or game meat, like rabbit, pheasant, or moose; that's one of the reasons why I prefer it with venison instead of beef or pork. Tourtière remains a staple in Québécois households, both during Réveillon *and throughout the year. It's part of our heritage, it's close to my heart, and it's important for me to keep it alive. Serve the* tourtière *along with pickled beets, gherkins, and ketchup.*

What you'll need:

9-inch (23 cm) pie plate

2 tablespoons (30 g) unsalted butter

1 small yellow onion, finely minced

1½ tablespoons (15 g) chopped garlic

½ cup (125 g) finely chopped button mushrooms

½ cup (125 mL) red wine (plus a glass for yourself)

1.3 pounds (600 g) ground venison

2½ teaspoons (8 g) kosher salt

1 teaspoon (3 g) Épices à Tourtière (recipe follows)

1 cup (225 g) grated potato (about 1 large)

5 ounces (150 g) back fat or pork belly, ground

1 batch Pâte Brisée (page 299)

1 egg yolk + 1 tablespoon (15 mL) homogenized milk (3.25% milk fat), lightly beaten for egg wash

Preheat your oven to 425°F (220°C), with the rack in the centre position.

In a large pot on medium heat, melt the butter. Sauté the onion and garlic, stirring often, for 4 minutes. Add the mushrooms and cook, stirring often, until all of the liquid has evaporated, about 5 minutes. Stir in the red wine and drink your glass while letting it cook off completely, about 10 minutes. Add the venison, salt, and *épices à tourtière*, and cook for 5 minutes, stirring to break up the chunks of meat.

Using your hands, squeeze all the water out of the grated potato. Stir it into the pot, along with the back fat, and cook for 20 minutes. Taste for seasoning. Remove from the heat and let cool at room temperature.

Divide the *pâte brisée* in half. On a lightly floured work surface, roll out each half into a ⅟₁₆-inch thick (2 mm) circle that fits into the pie plate. Lay one circle in the bottom and up the sides of the pie plate. Fill it with the venison mixture. Cover with the other dough circle. Trim off the excess dough and pinch or decoratively flute the edges with your fingers to seal. Brush the top with the egg wash. Using a paring knife, poke a few holes in the top crust in a design that pleases you—you're the artist.

Bake the tourtière for 15 minutes. Lower the temperature to 375°F (190°C) and bake for 45 to 55 minutes, until the pastry is a nice golden brown. Transfer to a wire rack and let cool for 30 minutes at room temperature before serving.

VARIATION *If you prefer to make single servings, follow our lead at the restaurant, where we make individual tourtières in the form of a dome (pithivier) and fill them with 5 ounces (160 g) of the ground venison mixture.*

continued

ÉPICES À TOURTIÈRE

Tourtière Spice Mix

Yield: ABOUT ⅓ CUP (75 ML)
Preparation time: 2 MINUTES

5 teaspoons (10 g) freshly grated
nutmeg

4½ teaspoons (10 g) ground cloves

4 teaspoons (30 g) freshly cracked
black pepper

3½ teaspoons (10 g) ground
cinnamon

1½ teaspoons (7 g) ground ginger

In a small bowl, combine all the ingredients. Transfer to an airtight container and store in a cool, dark place for up to 6 months; after that, the spices will start to lose their potency.

⚜

Côte de Porc, Pomme Purée, et Sauce Charcutière

Pork Chops with Potato Purée and Charcutière Sauce

Yield: 4 PORTIONS

Preparation time: 45 MINUTES + 12 HOURS BRINING + 1 HOUR TEMPERING

Cooking time: 1 HOUR + 10 TO 15 MINUTES RESTING

What you'll need:

Large cast-iron pan

Brine:

8 cups (2 L) water, divided

½ cup + 1 tablespoon (80 g) kosher salt

1 tablespoon (15 g) firmly packed brown sugar

5 black peppercorns

5 sprigs thyme

1 bay leaf

4 organic bone-in pork chops, 1 inch (2.5 cm) thick

Pomme Purée:

2.2 pounds (1 kg) fingerling or Yukon Gold potatoes

1 tablespoon + 2 teaspoons (25 g) kosher salt

¾ cup (175 mL) heavy or whipping cream (35% milk fat), warmed

1 cup (225 g) cold unsalted butter, diced

⇝ *This dish is, arguably, the most popular main course at the restaurant. And for good reason, as the flavours are very comforting. Pork chops can be dry and sad when they're overcooked, but the brine in this recipe both seasons them properly and helps keep them juicy. Pair the chops with the butteriest* pomme purée *you'll ever taste, gratinée them with a chunk of cheese, and serve them with mustard and a sauce full of gherkins for a flat-out match made in heaven.*

TO BRINE THE PORK CHOPS: In a small saucepan on high heat, combine 1 cup (250 mL) of the water with the salt, brown sugar, peppercorns, thyme, and bay leaf. Bring to a boil. Transfer to a deep bowl, stir in the remaining water, and refrigerate until cold. Add the pork chops to the brine, making sure they are submerged in the liquid. Brine in the fridge for 12 hours.

FOR THE POMME PURÉE: Place the potatoes and salt in a medium saucepan and add enough cold water to cover by about 1 inch (2.5 cm). Bring to a gentle simmer on medium heat. (The potatoes are cooked whole to prevent them from absorbing the water, thus allowing you to incorporate more butter and cream.) Cook until the potatoes are extremely tender when tested with a paring knife. Drain off the water and let the potatoes cool for a while. When they're cool enough to handle, peel the potatoes and cut them in half.

Lay a piece of parchment paper on a clean work surface. Place one potato half in a sieve and, using a stiff plastic scraper, press it through the sieve and onto the parchment paper. If you don't have a sieve, a ricer will do the job.

Once you've pressed all the potatoes, transfer them to a medium saucepan and warm them on medium-low heat. Using a stiff silicone spatula or a wooden spoon, incorporate one-third of the warm cream into the potatoes, then beat in a few cubes of butter until it is emulsified into the potatoes. Continue gradually stirring in the cream and butter to develop a creamy purée. Keep the heat low enough to incorporate the butter without losing the emulsion. If the purée begins to look oily, with the fat separating from

continued

Pork Chops:

Kosher salt and freshly cracked black pepper

2 tablespoons (30 mL) grapeseed oil

5 tablespoons (75 g) unsalted butter, cubed

3 sprigs thyme

3 cloves garlic (unpeeled), smashed

1 batch Sauce Charcutière (recipe follows)

4 ounces (110 g) Oka Classique cheese, cut into 4 portions

Chopped fresh chives, to garnish

the potatoes, the emulsion is breaking. To restore it, you may need to add hot water periodically, just as you would for Aïoli (page 295) or *Sauce Hollandaise* (page 307). Once you've emulsified all the butter and cream, pass the purée through the sieve again to give it an ultra-smooth texture. Taste for seasoning. Set aside.

FOR THE PORK CHOPS: Remove the pork chops from the fridge and temper them at room temperature for 1 hour (see tip).

Preheat your oven to 350°F (180°C), with the rack in the centre position.

Season the pork chops lightly with salt and pepper, mostly on the fat cap; remember that they've been brined and will already be seasoned. In a large cast-iron pan on high heat, heat the oil until hot. Add two pork chops (to avoid overcrowding) and sear nicely on both sides. Remove the seared chops to a baking sheet. Sear the remaining two chops. Return all the pork chops and any accumulated juices to the pan, lower the heat to medium, and add the butter, thyme, and garlic. Using a large spoon, start basting the chops with the butter. Continue basting for 3 to 4 minutes to allow the chops to absorb the butter and herb flavour.

Transfer the pork chops to a baking sheet and pour the thyme, garlic, and butter on top.

Bake the chops for 8 to 10 minutes or until a meat thermometer inserted in the thickest part of a chop registers 135°F (57°C). Transfer the chops to a plate or a tray and let rest for 10 to 15 minutes, until the internal temperature reaches 145°F (63°C). Move the oven rack to the top position and switch your oven to broil.

Meanwhile, gently reheat your *pomme purée* and *Sauce Charcutière.*

Place one piece of Oka cheese on each chop. Broil until the cheese is melted and starts to caramelize.

Spoon some *pomme purée* onto each plate as a base, and top it with a pork chop and a generous amount of sauce. Garnish with chives—*bon appétit*!

TIP *It's important to always—I really mean always—temper any meat before you cook it. Taking cold meat out of the fridge and putting it directly into the pan or oven will only lengthen the total cooking time and will produce an uneven doneness: well done on the outside and rare on the inside. Start with room-temperature meat to help ensure an even* cuisson *(doneness) all the way through.*

SAUCE CHARCUTIÈRE

Charcutière Sauce

Yield: ABOUT 1 CUP, ENOUGH
FOR 4 PEOPLE

Preparation time: 10 MINUTES

Cooking time: 15 MINUTES

3 ounces (85 g) thick-sliced smoked bacon, cut into ⅓-inch (0.75 cm) cubed lardons

2 tablespoons (30 mL) cold unsalted butter, cubed, divided

1 small shallot, finely minced

¼ cup (65 mL) white wine

1 tablespoon (15 mL) Dijon mustard

1 cup (250 mL) pork demi-glace (page 311)

12 gherkins, quartered lengthwise

½ teaspoon (2 g) kosher salt

¼ teaspoon freshly cracked black pepper

Splash of red wine vinegar

Line a plate with paper towel and have it ready beside the stove. In a small sauté pan on medium-high heat, sauté the bacon lardons until the fat is rendered and golden brown, about 4 minutes. Using a slotted spoon, place the bacon on the lined plate to soak up the excess fat.

In a small saucepan on medium heat, heat 1 tablespoon of butter until foamy. Lower the heat to medium and sweat the chopped shallot with the butter until tender and translucent but with no colouration, about 5 minutes. Deglaze the shallots with the white wine and reduce until there's almost no liquid left.

Mix in the mustard, then stir in the pork demi-glace and bring to a gentle simmer on medium heat. Stain the sauce through a fine sieve and put back into the saucepan. Stir in the bacon, gherkins, salt, and pepper. Cook gently for 3 to 4 minutes. Remove from the heat and whisk in the remaining butter and a splash of red wine vinegar to cut the richness of the sauce.

✢

IMAGE ON PAGE 198

Ris de Veau à la Grenobloise

Veal Sweetbreads with Butter and Caper Sauce

Yield: 4 PORTIONS

Preparation time: 45 MINUTES +
30 MINUTES SOAKING

Cooking time: 45 MINUTES

🥄 *I know a lot of people have their doubts about eating sweetbreads, but in Québec and France,* ris de veau *is commonly found on restaurant menus along with other offal dishes. Sweetbreads are an organ meat taken from an animal's thymus gland and pancreas;* ris de veau, *from veal, and* ris d'agneau, *from lamb are the most common. They definitely aren't bready, but they do taste kind of sweet. I love their subtle flavour and smooth, tender texture when you cook them right. The outside is wonderfully crispy, while the inside is juicy and almost creamy. I use sweetbreads in numerous ways: to make pâtés, terrines, sausages, and stews, or simply pan-fried in a lot of butter. That last preparation is definitely my favourite because they end up tasting kind of like a chicken nugget on steroids. I'm also partial to the* Grenobloise *preparation for sweetbreads, as the acidity provides a great counterpoint to their richness. When prepping sweetbreads at the restaurant, we soak them to remove any excess blood and press to flatten them, which helps achieve a better sear.*

4 veal sweetbreads (each about 5 ounces/150 g)

1 medium carrot, peeled and thinly sliced

1 medium onion, thinly sliced

Bouquet garni of parsley, thyme, and bay leaf (see tip, page 47)

Kosher salt

Juice of ½ lemon

12 ounces (350 g) cauliflower, cut into 1-inch (2.5 cm) chunks

4 cups (1 L) cold homogenized milk (3.25% milk fat)

½ cup (100 g) medium-grain white rice

3 tablespoons (45 mL) heavy or whipping cream (35% milk fat)

4 ounces (125 g) unsmoked bacon (such as pancetta), diced into ½-inch (1 cm) cubes

2 slices brioche

Place the sweetbreads in a large bowl, cover with cold water, and leave under running cold water for about 30 minutes.

Meanwhile, prepare a *court bouillon* by adding 6 cups (1.5 L) water to a medium saucepan, along with the carrot, onion, bouquet garni, 2 tablespoons (20 g) salt, and the lemon juice. Bring to a simmer on medium-high heat, then lower the heat to low and cook gently for 30 minutes. Strain the liquid through a tamis, discarding the solids.

Return the *court bouillon* to the saucepan and bring to a simmer on medium heat. Drain the sweetbreads, add them to the *court bouillon*, and poach for 3 minutes. Meanwhile, prepare an ice bath. Using a slotted spoon, immediately transfer the sweetbreads to the ice bath to stop the cooking. Once cool, take them out of the ice bath and, using a small paring knife, trim the sweetbreads to remove the membrane that covers them. Return them to the fridge.

TIP Court *is French for "short," and the name "*court bouillon*" refers to the quick preparation time for a simple broth that's used to poach fish, seafood, or chicken.*

3 tablespoons (45 mL) Beurre Clarifié (see tip, page 125)

4 tablespoons (40 g) all-purpose flour

Freshly cracked black pepper

4 tablespoons (60 mL) grapeseed oil

¼ cup (55 g) unsalted butter, cubed

1 cup (250 mL) chicken jus (reduced Chicken Stock, page 308)

2 tablespoons (30 mL) red wine vinegar or lemon juice

1½ tablespoons (50 g) small capers, rinsed

1 tablespoon (15 mL) chopped fresh curly parsley

Fried parsley, for garnish (optional)

Next up, making the cauliflower purée. Place the cauliflower in a medium pot and pour in the cold milk. Season with 1 tablespoon (10 g) salt and bring to a simmer on medium-high heat. As soon as the milk comes to a boil, add the rice and stir for 1 minute with a wooden spatula to ensure that it doesn't stick to the bottom of the pot. Lower the heat to low, half-cover with a lid, and cook gently for 20 minutes.

Drain the cauliflower and rice in a tamis, reserving the milk in case you need it. Transfer the cauliflower and rice to a blender, add the cream, and purée for a good 3 minutes. The purée should be very creamy. If it is too thick, add some of the reserved milk, 1 tablespoon (15 mL) at a time. Taste for seasoning. Transfer to a small saucepan, cover, and keep warm.

If you decide to make fried parsley, wash it clean and dry it on a clean dish-towel. Heat 4 cups (1 L) of canola oil in a deep pan to 375°F (190°C) on medium-high heat. Line a small baking sheet with paper towel. Put the parsley in the oil, watch out for oil splashing, and hold it in the oil for about 2 minutes until there are no more bubbles of moisture coming out. Transfer to the baking sheet so the paper towel can absorb the oil. Sprinkle with salt. Reserve.

In a medium skillet on medium heat, cook the bacon until crispy. Using a slotted spoon, transfer the bacon to a plate lined with a paper towel, keeping the rendered fat in the skillet.

Remove the crusts from the brioche slices and cut the bread into ½-inch (1 cm) cubes. Add the *beurre clarifié* to the bacon fat in the skillet. Fry the bread cubes on medium heat until golden brown. Transfer to a plate lined with a paper towel and set aside. Discard any leftover fat and clean the skillet.

Return the skillet to medium-high heat. Place the flour in a shallow dish. Season the sweetbreads with salt and pepper and dredge them in the flour. Make sure they are well coated, then shake them to remove any excess flour. Add the oil to the skillet; once it's really hot, carefully place the sweetbreads in the pan. Don't play with them or flip them—you want the sweetbreads to develop a nice golden-brown crust. Searing the first side will take 5 to 6 minutes. Once you have a good crust, flip the sweetbreads over, lower the heat to medium, and add half of the butter. Cook the sweetbreads on the second side for 4 minutes, constantly basting them with butter. Insert the tip of a paring knife in the centre of a sweetbread and test it on your lower lip to make sure it's warm. Transfer the sweetbreads to a plate and cover to keep them warm.

continued

Discard the oil and add the remaining butter to the skillet. Cook on medium heat until the butter gives off a nutty smell and becomes a light-golden colour, 2 to 3 minutes. Stir in the bacon, chicken jus, vinegar, capers, and parsley, and return the sweetbreads to the pan. Heat everything together for 1 minute.

To serve, place a good spoonful of cauliflower purée on each serving plate and top with a sweetbread. Spoon the sauce over the sweetbread. Sprinkle with the brioche croutons and garnish with fried parsley.

TIP *I've seen recipes that use potatoes, celeriac, or more cream to give a cauliflower purée more body, but using rice allows the purée to keep its proper cauliflower flavour while still being thick and creamy.*

⚜

IMAGE ON PAGE 199

Cailles en Sarcophage

Stuffed Quails in Puff Pastry

Yield: 6 PORTIONS

Preparation time: 3 HOURS + 1 HOUR OR OVERNIGHT CHILLING

Cooking time: 1½ HOURS

❧ *This dish has become one of our menu icons at St. Lawrence, and I firmly believe that it helped put us on the map. I didn't come up with this recipe; in fact, I discovered it watching a Danish movie called* Babette's Feast. *Set in late nineteenth-century Denmark, the plot centres on a French woman named Babette who carves out a life for herself as a housemaid and cook in a tiny remote community. After receiving word of winning 10,000 francs in her home country, she arranges to cook a "real French dinner" for a few townspeople.* Cailles en sarcophage *was on her menu, stuffed with foie gras and black truffles, served in a puff pastry case, and garnished with figs and sauce. The scenes of Babette cooking the quail were absolutely beautiful; I was amazed, and I had to reproduce it. Though this dish is not easy to execute and the ingredients are rather expensive, it is incredibly special.* Babette's Feast *taught me something: in a world where most chefs are only interested in feeding their ego, the best gift a cook can give is spending money, time, and energy cooking for your guests, friends, or family.*

What you'll need:

4-inch (10 cm) round pastry cutter (preferably fluted)

2½-inch (6 cm) round pastry cutter

Four 2-inch-high (5 cm) ring moulds

Puff Pastry Cases:

1.1 pounds (500 g) Pâte Feuilleté Rapide (page 300, or store-bought puff pastry), defrosted

1 egg yolk + 1 tablespoon (15 mL) homogenized milk (3.25% milk fat), lightly beaten for egg wash

Brined Quails:

4 cups (1 L) water

⅓ cup + 1 tablespoon (50 g) kosher salt

1 tablespoon (12 g) firmly packed brown sugar

2 sprigs thyme

1 bay leaf

6 jumbo quails, deboned

FOR THE PUFF PASTRY CASES: On a lightly floured work surface, roll out the puff pastry dough to ⅛ inch (3 mm) thick. Using the larger pastry cutter, cut the dough into discs, slightly twisting the cutter on your worktop to make sure the disc is cut in a perfectly neat shape. The disc will detach easily from the puff pastry dough sheet. Cut twelve discs, for a total of six cases.

Line a baking sheet with a silicone baking mat. Arrange six discs on the mat and, using a pastry brush, glaze them lightly with egg wash.

Using the smaller pastry cutter, cut a hole in the centre of each of the discs remaining on your worktop, creating six pastry dough rings (keep the scraps in your freezer to make *fleurons*). Carefully place one ring on top of each disc. Glaze with egg wash and refrigerate for at least 1 hour before baking. (Ideally, you'd start the recipe the day before and refrigerate the dough overnight to prevent it from shrinking during baking.) Reserve the remaining egg wash.

FOR THE BRINED QUAILS: Meanwhile, in a small saucepan on high heat, combine 1 cup (250 mL) of the water with the salt, brown sugar, and herbs. Bring to a boil. Transfer to a deep bowl, stir in the remaining water, and

continued

Sausage Stuffing:

9 ounces (250 g) ground pork, preferably from the shoulder

1 clove garlic, chopped

1 tablespoon (15 mL) chopped fresh flat-leaf parsley

1 tablespoon (15 mL) breadcrumbs

1 teaspoon (3 g) kosher salt

1 tablespoon (15 mL) white wine

1 teaspoon (5 mL) cognac

Sauce:

2 tablespoons (30 g) unsalted butter

2 shallots, finely chopped

2 tablespoons (30 mL) cognac or brandy

1 cup (250 mL) white wine

4 cups (1 L) quail stock (made from the bones) or Chicken Stock (page 308, or store-bought)

1 teaspoon (5 mL) honey

Kosher salt and freshly cracked black pepper, to taste

1 tablespoon (8 g) cornstarch (optional)

2 tablespoons (30 mL) water (optional)

Assembly:

4 ounces (125 g) foie gras terrine or torchon (I suggest Rougié if using store-bought)

Kosher salt and freshly cracked black pepper

2 tablespoons (30 g) unsalted butter

36 seedless green grapes, peeled if you have the patience (you can also substitute 6 fresh figs)

Mustard greens or arugula, to garnish

refrigerate until cold. Add the quails to the brine, making sure they are submerged in the liquid. Brine in the fridge for 1 hour while you prepare the remaining ingredients.

TO BAKE THE PUFF PASTRY CASES: Preheat your oven to 400°F (200°C), with the rack in the centre position.

Remove the dough from the fridge and brush with more egg wash. Place a ring mould in each corner of the baking sheet and rest a second baking sheet on top of the ring moulds. (This will help control the rise of the puff pastry cases while baking, so they don't rise too high or unevenly.) Bake for 10 minutes, then lower the heat to 350°F (180°C) and bake for 15 minutes. Remove the top baking sheet and bake for 10 minutes or until the base of the pastry cases is well cooked. Transfer to a wire rack and let cool.

FOR THE SAUSAGE STUFFING: In a medium mixing bowl, using your hands, mix all the ingredients until fully incorporated. Don't overwork the sausage mixture or it will be tough.

FOR THE SAUCE: In a medium saucepan on medium-high heat, melt the butter. Sweat the shallots for 3 minutes, until soft. Deglaze the pan with the cognac, use a long match to light it, and flambé to cook off the alcohol (page 94). When the flames die down, stir in the white wine and reduce to ¼ cup (60 mL). Add the stock and reduce until you have 2 cups (500 mL) of sauce. Add the honey and season with a good pinch of salt and pepper.

If the sauce is too thin for your liking, you can add a cornstarch slurry to it. In a small bowl, combine the cornstarch and water. Bring the sauce back to a simmer and whisk in the slurry a little at a time until your sauce is the desired consistency. Remove from the heat and keep warm.

TO ASSEMBLE: Preheat your oven to 425°F (220°C), with the rack in the centre position. Line a baking sheet with a silicone mat or parchment paper and spray with oil.

Remove the quails from the brine and pat dry. Cut the foie gras terrine into six portions, and divide the sausage stuffing into six portions. Encase each portion of foie gras terrine in sausage mixture and stuff into a quail. Reshape the quails to their original form as much as possible and transfer to the baking sheet. Gently truss each quail with butcher's twine, starting from the back and making one continuous loop around to the front of the bird and back again before tying a knot. This will help the birds hold their shape during cooking. Season the outside of the quails with a little bit of

continued

salt and pepper.

Bake for 20 to 25 minutes, depending on the size of the quails, until a meat thermometer inserted in the centre of the quails registers 135°F (57°C). Tent the quails with foil and let rest for 10 minutes.

Meanwhile, in a sauté pan on medium-high heat, melt the butter. Add the grapes, lower the heat to medium-low, and cook gently for 4 to 5 minutes, until the grapes are warm all the way through. Pour the sauce into the pan, stir to combine, and keep warm.

Place the puff pastry cases back in the oven to warm up for 2 minutes from the residual heat of the baking.

Place a puff pastry case on each serving plate. Cut the twine from the quails and transfer each one to its dedicated *sarcophage* (puff pastry case). Spoon sauce over the quails, along with six grapes per plate. Garnish with a few leaves of mustard greens.

⚜

Ballotine de Canard et Sauce à l'Orange

Duck Roulade with Orange Sauce

Yield: 4 PORTIONS

Preparation time: 2 HOURS

Cooking time: 3 HOURS +
30 MINUTES RESTING

🍴 Ballotine *is a favourite technique of mine because it uses all the parts of an animal, cost-effectively serving more people by stretching your protein into more portions. The French word* ballotine *means "a package of goods," and it's basically a piece of meat that has been deboned, stuffed, and rolled into a cylinder to be roasted, braised, or poached. Many people have asked me what the difference is between a* ballotine *and a* galantine. *Though prepared the same way, a* galantine *is always poached in a stock, cooled, sliced thinly, and served cold, whereas a* ballotine *is served hot, more like a roast. At the restaurant, we serve the* ballotine *with* Pommes Duchesse *(page 181) and roasted endives.*

One 6-pound (2.75 kg) whole Grade A duck, preferably from Brome Lake

3 tablespoons (25 g) finely chopped garlic

3 tablespoons (25 g) finely chopped shallots

¾ cup (175 mL) red wine

2 tablespoons (30 mL) cognac or brandy

3.5 ounces (100 g) pork back fat, diced into ⅛-inch (3 mm) cubes

2 teaspoons (3 g) chopped fresh sage leaves

1 teaspoon (4 g) kosher salt

½ teaspoon (1 g) freshly cracked black pepper

⅛ teaspoon (1 g) curing salt

Grated zest of 1 orange, divided

1 egg white

1 bunch green Swiss chard

2 tablespoons (30 mL) maple syrup

2 tablespoons (30 mL) red wine vinegar

1 cup (250 mL) fresh orange juice

1 cup (250 mL) duck demi-glace (reduced Duck Stock, page 311)

1 tablespoon (15 g) cold unsalted butter

Start by breaking down the duck, deboning and skinning the breasts and legs. (Save the bones for making stock, and keep the skin for rendering duck fat.) Dice the duck leg meat into ⅓-inch (1 cm) cubes, transfer to a plate, and freeze for 10 minutes. Take the duck out of the freezer once the meat is very cold but not frozen. Using a food processor, pulse the meat to grind it; you should have around 11 ounces (300 g) of ground duck meat. (Alternatively, you can simplify the whole process by asking your butcher for two duck breasts and the meat of two duck legs, preferably ground for the legs.) Set the ground meat and duck breasts aside.

In a small saucepan, combine the garlic, shallots, red wine, and cognac. Bring to a simmer on medium-high heat, then lower the heat to medium-low and cook until all of the liquid has evaporated. Let this reduction cool.

In a medium bowl, using your hands, mix together the ground leg meat, pork back fat, sage, kosher salt, pepper, curing salt, half the orange zest, and the egg white until well combined; don't overmix. Essentially, you're making a farce (see tip). Add the reduction to the farce, mix well, and refrigerate until needed.

Using a paring knife, remove the stems from the Swiss chard while keeping the leaves whole. Bring a medium pot of salted water to a boil on medium-high heat. Prepare an ice bath. Blanch the Swiss chard leaves in the boiling water for 20 seconds, then immediately transfer them to the ice bath to stop the cooking. Remove the Swiss chard from the ice bath and blot the leaves on a kitchen towel to remove all excess water.

continued

On a clean work surface, lay out a 24 by 12-inch (60 by 30 cm) rectangle of plastic wrap. Arrange the Swiss chard leaves in the middle of the plastic wrap, overlapping each other, to create a 14 by 8-inch (35 by 20 cm) rectangle. Spread half of the farce along the chard in an even layer, leaving a 4-inch (10 cm) border at the top and bottom of the chard. Lay the two duck breasts down the centre of the farce in a straight line and spread the remaining farce evenly over top. Starting with the long side of the rectangle closest to you, use the plastic wrap to help you roll the Swiss chard and farce forward into a cylinder surrounded by plastic wrap, keeping everything nice and tight. Tie each end of the roll in a knot or tie off the ends with butcher's twine. Using the tip of a paring knife, poke several holes down one side of the *ballotine*. Repeat the process on the opposite side. Wrap the *ballotine* one more time in plastic wrap to make sure you have an evenly packed cylinder that is very tight. At the end, you should have a ballotine about 10 inches (25 cm) in length.

I can suggest two methods for cooking the *ballotine*. The goal is to bring the internal temperature to 145°F (63°C), ensuring that the farce is properly cooked while the centre of the breasts remains pink (medium doneness). If you have a home circulator for sous vide cooking, you can cook the *ballotine* for 3 hours at 145°F (63°C). Alternatively, you can use a steamer that's large enough to fit the *ballotine* and steam it until it reaches the desired internal temperature. With either method, make absolutely sure that your thermometer is accurate. Once the *ballotine* is cooked, let it rest at room temperature for 30 minutes before removing the plastic wrap and slicing into it.

Meanwhile, in a small saucepan on medium-high heat, bring the maple syrup to a boil. Add the vinegar and boil until the liquid is reduced by half. Add the orange juice, return to a boil, and reduce to about ⅓ cup (75 mL) sauce. Stir in the demi-glace and the remaining orange zest, and bring to a simmer. Remove from the heat, taste for seasoning, and whisk in the butter.

Slice the *ballotine*, allocating two slices per guest, and serve with a generous amount of sauce.

TIP *From the French word* farcir, *which means "to stuff," a farce is a savoury stuffing or forcemeat: raw meat or fish that has been finely ground, seasoned, and emulsified with fat. These mixtures are used to make sausages, terrines, pâtés, stuffed pastas, and quenelles.*

Poisson en Croûte et Sauce Choron

Fish in Pastry with Choron Sauce

Yield: 4 PORTIONS

Preparation time: 2½ HOURS + 65 MINUTES CHILLING

Cooking time: 30 TO 40 MINUTES + 5 TO 10 MINUTES COOLING

While watching a video of the Roux brothers making beef Wellington, I picked up a trick that I realized would apply perfectly to making poisson en croûte. *Encasing the chard-wrapped fish and* mousseline *in crêpes would produce a crisper crust, as the added layer prevents the steam from making the pastry crust soggy while the fish cooks. I know it takes time to make this amazing dish, but don't be daunted. You can do the bulk of the prep work the day before: prepare the fish in pastry and refrigerate it overnight. The next day, take it out of the fridge and give it an egg wash before transferring it straight into the oven, adding an extra 10 minutes of baking time. I use cod for this recipe because it's my favourite local fish, but any fish you prefer would do, really. The best one, in my opinion, if you can find it at your fishmonger, is* loup de mer—*sea bass in English. To this day, I still daydream about the* loup de mer en croûte *I had at Paul Bocuse's iconic L'Auberge du Pont de Collonges in Lyon, one of the best dishes I've ever had in my life.*

1 large cod fillet, about 1.6 pounds (700 g), skin and pin bones removed

1 teaspoon (4 g) kosher salt

1 batch Fish Mousseline (recipe follows)

4 Crêpes aux Herbes (recipe follows)

1 bunch green Swiss chard or 36 large spinach leaves

4 tablespoons (20 g) chopped tender fennel fronds

1 egg yolk + 1 tablespoon (15 mL) homogenized milk (3.25% milk fat), lightly beaten for egg wash

1.3 pounds (600 g) Pâte Feuilleté Rapide (page 300, or store-bought)

1 batch Sauce Choron (variation, page 305)

Beurre Clarifié (see tip, page 125), to glaze (optional)

Using a sharp knife, trim the fish into an even fillet that's 1 inch (2.5 cm) thick and weighs 1.2 pounds (550 g). Keep 5 ounces (150 g) of the fish trimmings for the *mousseline*. Season the fillet on both sides with the salt and refrigerate until needed.

Make the fish *mousseline* and the herb crêpes.

Using a paring knife, remove the stems from the Swiss chard while keeping the leaves whole. Bring a pot of salted water to a boil on medium-high heat. Prepare an ice bath. Blanch the Swiss chard leaves in the boiling water for 20 seconds, then immediately transfer them to the ice bath to stop the cooking. Remove the Swiss chard from the ice bath and wrap in a damp dishtowel.

On a clean work surface, lay out a sheet of plastic wrap large enough to cover the fish. Arrange the crêpes in a line on the plastic wrap, slightly overlapping each other by about 1 inch (2 cm). Cover the crêpes with the blanched Swiss chard. Pipe and spread half of the fish *mousseline* along the bottom edge of the chard, forming a rectangle large enough to lay the fish fillet on. Sprinkle half of the fennel fronds on top of the fish *mousseline*, then lay the fish on top. Sprinkle the remaining fennel fronds over the

continued

fillet, then pipe and spread the remaining fish *mousseline* over top. Use the plastic wrap to help you roll the crêpes up over the fish until the fillet is snugly covered, free of any gaps. Don't let the crêpes overlap—the fish should be enclosed in a single layer of crêpes. Using kitchen scissors, cut off the excess. Tightly wrap the rolled fish in the plastic wrap and tie each end securely in a knot. Chill in the fridge for 20 minutes.

Preheat your oven to 425°F (220°C), with the rack in the centre position. Line a large baking sheet with parchment paper and spray with cooking oil.

On a lightly floured work surface, roll out one-third of the puff pastry into a 16 by 6-inch (40 by 15 cm) rectangle that's ¼ inch (5 mm) thick. Pick the pastry up by rolling it loosely around the rolling pin and then unrolling it onto the lined baking sheet. Remove the fish from the fridge, unwrap the plastic wrap, and place the rolled fish in the centre of the pastry. Brush the pastry around the rolled fish with egg wash.

Roll out the remaining puff pastry into a 22 by 10-inch (55 by 25 cm) rectangle that's ¼ inch (5 mm) thick. Pick the pastry up by rolling it loosely around the rolling pin and then laying it over the fish. Apply slight pressure with your hands to make sure there are no air pockets between the fish and the pastry, and press with your fingers to seal the edges at the base of the pastry. Put the baking sheet in the fridge for 15 minutes to firm up the pastry before you start to decorate it.

Using a very sharp paring knife, cut off the excess pastry around the fish, leaving a 1-inch (2.5 cm) border as well as two fins and a tail, to accentuate the fish's shape. With the knife tip, draw very light semicircular lines on the pastry to look like fish scales. Lightly draw eyes on the head and mark linear rays on the fins and tail and around the borders. Brush the pastry all over with egg wash and chill it in the fridge for 30 minutes.

Take the pan out of the fridge and apply a final coat of egg wash over the pastry. With your paring knife, make a few incisions in the pastry to let the steam out during cooking.

Bake for 30 to 40 minutes, until the pastry is golden brown and a meat thermometer inserted in the centre of the fish registers 130°F (54°C). (Or insert the tip of a paring knife into the centre, from the side, and make sure it's warm to the touch when you pull it out.) Use a wide spatula to slide the fish carefully onto a wire rack. Let cool for 5 to 10 minutes before serving.

Meanwhile, prepare the sauce Choron.

Brush the pastry with the *beurre clarifié* to give it extra shine. Present the fish whole on a platter to impress your guests, then cut it into slices using a serrated knife. Plate the slices individually and pour on some of the sauce. Make sure to bring the rest of the sauce to the table in a gravy boat—it's pretty irresistible.

✤

MOUSSELINE DE POISSON

Fish Mousse

Yield: 2 CUPS

Preparation time: 15 MINUTES

5 ounces (150 g) fish trimmings, cubed and cold

3.5 ounces (100 g) scallops, cubed and cold (about 3 pieces)

1 egg white

½ cup (125 g) cold heavy or whipping cream (35% milk fat)

1 teaspoon (3 g) kosher salt

1 tablespoon (15 g) all-purpose flour, sifted

In a food processor, combine the fish, scallops, egg white, cream, and salt, and pulse until blended and smooth. Pass the mixture through a sieve into a medium mixing bowl to make sure there are no lumps. Using a silicone spatula, fold in the sifted flour until well incorporated. Transfer the *mousseline* to a piping bag with a plain tip. Cover and refrigerate until you are ready to assemble the *poisson en croûte*.

⚜

CRÊPES AUX HERBES

Herb Crêpes

Yield: FOUR 9-INCH (23 CM) CRÊPES

Preparation time: 15 MINUTES + 1 HOUR CHILLING

Cooking time: 15 MINUTES

What you'll need:

9-inch (23 cm) non-stick crêpe pan

⅔ cup (150 mL) homogenized milk (3.25% milk fat)

1 egg

½ cup (65 g) all-purpose flour, sifted

1 tablespoon (4 g) finely chopped fresh flat-leaf parsley

1 tablespoon (4 g) finely chopped fresh chervil

1 tablespoon (4 g) finely chopped fresh chives

Pinch (1 g) kosher salt

2 tablespoons (25 g) unsalted butter, melted

Grapeseed oil, for cooking

In a medium mixing bowl, whisk together the milk and egg. While whisking constantly, gradually add the sifted flour. Whisk in the herbs, salt, and butter. Chill in the fridge for 1 hour.

In the crêpe pan, heat a light coating of oil on medium-high heat. Pour in enough batter to thinly coat the bottom of the pan, swirling the pan as you pour in the batter to help ensure an even coating. Cook the crêpe for 1 to 2 minutes on the first side, until it lifts from the pan easily. Flip it over and cook for 1 minute on the other side. Be careful that it doesn't take on too much colour. As you finish cooking each crêpe, transfer it to a plate, stacking them on top of one another. Repeat to make four crêpes, lightly oiling the pan between each one.

⚜

Pommes Aligot

Aligot Mashed Potatoes

Yield: 6 PORTIONS
Preparation time: 15 MINUTES
Cooking time: 45 MINUTES

2.2 pounds (1 kg) fingerling or Yukon Gold potatoes, peeled

9 ounces (250 g) fresh cheese curds

1 clove garlic

¾ cup (175 mL) heavy or whipping cream (35% milk fat), warmed

½ cup (115 g) cold unsalted butter, cubed

9 ounces (250 g) Gruyère cheese, grated

1 tablespoon (10 g) kosher salt

What's more comforting and stick-to-your-ribs delicious than the combo of potatoes and cheese? Then again, you could add poutine gravy to them and make it a threesome. Pommes Aligot is cheesy mashed potatoes with the ultimate stretchy cheese pull, just like biting into a great grilled cheese sandwich. I'm certain it was, at some point, an Instagram phenomenon, as it makes incredible pictures that melt people's hearts. Though it's traditionally made with Tomme de Laguiole, this cheese is extremely hard to find outside the south of France, and we substitute Québec cheese curds and Gruyère at the restaurant for that very reason. While the version we make at St. Lawrence isn't quite traditional, I've never felt bad about using Québec cheese curds for anything, really.

Place the potatoes in a large pot and add enough cold salted water to cover. Bring to a simmer on medium-high heat. Lower the heat to medium-low and cook until the potatoes are fork-tender, 20 to 30 minutes. Drain into a colander and let the potatoes release their steam for 5 minutes.

Meanwhile, using a food processor, shred the cheese curds into small chunks (this will help them melt better). Using a rasp grater (such as a Microplane), grate the garlic.

Using a ricer or food mill, finely mash the potatoes. Return the potatoes to the warm pot, along with the grated garlic. On medium heat, add the cream and butter, and stir slowly with a wooden spoon until fully incorporated. While stirring constantly, gradually add the cheese curds and Gruyère, little by little. You'll have to put more muscle into stirring as the purée gets thicker and thicker. Once all the cheese is mixed in, the purée should have a stringy and elastic texture. It's usually the moment when you start showing off to everyone around you and taking selfies. Season with the salt and serve right away.

VARIATION *If you can't track down cheese curds, you can use fresh bocconcini mozzarella balls or regular mozzarella instead. Just be judicious when adding salt, as the salt level is usually high in those babies.*

EVERY AFTERNOON AT 4:00 pm, the whole St. Lawrence crew gathers around a few tables and the bar seats for staff meal before evening service—it's a key moment in our day. Our team is one big family. They're people we can count on and trust, people we look forward to seeing every day, even when times are tough.

St. Lawrence staff meals are really good. That said, at the beginning they weren't because people didn't really understand how much care and effort they should put into preparing them. Everyone in the back-of-house crew takes a turn, but at the beginning I always make sure to step up to the plate soon after a new member of the team starts so they can see the extra work that should go into such an important part of our restaurant family's routine. From the very first day, they need to know that they have to plan ahead, organize their work, and make staff meal a priority.

I've worked hard to develop this culture; it gives everyone on the kitchen line a chance to shine, to show off the cuisine of their homeland if they're from another country and share their culture's food with the rest of the team. There have been curries, steamed soft bao with pork belly and slaw, sheet pizza made with beautiful dough, scratch-made pies. Couscous with lamb stew and vegetables. St. Lawrence doesn't have the luxury of having a pastry chef who can throw a dessert in there—we don't really eat dessert with staff meal, but that'd be a treat.

When you think about it, the structure of our jobs in the kitchen is that we work all day to prepare ourselves for working all night. There's no other job like it. Our day starts between 9:30 to 10:00 am, and we work for six hours before having staff meal and going back to work for another six hours. Staff meal splits our day in half and brings us a moment of joy. We're all working so hard and we all anticipate sitting down for at least 15 minutes to enjoy something that's hearty and flavourful, a moment when we can just relax and tell stories before work. And grabbing staff meal to eat at your station army-style while you work is a total no go. If people aren't sitting down by 4:15 pm, I or one of the sous-chefs will tell them to put their shit down and go have staff meal. Some people try to work right through without taking the time—I know it's a lot of pressure to be 100% ready before service, but going straight through with zero break doesn't set you up for success.

Mille-Feuille Choco-Café

Chocolate and Coffee Mille-Feuille

Yield: 6 PORTIONS

Preparation time: 45 MINUTES +
3 HOURS CHILLING

Cooking time: 25 TO 30 MINUTES
+ 10 MINUTES RESTING

What you'll need:

2 piping bags, each with a large
round tip

Chocolate Ganache:

1 sheet gelatin

1 cup (130 g) 65% to 70% chocolate,
chopped into small pieces

½ cup (125 mL) homogenized milk
(3.25% milk fat)

½ cup (125 mL) heavy or whipping
cream (35% milk fat)

3 egg yolks

1 tablespoon (15 g) granulated sugar

Crème Pâtissière:

1 sheet gelatin

1 cup (250 g) homogenized milk
(3.25% milk fat)

3 egg yolks

¼ cup (25 g) cornstarch

2 tablespoons (30 g) granulated
sugar

⅓ cup (75 g) cold unsalted butter,
diced into small cubes

2 tablespoons (30 mL) reduced
espresso (reduced from a double
shot)

2 tablespoons (50 g) store-bought
hazelnut praline paste or chopped
roasted hazelnuts

➤ *Mille-feuille is a classic French dessert that's found in almost any respectable Parisian patisserie. One of my favourite ways to end a simple weekday dinner is to eat a small piece of dark chocolate while sipping an espresso; this inspired me to move away from the classic vanilla mille-feuille and play with the flavours. The weak point with mille-feuille is that, once you put it together, the pastry starts to absorb moisture from the pastry cream and loses its flakiness. It's better to keep the puff pastry and cream separate and assemble the dessert at the last minute. If you undertake making your own homemade puff pastry dough, you'll be even more proud of the final outcome, but a good store-bought pastry dough will save you a lot of time.*

Day 1

FOR THE CHOCOLATE GANACHE: In a small bowl, soak the gelatin sheet in cold water for 10 minutes. Place the chocolate in a medium mixing bowl and set aside.

In a small saucepan on medium heat, bring the milk and cream to a simmer, then remove from the heat.

In a small mixing bowl, whisk the egg yolks and sugar for 1 minute. While whisking constantly, very slowly pour in a little bit of the hot milk mixture. Continue pouring and whisking until fully incorporated. Return the mixture to the saucepan and heat it to 185°F (85°C) on medium heat. It should coat the back of a spoon. Whisk in the softened gelatin.

Pour the milk mixture through a tamis directly into the bowl of chocolate. Whisk until the ganache is homogeneous and smooth. Place a piece of plastic wrap directly on top of the ganache to prevent a skin from forming on the surface. Refrigerate until set, about 3 hours.

FOR THE CRÈME PÂTISSIÈRE: Meanwhile, in a small bowl, soak the gelatin sheet in cold water for 10 minutes.

In a medium saucepan on medium heat, bring the milk to a simmer, then remove from the heat.

In a medium mixing bowl, whisk the egg yolks, cornstarch, and sugar for 1 minute. While whisking constantly, slowly pour a little of the hot milk into the egg yolk mixture; then, still whisking, add the rest of it until fully

½ batch of Pâte Feuilleté Rapide (page 300) or 1.1 pounds (500 g) store-bought puff pastry

Icing sugar, for dusting

incorporated. Return the mixture to the saucepan, place on medium-low heat, and whisk until the mixture thickens and looks like a custard. Be sure that you're whisking right to the bottom of the pot, to prevent the custard from sticking. Turn off the heat and whisk in the softened gelatin, butter, espresso, and praline.

Transfer the pastry cream to a container and place a piece of plastic wrap directly on top of the cream to prevent a skin from forming on the surface. Refrigerate until set, about 3 hours.

Day 2

TO ASSEMBLE AND FINISH: While the ganache and pastry cream are chilling, line a baking sheet with parchment paper. On a lightly floured work surface, roll out the puff pastry dough into a 10 by 12-inch (25 by 30 cm) rectangle that's ⅛ inch (3 mm) thick. Using a sharp knife, cut the rectangle into three 4 by 10-inch (10 by 25 cm) strips. Transfer the strips to the lined baking sheet and refrigerate for at least 1 hour to help prevent shrinkage.

Preheat your oven to 425°F (220°C), with the rack in the centre position.

Remove the puff pastry dough from the fridge and prick the surface with a fork to prevent it from puffing up too much while baking. Bake for 25 to 30 minutes, until the pastry is a beautiful hazelnut brown. Remove it from the oven and place another baking sheet of the same size directly on top of the pastry for 10 minutes to tighten it. Remove the top pan and transfer the puff pastry to a wire rack to cool.

Transfer the chocolate ganache to one piping bag and the pastry cream to the other. Lay one strip of puff pastry on a wooden board. Pipe either long lines or dots of chocolate ganache over the pastry, covering the entire strip. Place a second pastry strip on top of the ganache, pressing down gently. Pipe lines or dots of pastry cream over that strip. Top the pastry cream with the last strip of puff pastry, pressing down gently. Dust generously with icing sugar. Using a serrated knife, trim all the edges to make it look pretty.

Bring the mille-feuille to the table and slice it carefully in front of your guests.

✤

IMAGE ON PAGE 220

LEFT: MILLE-FEUILLE CHOCO-CAFÉ, PAGE 218   RIGHT: RIZ AU LAIT ET CARAMEL SALÉ, PAGE 222

Riz au Lait et Caramel Salé

Rice Pudding and Salted Caramel

Yield: 8 PORTIONS
Preparation time: 1 HOUR
Cooking time: 1½ HOURS

❧ I won't lie to you: my memories of rice pudding are not great. I've definitely had more bad rice puddings than good ones, as it's often way too thick and heavy. The first time I had a truly great rice pudding, one that actually made me say "Wow!" out loud, was at L'Ami Jean in Paris—it tasted like a giant bowl of vanilla crème Chantilly with grains of rice in it. Paired with a salted caramel and a mix of caramelized nuts on the side, it was heaven. The generous portion, a massive bowl of it, was enough for four people and would normally scare a table of two. But we dove right in and ended up eating the whole thing, and my wife had to stop me from ordering a second one! Don't go fancy or super spendy when buying rice for this recipe—truth be told, cheap-ass rice works best for it.

Pets de Soeur (Nun's Farts):

8 ounces (225 g) Pâte Brisée (page 299) or reserved trims from your freezer

¼ cup (55 g) softened unsalted butter

½ cup (80 g) firmly packed brown sugar

¼ teaspoon (1 mL) ground cinnamon

Rice Pudding:

2 cups (500 mL) homogenized milk (3.25% milk fat)

¾ cup (175 mL) water

¾ cup (175 g) Arborio rice

½ cup + 2 tablespoons (125 g) granulated sugar

1¼ cups (300 mL) heavy or whipping cream (35% milk fat)

1 vanilla bean, split and scraped, or 1 teaspoon (5 mL) vanilla extract

FOR THE PETS DE SOEUR: On a floured work surface, roll out the pastry into a 10 by 4-inch (25 by 10 cm) rectangle that's ⅛ inch (3 mm) thick. Spread the butter over the entire surface of the dough, then sprinkle with the brown sugar and cinnamon. Roll the dough into a cylinder to enclose the filling. Place the cylinder on a baking sheet and freeze until the dough is semi-frozen, about 1 hour.

FOR THE RICE PUDDING: Meanwhile, preheat your oven to 250°F (120°C), with the rack in the centre position.

In a medium ovenproof saucepan on medium heat, combine the milk and water and bring to a simmer. Whisk in the rice, cover with a lid, and transfer to the oven. After 20 minutes, remove the pot from the oven and whisk the rice vigorously to separate the grains and ensure the rice doesn't stick to the bottom of the pot. Cover and continue cooking in the oven for another 20 minutes. Whisk the rice again; at this point, the mixture should be thick and the rice should be tender. If not, cover the pot, return it to the oven, and continue cooking for another 10 minutes.

Transfer the pot to the stovetop and whisk in the sugar until it dissolves; the mixture will thin out a little. Cook, uncovered, on low heat for 20 minutes or until it thickens again, stirring often to make sure it doesn't burn at the bottom of the pot.

Transfer the rice mixture to a large bowl set over ice and let cool completely at room temperature. Using a rubber spatula, work the cold rice

Salted Caramel:

½ cup + 1 teaspoon (115 g) granulated sugar

2 tablespoons (30 mL) water

A few drops of fresh lemon juice

½ cup (125 mL) heavy or whipping cream (35% milk fat)

¼ cup (55 g) unsalted butter, cubed

1 teaspoon (4 g) kosher salt

½ sheet gelatin, soaked in cold water for 10 minutes (optional)

3 tablespoons (45 mL) Crème Fraîche (page 296, or store-bought) or whipped cream

Pecans:

⅓ cup (65 g) granulated sugar

1 tablespoon (15 mL) water

1 cup (100 g) pecan halves, toasted (see Salade d'Endives on page 189)

IMAGE ON PAGE 221

to make sure all the grains are separated from each other. Take your time, as this is a crucial step for the perfect texture.

In a separate bowl, whip the cream by hand with the vanilla until medium peaks form (see tip). Gently fold the whipped cream, one-third at a time, into the rice mixture. Cover and refrigerate until needed, for up to 2 hours.

FOR THE SALTED CARAMEL: In a medium saucepan on medium-high heat, heat the sugar, water, and lemon juice until the mixture is a deep amber colour, about 8 to 10 minutes. Remove from the heat and gradually whisk in the cream—watch yourself, because it will bubble like crazy. Whisk until the caramel is smooth, then whisk in the butter, salt, and gelatin.

Transfer the caramel to a bowl, cover with plastic wrap, and refrigerate until very cold. Stir in the crème fraîche until fully incorporated. Cover and refrigerate until needed, for up to 24 hours.

FOR THE PECANS: In a small pot on medium-high heat, heat the sugar and water, stirring until the sugar is dissolved. Add the pecans and cook, stirring, until they are well coated in a light-golden-brown caramel. Pour out onto a silicone baking mat or parchment paper and let cool. Separate the pecans and set aside.

TO BAKE: Preheat your oven to 375°F (190°C), with the rack in the centre position. Line a baking sheet with parchment paper.

Cut the semi-frozen pastry cylinder into slices about ¼ inch (5 mm) thick and lay them on the lined baking sheet 1 inch (2.5 cm) apart. Bake for 12 to 15 minutes or until golden brown. Let cool completely. (The *pets de soeur* can be stored in an airtight container at room temperature for up to 3 days).

TO SERVE: You could spoon out the rice pudding into individual serving bowls, but I prefer bringing the entire bowl to the dinner table and scooping it out for everyone—it's all about the drama. Serve the rice pudding with a few handfuls of caramelized pecans, some *pets de soeur*, and a spoonful of salted caramel.

TIP   *When you're making a whipped cream or a meringue, you'll progress through different stages while you're whisking. Soft peaks barely hold their shape, and the peaks will flop over immediately when you lift the whisk. Medium peaks hold their shape pretty well, except that the tip of the peak curls over on itself when you lift the whisk. Stiff peaks stand straight up.*

Tarte au Citron Flambée au Pastis

Lemon Tart Flambéed with Pastis

Yield: ONE 9-INCH (23 CM) TART, 8 TO 10 PORTIONS

Preparation time: 45 MINUTES

Cooking time: 40 MINUTES + 3 HOURS RESTING

🐟 *For this classic lemon tart, the lemony custard is poured into the baked tart shell and then set in the fridge, so there's no need to worry about an undercooked crust or an overcooked filling. It's a fairly quick and simple dessert to make, and it's always hugely popular. At St. Lawrence, we like putting a Swiss meringue on top and torching it slightly, for two good reasons: first because it tastes like marshmallows, and second because we always have a good amount of leftover egg whites that we need to use up. And the dramatic flambé at the table never fails to get oohs and ahs from our guests—people love fire!*

What you'll need:

Hand blender

Stand mixer fitted with the whisk attachment

Piping bag with a star tip

Kitchen torch

Tart Shell:

1 batch Pâte Sucrée (page 302)

Lemon Curd:

6 large eggs (10.5 ounces/300 g)

1 cup (200 g) granulated sugar

Zest of 1 lemon

¾ cup (175 mL) fresh lemon juice

1 sheet gelatin

1 cup (240 g) cold unsalted butter, cubed

Swiss Meringue:

4 egg whites (5.5 ounces/160 g)

¾ cup (150 g) granulated sugar

A few drops fresh lemon juice

Serving:

¼ cup (50 g) granulated sugar, to caramelize

¼ cup (60 mL) brandy

¼ cup (60 mL) Pastis (preferably Ricard)

FOR THE TART SHELL: The day before, make the *pâte sucrée*. The day of, make the tart shell as directed on page 302.

FOR THE LEMON CURD: In a small bowl, soak the gelatin sheet in cold water for 10 minutes.

Meanwhile, in a mixing bowl, whisk the eggs with the sugar until fully incorporated, then whisk in the lemon zest and juice.

Transfer the egg mixture to a medium pot on medium-high heat. Bring it to a boil, whisking constantly to make sure the mixture doesn't stick to the bottom of the pot. It will thicken and look like a curd. Don't be scared—it won't turn into scrambled eggs.

Remove the pot from the heat, squeeze all the water out of the gelatin, and whisk it into the lemon curd. Let cool to 150°F (66°C). Using a hand blender, start incorporating the cubes of cold butter a little at a time. Once the butter is fully incorporated, pass the lemon curd through a tamis and pour it into the baked tart shell; it should be filled nearly to the top of the pie crust and almost feel like it's going to overflow. (You might have some leftover lemon curd. Keep it in a small airtight container in the fridge for when you have a snack attack.). Let set in the fridge for at least 3 hours.

FOR THE SWISS MERINGUE: Don't begin making the Swiss meringue until 2 hours before you're ready to pipe so that it retains its fluffiness. Start by filling a medium saucepan one-quarter full with water. Set the pan on medium-high heat and bring the water to a simmer.

continued

In a medium heatproof mixing bowl, combine the egg whites, sugar, and lemon juice. Place the bowl over the pan of simmering water and whisk constantly until the sugar is dissolved and the whites are quite hot to the touch, about 5 minutes. You can test it by rubbing a bit of the mixture between your fingers and making sure you don't feel any grains of sugar.

Transfer the egg white mixture to the bowl of a stand mixer fitted with the whisk and whip on medium speed until glossy peaks form, about 5 minutes. Using a rubber spatula, transfer the meringue to a piping bag with a star tip.

TO SERVE: Cut the tart into eight to ten slices. Sprinkle a thin layer of sugar on top of each slice and brûlée them with a kitchen torch until nicely caramelized. Channel your artistic flair and decorate the slices with piped rosettes of meringue.

In a small saucepan on medium-high heat, heat up the brandy and pastis to a low simmer and light it on fire. Let the alcohol burn off for at least 1½ minutes, then, in front of your guests, pour the flaming alcohol over the tart slices.

TIP *When it comes to the quantity of eggs you'll need for this recipe, make sure you measure by weight. There's often variation in the weights of egg sizes, depending on the producer, especially when it comes to the size of the yolks. So it's definitely better to weigh them.*

⚜

Babas au Sortilège

Baba Cakes with Sortilège Maple Liquor

Yield: 12 PORTIONS

Preparation time: 1 HOUR +
1½ HOURS PROOFING

Cooking time: 30 MINUTES

➤ *A* baba *is a cake made from savarin dough, very similar to a brioche, that's fully saturated in a rum syrup after baking. Historically, it was usually prepared for religious celebrations, like Christmas or Easter. I really enjoy the simple flavour of a moist and boozy wet cake with whipped cream—it makes you feel especially grown-up. In this recipe, I've swapped the traditional rum for Sortilège, a maple whisky from Québec, which is how we serve this version of the traditional dessert at St. Lawrence, especially for our yearly* Cabane à Sucre *menu event. I always enjoy raisins in a brioche, and I often associate maple with apples, so having the compote as an accompaniment makes a lot of sense to me.*

What you'll need:

Stand mixer fitted with the paddle attachment

Twelve 2-inch (5 cm) metal or Silicone dariole moulds (see tip) or small ramekins

Babas:

3 tablespoons (45 mL) homogenized milk (3.25% milk fat)

1½ teaspoons (6 g) active dry yeast

1⅓ cups (200 g) all-purpose flour

1 teaspoon (3 g) kosher salt

2 teaspoons (14 g) honey

3 eggs

⅓ cup (75 g) softened unsalted butter + more for buttering the moulds

Apple and Raisin Compote:

¼ cup (40 g) golden raisins

3 Granny Smith apples, peeled and diced into ½-inch (1 cm) cubes (about 2 cups/500 mL)

Juice of 1 lemon

½ cup (100 g) granulated sugar

½ cup (125 mL) water

FOR THE BABAS: In a small saucepan on low heat, heat up the milk slowly, making sure the temperature doesn't go above 86°F (30°C). Stir in the yeast until fully dissolved.

Place the flour, salt, and honey into the bowl of a stand mixer fitted with the paddle. Pour in the yeast mixture, add one egg, and mix together at medium speed until completely combined. Trickle in the remaining eggs, one at a time, mixing until each addition is fully incorporated before pouring in more. Start adding small pieces of butter to the bowl, a few at a time, and mix until the dough is homogeneous and pulls away from the sides of the bowl. The dough should be smooth, shiny, and elastic. Transfer to a bowl, cover with a plastic film and let proof at room temperature for 1 hour until doubled in size.

Place the raisins in a small bowl, cover with warm water, and let soak for 1 hour.

Grease the dariole moulds with butter or baking spray. Transfer the dough to a clean surface. Portion out 1.5-ounce (45 g) pieces of dough (about 2 tablespoons/30 mL) and spoon them into the moulds, filling them no more than halfway up the sides. Let the dough proof at room temperature until it doubles in size, about 30 minutes, depending on the temperature of the room. When finished proofing, the dough should be about ⅛ inch (3 mm) from the top of the moulds.

Meanwhile, preheat your oven to 375°F (190°C), with the rack in the centre position.

continued

Syrup:

1¾ cups (375 g) granulated sugar

3 cups (750 mL) water

1 vanilla bean, split and scraped, or
1 teaspoon (5 mL) vanilla extract

Grated zest and juice of 2 oranges

Grated zest and juice of 1 lemon

½ cup (125 mL) Sortilège (or rum),
plus more for drizzling

Crème Chantilly:

1½ cups (375 mL) heavy or
whipping cream (35% milk fat)

1 tablespoon (8 g) icing sugar

1 vanilla bean, split and scraped, or
½ teaspoon (2 mL) vanilla extract

Bake the babas for 15 minutes or until a skewer inserted into the centre of a baba comes out clean. Let cool in the moulds for 10 minutes, then unmould the babas onto a wire rack to cool completely. The babas are ready to be soaked, but you can store them in an airtight container for up to 3 days. Freeze any extras for another dinner party.

FOR THE APPLE AND RAISIN COMPOTE: Drain the raisins and add the apples and lemon juice to the bowl, tossing to coat. In a small saucepan on medium heat, combine the sugar and water. Bring to a simmer, then stir in the apple mixture. Cook, stirring occasionally with a wooden spoon, until most of the liquid has evaporated, the apples are cooked, and the raisins are plump. Transfer to a container and let cool completely, then cover and refrigerate until needed.

FOR THE SYRUP: In a large saucepan, combine the sugar, water, and vanilla. Bring to a boil. Remove from the heat and stir in the lemon and orange zest and juice. Let cool completely, then stir in the Sortilège. (The syrup can be made up to 1 week ahead and refrigerated in an airtight container until needed.)

Have a baking sheet ready. In a large pot on medium heat, bring the syrup to 104°F (40°C). Drop the babas into the syrup and let them soak it up for 2 minutes, then gently flip them over and let soak until the babas feel spongy and are well saturated with syrup but not breaking apart. Using a slotted spoon, transfer the babas to the pan to cool. Reserve the remaining syrup.

FOR THE CRÈME CHANTILLY: Meanwhile, in your stand mixer fitted with the whisk attachment, whip the cream, icing sugar, and vanilla until soft peaks form.

Slice each baba vertically through the centre, stopping halfway down so that it remains hinged at the bottom. Use your finger to carefully open up the babas up. Lay out individual serving bowls; you'll be serving one baba per person. Place a spoonful of the compote in each serving bowl and rest a baba on top. Slowly pour syrup on each baba to ensure that the centre is fully soaked. You should have a thin layer of syrup at the bottom of each bowl. Spoon a dollop of *crème Chantilly* into the baba's cavity, and drizzle on a little more Sortilège if you like your dessert to be boozy—I won't judge.

TIP *A dariole mould is a small, slightly tapered cylindrical mould shaped like a flowerpot. They're a versatile addition to your kitchen kit, great for making individual treats like panna cottas, cakes, and puddings, but equally great for little quiches, pâtés, and terrines.*

TIP *Before soaking the babas, set aside any extra ones and freeze them for another dinner party.*

Soufflé Glacé à L'Orange et Grand Marnier

Frozen Orange Soufflé with Grand Marnier

Yield: 4 PORTIONS

Preparation time: 1 HOUR +
6 HOURS FREEZING

Cooking time: 10 MINUTES

This make-ahead dessert is a perfect way to finish an elegant dinner, especially in the warm summer months. All you need is little bit of freezer space. The frozen soufflés have a dramatic appearance: they look like hot soufflés fresh out of the oven, but they are, in fact, ice cream. Putting parchment paper around the ramekins holds the custard in place vertically while it's freezing, and the height of the end result will be visually appealing. Though this recipe doesn't really need the Grand Marnier, I prefer incorporating the orange liqueur, as it offsets the richness and sweetness of the frozen soufflé.

What you'll need:

Stand mixer fitted with the whisk attachment

Four ¾-cup (175 mL) ramekins or soufflé dishes

Grated zest of 2 oranges

1 cup (250 mL) fresh orange juice (5 to 6 oranges)

½ cup (100 g) granulated sugar

10 egg yolks (5 ounces/150 g)

1¼ cups (325 mL) heavy or whipping cream (35% milk fat)

⅓ cup (75 mL) Grand Marnier

Icing sugar, to dust

Orange segments or candied oranges, to garnish (optional)

In a small pot on medium-high heat, bring the orange zest, orange juice, and sugar to a consistent boil. With the help of a good thermometer (such as a candy thermometer), bring the mixture to 220°F (105°C).

Using a stand mixer fitted with the whisk, whisk the egg yolks rapidly on high speed, then pour in the boiling orange syrup slowly and gradually. Continue whisking until the mixture is completely cold and doubled in volume.

In a separate bowl, whip the cream by hand to soft peaks. Using a rubber spatula, gently fold the whipped cream into the egg yolk mixture, along with the Grand Marnier.

Cut four 12 by 3-inch (30 by 7 cm) strips of parchment paper. Wrap one strip around the top rim of each ramekin and secure it with an elastic band or tape. The paper should come up above the rim by 1½ inches (4 cm) or so; it will help the soufflé custard to stay in place as it freezes.

Using a spoon, divide the soufflé mixture among the prepared ramekins. Place the soufflés in the freezer for 6 hours.

To serve, remove the parchment paper, dust the frozen soufflés with icing sugar, and garnish with orange segments.

TIP *After 6 hours in the freezer, the soufflé will start to lose its light texture and become harder and harder. Best to plan ahead so your dessert course hits the table right around that mark.*

HOME COOKING

FOR ME, COOKING AT home is very much inspired by the best seasonal ingredients available. I like to keep things simple so that my two daughters, Aïla and Florence, can be involved in prep, and I build our family meals around what the kids like to eat. Aïla and Flo aren't quite yet at the age where they'll appreciate dishes like rabbit in mustard sauce or *poulet à la crème*, but hopefully they'll become more adventurous eaters as they get older.

Pasta is a popular choice with the girls—my daughters are especially fond of being by my side when we do *pasta alla chitarra* from scratch. When we sit down at the table, it makes it extra special to be able to say, "Thank you, girls, for helping me make the pasta." For dessert, chocolate mousse definitely wins by a mile, especially when it comes to having two mini sous-chefs in the kitchen. And the golden prize of licking the spatula with the leftover mousse always brings a lot of smiles.

As a kid in my mom's kitchen, I was in charge of the vegetables, whether it was cleaning them a certain way or cutting them to a particular size. Aïla has her own mini chef's knife, and she's right in there when I ask her to make a crudité plate. She cuts up the carrots, cucumbers, broccoli, and celery while Florence whisks the dressing—sure, it takes about an hour for them to put everything together, but our shared joy comes from them learning the process alongside me.

Artichauts à la Vinaigrette

Artichokes with Mustard Vinaigrette

Yield: 4 PORTIONS

Preparation time: 15 MINUTES

Cooking time: 20 TO 30 MINUTES

Artichokes aren't an easy vegetable to introduce to kids—they're definitely outside the box. But one of my favourite childhood dishes was this simple boiled artichoke vinaigrette dish that Mom used to make. It's a great starter, and it's also perfect for sunny picnics on the beach. I remember how much fun I had eating the artichokes as a young boy, going through all the leaves one by one, dipping them in the vinaigrette, and pulling them through my teeth to scrape off the flesh. Then there was the big prize: eating the artichoke heart was always something special. Now I prepare this dish at home for my daughters, and they absolutely love it too. Maybe not for the artichoke flavour itself, but more for the concept of the dish, which shows that eating can be a lot of fun.

4 large globe artichokes

1 lemon

1 cup (250 mL) Vinaigrette Classique (recipe follows)

Snap or cut off the artichoke stalks. (I prefer to snap them, as the chewy strings slide out of the artichoke hearts and leave them tender and clean.) Cut 4 slices from the centre of the lemon that are about ¼-inch (6 mm) thick. Using butcher's twine, attach 1 lemon slice to the bottom of each artichoke; this will give flavour and prevent oxidization.

In a large pot on medium-high heat, bring salted water to a boil. Add the artichokes, lower the heat to medium and simmer for 20 to 25 minutes or until a leaf detaches easily when gently pulled. Turn off the heat and drain the water.

Lift the artichokes out of the pot, rest them tips-down on a wire rack, and let them drain completely, about 5 minutes. Remove the twine and lemon slices and discard. Serve the dressing alongside the cooled artichokes for dipping.

⚜

VINAIGRETTE CLASSIQUE

Classic French Vinaigrette

Yield: 1½ CUPS (375 ML)

Preparation time: 20 MINUTES

1 large shallot, minced

¼ cup (60 mL) fresh lemon juice

1 teaspoon (3 g) kosher salt

1 large clove garlic, finely grated

2 teaspoons (10 mL) Dijon mustard

2 teaspoons (10 mL) grainy Dijon mustard

2 teaspoons (10 mL) honey

½ cup (125 mL) extra-virgin olive oil

½ cup (125 mL) grapeseed oil

2 sprigs thyme, leaves only

Big pinch freshly cracked black pepper

In a bowl, soak the minced shallot in cold water for 5 minutes, then drain the water. In a medium mixing bowl, whisk together the lemon juice and salt until the salt is dissolved. Add the shallot, garlic, Dijon mustard, grainy Dijon mustard, and honey. Mix well. Combine the olive oil and grapeseed oil, and drizzle slowly into the dressing while whisking constantly to emulsify. Whisk in the thyme and pepper. Taste for seasoning.

Brandade de Morue
Salt Cod Brandade

Yield: 6 PORTIONS

Preparation time: 30 MINUTES +
48 HOURS SOAKING

Cooking time: 30 MINUTES

❧ *If you open my home fridge, you'll almost always find a piece of salt cod on the shelf (though it can definitely be stored in your pantry). I love both the history of this fish and the concept of preserving it. Brandade is a wonderful dish from the south of France, and many other countries have a version of it. In this case, the salt cod is mixed with silky mashed potatoes to create an excellent dip that's perfect for any party. There is some debate: traditionalists insist that cod alone is enough to create the smooth texture, while others enjoy the dimension added by the potatoes. Either way, it's a wonderful preparation.*

What you'll need:

Stand mixer fitted with the paddle attachment

10 ounces (275 g) salted cod

1½ cups (375 mL) homogenized milk (3.25% milk fat)

1 cup (250 mL) water

1 bay leaf

1 sprig thyme

9 ounces (250 g) fingerling or Yukon Gold potatoes

3 cloves garlic

1 cup (250 mL) heavy or whipping cream (35% milk fat)

3 tablespoons (45 mL) extra-virgin olive oil, plus more for drizzling

Juice of 1 lemon

Freshly cracked black pepper and cayenne pepper, to taste

Toasted French baguette slices, for serving

Black olives, for serving

Place the salt cod in an airtight container and cover generously with cold water. Cover and let soak in the fridge for 48 hours, changing the water every 12 hours or so.

Using a sharp knife, split the cod in half lengthwise. Place it in a small saucepan and add the milk, water, bay leaf, and thyme. On medium-low heat, bring the liquid to 185°F (85°C) and poach the fish for 20 minutes or until tender and falling apart. Line a plate with a paper towel. Remove the fish from the liquid and drain on the paper towel until cool. Discard the liquid.

While the fish is cooking, place the potatoes in a medium pot and cover with cold water. Bring to a simmer on medium-high heat and cook until tender, about 20 minutes.

Meanwhile, using a Microplane, grate the garlic into a small saucepan. Add the cream, and bring to a boil on medium heat. Remove from the heat and let cool.

Remove any bones and skin from the cod. Place the cod, potatoes, and ½ cup (125 mL) of the cream mixture in the bowl of a stand mixer fitted with the paddle attachment. Beat on low speed for 30 seconds, until the mixture is combined and smooth; it will be thick.

Transfer the cod mixture to a medium pot on low heat. Using a wooden spoon, start working the fish mixture against the side of the pot. While stirring constantly, pour in the remaining cream in a thin and steady stream until the cod has absorbed all the liquid. Stir in the oil, lemon juice, pepper, and cayenne. Taste for seasoning. Transfer the *brandade* to a serving bowl and drizzle more oil on top. Serve the baguette toasts and olives on the side.

⚜

Cervelle de Canut

Fresh Cheese with Herbs

Yield: 6 TO 8 PORTIONS
Preparation time: 15 MINUTES
Cooking time: 20 MINUTES

Cervelle de canut is basically the Boursin of France, an herbed fresh farmer's cheese spread that's a speciality of Lyon. The name is kind of weird, as it literally means "silk worker's brain," named after nineteenth-century Lyonnaise silk workers, who were called canuts. *Sadly, the name reflects the low opinion of the people towards these workers. Happily for us, though, it's delicious—creamy, fragrant, and fresh at the same time. Cervelle de canut is one of my family's favourite dishes. It's a great make-ahead appetizer that you can pop out of the fridge once your guests arrive. Use a full-fat cream cheese for the dish, or it will be too runny and less delicious.*

Cheese:

1 large shallot, finely chopped

1 clove garlic, grated

2 tablespoons (10 g) chopped fresh flat-leaf parsley

2 tablespoons (10 g) chopped fresh chives

1 tablespoon (5 g) chopped fresh tarragon

1 teaspoon (3 g) chopped fresh dill

1 teaspoon (3 g) kosher salt

¼ teaspoon (1 g) freshly cracked black pepper

⅓ cup (75 mL) Crème Fraîche (page 296, or store-bought) or high-fat sour cream

1.1 pounds (500 g) full-fat cream cheese

Crostini:

2 tablespoons (30 g) unsalted butter, melted

2 tablespoons (30 mL) extra-virgin olive oil

1 teaspoon (5 mL) chopped garlic

1 teaspoon (3 g) kosher salt

1 teaspoon (5 mL) fresh thyme leaves

1 French baguette, cut into ¼-inch (5 mm) slices

FOR THE CHEESE: Rinse the shallot under cold water to remove the raw onion taste. In a medium mixing bowl, stir together the shallot, garlic, parsley, chives, tarragon, dill, salt, and pepper. Add the crème fraîche and mix until fully incorporated. Using a rubber spatula, gently fold in the cream cheese until the herbs and aromatics are evenly distributed. Don't overmix. Spoon the mixture into a small airtight container, cover, and store in the fridge for up to 1 week.

FOR THE CROSTINI: Preheat your oven to 350°F (180°C), with the rack in the centre position. Line a baking sheet with a silicone mat or parchment paper.

In a small bowl, mix together the butter, oil, garlic, salt, and thyme. Lay out the bread slices on the lined baking sheet and brush each slice on both sides with the butter mixture.

Bake for 10 minutes, then flip the slices over and bake for another 10 minutes. The crostini should be golden brown and crispy, but not dried out and rock hard.

Transfer the crostini to a serving plate and serve with the cheese to spread on top.

Tarte Flambée–Flammekueche

Alsatian Thin-Crust "Pizza"

Yield: 6 INDIVIDUAL PIZZAS OR 2 LARGE PIZZAS

Preparation time: 45 MINUTES + 1½ TO 2 HOURS RISING

Cooking time: 25 TO 40 MINUTES

What you'll need:

Stand mixer fitted with the dough hook attachment

Pizza stone (optional but preferable)

Pizza paddle

Dough:

¾ cup + 2 tablespoons (205 mL) homogenized milk (3.25% milk fat)

2 teaspoons (12 g) granulated sugar

4 teaspoons (20 g) unsalted butter

1½ teaspoons (6 g) active dry yeast

2 cups (300 g) all-purpose flour

1 teaspoon (3 g) kosher salt

Cream Topping:

1 cup (250 mL) *fromage blanc* or softened full-fat cream cheese

½ cup (125 mL) Crème Fraîche (page 296, or store-bought)

1 egg yolk

1 tablespoon (10 g) all-purpose flour

¼ teaspoon (1 mL) freshly grated nutmeg

Good pinch kosher salt

Freshly cracked black pepper

Tarte Flambée:

8 thick slices (12 ounces/350 g) smoked bacon, cut into lardons

1 small yellow onion, very thinly sliced

2 tablespoons (30 mL) finely sliced fresh chives

❧ Tarte flambée *is an Alsatian flatbread topped with* fromage blanc, *onions, and bacon. It looks like a pizza and it cooks like a pizza, but don't tell that to a Franco-German Alsatian. Judging by the name, they want it to be a tart that's cooked at high temperature—fair enough! I had my first* tarte flambée *in Strasbourg, and it was everything I imagined it would be. Because of its proximity to the German border, France's Alsace region has developed a unique identity, with its own cuisine. We Québécois share a number of similarities with Alsatians, each of us living within a unique cultural pocket in our respective countries. We definitely have the same love for beer, and our cuisines are robust and generous, with lots of slow-simmered dishes featuring ham, sausages, and other cuts of cured pork. I felt truly at home in Alsace, and this dish brings back all the great memories from that trip every time I make it.*

FOR THE DOUGH: In a small pot on low heat, heat the milk, sugar, and butter, stirring until the butter is melted and the sugar is dissolved. Let cool to body temperature (98°F/37°C), then whisk in the yeast and let stand for 10 minutes.

In the bowl of a stand mixer fitted with the dough hook, combine the flour and salt. With the mixer running on medium speed, slowly pour in the milk mixture and mix for 8 minutes, until the dough is smooth and elastic.

While the dough is mixing, lightly oil a medium bowl. Form the dough into a ball, place it in the oiled bowl, and cover the bowl with plastic wrap. Let rise at room temperature for 1½ to 2 hours.

If you're making individual tartes, divide the dough into six equal portions. Roll each portion into a little ball with the palm of your hand, as if you're making dinner rolls. Lightly flour a work surface. Using a small rolling pin, roll out each ball into an 8 to 10-inch (20 to 25 cm) long sheet that's ⅛ inch (3 mm) thick. Sprinkle some flour on the dough to prevent it from sticking. Line a baking sheet with parchment paper and transfer the dough onto it. Alternate layers of parchment paper and dough until you've rolled out all six portions. Let stand for 30 minutes.

If you're making larger pizzas, divide the dough into two portions. Lightly flour a work surface. Using a rolling pin, roll out each portion to ⅛ inch

continued

(3 mm) thick. Line a baking sheet with parchment paper and transfer the dough to the pan, layering them with a sheet of parchment between them. Let stand for 30 minutes at room temperature.

FOR THE CREAM TOPPING: Meanwhile, in a medium bowl, whisk together the *fromage blanc*, crème fraîche, egg yolk, flour, nutmeg, salt, and pepper until fully combined. Set aside.

FOR THE TARTE FLAMBÉE: Preheat your oven to 500°F (260°C), with the rack in the lowest position. It's better to use a pizza stone if you have one; if not, place an upside-down baking sheet on the rack. (You might want to heat up the pizza stone for 1 hour before baking, to make sure you get a crispy crust.)

In a large sauté pan on high heat, cook the bacon until caramelized. Using a slotted spoon, transfer the bacon to a baking sheet lined with paper towels to drain. Discard the fat.

Transfer one or two portions of dough to a lightly floured pizza paddle. Spread the cream topping in a thin even layer over the dough, leaving a small border around the edges. Distribute some of the bacon and onion evenly on top. Slide the tarte onto the baking stone and bake until crispy on the bottom and lightly browned on top, around 6 to 7 minutes for an individual tarte or 12 to 15 minutes for a larger tarte. If you're baking individual tartes in batches, you can place the finished tartes on two baking sheets, put them back in the oven for 3 to 4 minutes to reheat, and serve them all at once if that works better for you. Sprinkle the chives on top to garnish. Eat. Repeat.

TIP *If you're too pressed for time to make the dough, substitute a good store-bought puff pastry. It's not traditional by any means, but will still be very tasty.*

✤

Quiche Lorraine

Yield: 8 PORTIONS

Preparation time: 45 MINUTES +
20 MINUTES CHILLING

Cooking time: 3½ HOURS +
2 HOURS COOLING

This quiche is the real deal. I'm usually so annoyed by the American-style quiche; more often than not, it's done with factory-made pie shells that end up being soggy, and filled with overcooked custard. No, this is a high-sided pie, with fully cooked flaky pastry and a beautiful light and fluffy custard. It's funny how every time a cook in my kitchen announces that staff meal will be quiche, my first instinct is to panic a little, especially when they plan to start cooking it an hour beforehand. Quiche isn't a recipe you can casually throw together; it's definitely not something you'll be whipping up in a rush for a weeknight dinner. But if you take your time and take on the challenge, I can pretty much guarantee this will be the best quiche you'll ever have. Serve it with a nice green salad.

What you'll need:
Heavy-bottomed cast-iron pan
9 by 2-inch (23 × 5 cm) cake ring

1 pound (450 g) leeks (white and light green parts only), thinly sliced
½ cup (115 g) unsalted butter, cubed
¼ cup (60 mL) water
1½ teaspoons (5 g) kosher salt
2 bay leaves
8 ounces (225 g) smoked bacon, cut into lardons
Grapeseed oil, for brushing
½ batch Pâte à Pâté (page 298)
1¼ cups (300 mL) homogenized milk (3.25% milk fat)
1¼ cups (300 mL) heavy or whipping cream (35% milk fat)
7 eggs (13.3 ounces/385 g)
1 teaspoon (3 g) kosher salt
⅛ teaspoon (1 g) freshly cracked black pepper
Freshly grated nutmeg, to taste
¾ cup (130 g) grated Gruyère cheese

In a heavy-bottomed pot on low heat, combine the leeks, butter, water, salt, and bay leaves. Cover and cook gently for about 1 hour to confit the leeks, stirring every 15 minutes. The leeks should become very soft but should not take on any colour. Remove from the heat.

In a heavy-bottomed cast-iron pan, cook the bacon on medium-high heat for 5 to 10 minutes, until the fat has rendered. Using a slotted spoon, transfer the bacon to a small baking sheet lined with paper towels to drain. Stir the bacon into the leek confit and set aside.

Lightly brush the inside of the cake ring with oil and place it on a baking sheet.

On a floured work surface, lay out the *pâte à pâté* and rub it on both sides with flour. Using a rolling pin, roll out the dough into a 14-inch (35 cm) circle that's ¼ inch (5 mm) thick—yes, this is a fairly thick crust. It's important to work quickly so the dough doesn't get too soft. Roll the dough up loosely onto the rolling pin and hold it over the pan, centring it over the cake ring. Carefully lower the dough into the pan, pressing it gently into the bottom and against the sides of the cake ring. Trim any dough that extends more than an inch (2.5 cm) over the edges of the ring. Fold the excess dough over against the outside of the ring. (This will prevent the crust from shrinking down the sides as it bakes; you'll be removing the excess crust after the quiche is baked.) Carefully check for any cracks or holes in the dough and patch with the trimmed dough if necessary. Place in the freezer for at least 20 minutes to resolidify the butter.

continued

Preheat your oven to 375°F (190°C), with the rack in the centre position.

Line the chilled quiche shell with parchment paper and pour in dried beans to fill the shell completely. Blind bake for 40 to 45 minutes, until the edges of the pastry are lightly browned but the bottom is still light in colour. Remove from the oven, leaving the oven on, and let cool completely. Look again for any cracks (you don't want the custard to escape from the shell) and patch with pieces of raw dough if necessary.

Meanwhile, to make the custard, combine the milk and cream in a large saucepan on medium heat and bring to a slow simmer. Remove from the heat and let cool for 15 minutes.

Pour the milk mixture into a blender and add the eggs, salt, pepper, and nutmeg. Blend on low speed to mix, then increase the speed to high and blend until the custard is light and foamy, about 30 seconds.

Evenly distribute one-third of the Gruyère and half of the leek confit in the baked quiche shell (still on the baking sheet). Pour in enough of the custard to cover the ingredients and fill the shell about halfway. Top with the remaining leek confit and another third of the cheese. Fill the shell all the way to the top with the remaining custard and sprinkle with the remaining cheese.

Bake for 1½ hours, until the top of the quiche is browned and the custard is set when the pan is jiggled. Let cool completely on a wire rack, about 2 hours.

Using a serrated knife, cut away the excess crust from the top edge. Gently remove the cake ring, working it free in spots with a small knife if necessary. Using a long serrated knife, and supporting the sides of the crust with your opposite hand, carefully cut through the outer edge of the crust. Switch to a long slicing knife and cut through the custard and bottom crust. Repeat, cutting the quiche into eight pieces. The quiche is ready to eat, but if you prefer it hot, place the pieces on the baking sheet and put it back in the oven for 10 minutes or until warmed through.

⚜

Saumon à la Nage

Poached Salmon in Court Bouillon

Yield: 4 PORTIONS

Preparation time: 25 MINUTES + 30 MINUTES CURING

Cooking time: 40 MINUTES

Cooking fish à la nage *is a beautiful preparation. A* nage, *or* court bouillon—*French for "quick broth"—is an aromatic, flavourful liquid used to poach many kinds of fish and shellfish. It gives you a superb broth and cooks the fish slowly, without the aggression of a hot pan. To save time on the day you'll be serving the dish, prepare the bouillon in advance and keep it for up to three days in the fridge. The fish can be served either warm, directly out of the broth, or chilled. I quite like this light and healthy dish with its delicate, subtle flavours that let the ingredients speak for themselves. But if you're anything like me, you'll think it needs a bit of fat. That's why I propose a Béarnaise or Hollandaise sauce as a garnish or to serve on the side—that's totally optional.*

4 salmon fillets (each 6 ounces/ 175 g), skinned and deboned

2 teaspoons (6 g) kosher salt

Court Bouillon:

3 shallots

1 medium carrot, peeled

1 leek (white part only)

1 stalk celery

½ bulb fennel, peeled

3 tablespoons (45 g) unsalted butter

1 cup (250 mL) white wine

2 tablespoons (30 mL) white wine vinegar

4 cups (1 L) water

Bouquet garni of parsley, thyme, and bay leaf (see tip, page 47)

3 strips lemon peel

1 clove garlic, lightly crushed

1½ tablespoons (15 g) kosher salt

Freshly cracked black pepper, to taste

Garnish:

Sauce Béarnaise or Sauce Hollandaise (page 305 or 307), optional

2 tablespoons (30 mL) finely chopped fresh chives

Season the pieces of salmon on both side with the salt. Let stand at room temperature for 30 minutes.

FOR THE COURT BOUILLON: Meanwhile, slice the shallots, carrot, leek, celery, and fennel into ⅛-inch-thick (3 mm) rounds.

In a large pot on medium-high heat, heat the butter until foamy. Add the sliced vegetables, lower the heat to medium, and sweat gently for 10 minutes, ensuring they don't take on any colouration. Pour in the wine and vinegar, bring to a simmer, and cook for 1 minute to remove the alcohol taste. Add the water, bouquet garni, lemon peel, garlic, salt, and pepper, lower the heat and simmer very gently for 20 minutes. This is a very delicate broth, so don't rush it and don't hammer on the heat. The vegetables should still have a bite when cooked. Remove from the heat and with a slotted spoon discard the bouquet garni, lemon peel, and garlic.

Meanwhile, if desired, prepare your Béarnaise or Hollandaise sauce. Keep warm with a lid on while you cook the salmon.

Carefully add the salmon to the broth and return to a gentle simmer. Lower the heat and cook gently for 8 to 10 minutes, depending on how thick the fillets are and how well done you like your salmon. You don't want the poaching liquid to boil or even simmer; gentle cooking is the goal.

FOR THE GARNISH: Serve the fish in individual bowls, along with some of the bouillon and vegetables, topped with sauce and chives.

⚜

Moules Marinière

Mussels in White Wine, Dijon, and Crème Fraîche

Yield: 4 PORTIONS
Preparation time: 30 MINUTES
Cooking time: 15 MINUTES

I've always loved mussels. There's really nothing else like them, and moules-frites is unquestionably in my top five favourite dishes. As an added bonus, the nectar you end up with after cooking them is much better for making sauces or soups than a traditional fish stock. Dara and I were fortunate to eat many top-tier meals while travelling through France, but the best one was at the market in Bordeaux. The market is usually the first place I want to visit whenever I'm in an unknown city, because it gives me a really great sense of place. I gravitated to a tiny little spot serving moules-frites for lunch with only three different preparations on their concise menu. I chose my favourite and perhaps the simplest: moules marinière. Lunch was, in a word, phenomenal. The mussels were fresh, the well-salted french fries were piping hot, and we washed it all down with a great bottle of Muscadet that cost less than ten euros. Along with the happy, bustling ambience, it was arguably our best and cheapest meal of the whole trip—proof positive that you don't need to go to a fancy restaurant with three Michelin stars to have the best dining experience.

2 tablespoons (30 g) unsalted butter

2 shallots, thinly sliced

½ cup (125 mL) dry white wine

2 tablespoons (30 mL) Dijon mustard

2 bay leaves

2 sprigs thyme

3 pounds (1.4 kg) mussels, scrubbed and debearded (see Quenelle de Morue, page 183)

½ cup (125 mL) loosely packed *fines herbes* leaves (chervil, parsley, and tarragon)

½ cup (125 mL) Crème Fraîche (page 296, or store-bought)

Juice of ½ small lemon

Crusty French baguette, for serving

In a large pot, melt the butter on medium heat. Add the shallots and cook, stirring, until soft, about 5 minutes. Deglaze the pan with wine, bring to a boil, and cook for 1 minute to remove the alcohol taste. Whisk in the mustard, bay leaves, and thyme. Increase the heat to medium-high, add the mussels, and cover tightly. Shake the pot every minute until all the mussels have opened, 5 to 7 minutes. Using a slotted spoon, transfer the opened mussels to a serving dish. Discard mussels that have not opened after 8 minutes.

Remove the pot from the heat and whisk in the *fines herbes*, crème fraîche, and lemon juice. Pour the liquid over the mussels and serve immediately with a nice crusty baguette.

TIP *Mussels should smell like the ocean and sea air, briny and fresh. They should not smell fishy at all, and their shells should be tightly closed. If you find any mussels in your bag with open shells, gently tap them on the counter, wait a minute, and see if they close. Any mussels that don't close readily are probably dead; be sure to toss these out. Also discard any mussels with broken shells. Before cooking the mussels, scrub them in a bowl under cold running water and pull off any beards.*

POMMES FRITES AU FOUR

Crispy Oven Fries

Yield: 4 portions

Preparation time: 15 TO 20 MINUTES

Cooking time: 55 TO 60 MINUTES

4 large Russet potatoes, cleaned and scrubbed

1 tablespoon (15 mL) white vinegar

2 tablespoons (20 g) kosher salt

4 cups (1 L) water

½ cup (125 mL) grapeseed oil

Don't peel the potatoes—instead, trim all the rounded edges until you end up with a rectangle. This way the fries will be more evenly sized, which helps the cooking process, and you get to keep a little bit of the skin, which gives them flavour. Cut the potatoes into ⅓-inch (¾ cm) matchsticks, and rinse the fries in cold water to remove the starch.

Add the potatoes, white vinegar, salt, and water to a medium pot on high heat. The vinegar will prevent the potatoes from breaking down too much during the cooking process and overcooking. Bring to a simmer, then lower the heat to medium-low and continue cooking for 10 minutes until the potatoes are three-quarters cooked. Gently drain into a colander, being careful that you don't break the potatoes. Let the potatoes sit in the colander until no more steam is coming out of them.

Preheat your oven to 425°F (220°C), with the rack in the centre position.

Line a baking tray with a silicone mat. Transfer the potatoes to a mixing bowl and gently coat them with the oil. It might seem like a lot, but that's what it takes. Distribute the fries evenly on the baking tray and bake until they're crispy and golden brown, 45 to 50 minutes. Taste a french fry for salt level and adjust the seasoning if needed.

⚜

IT'S BEEN IMPORTANT for me to have my daughters, Aïla and Florence, in the kitchen from a young age so they see the cooking process while they're kids. This way, cooking will feel natural to them while they're growing up. We were with a group of friends one day, all of us chatting about the kind of food we make at home. When it came to talking about favourite meals and ready-made dishes easily found at the supermarket, my eldest daughter Aïla piped up and said, "Why don't you just make it instead of buying it at the grocery store?" One of my friends replied, "Well, I know your father cooks like that, but it's not really my thing."

I don't see cooking as too much work, but so many other people seem to say just that. Take making pancakes for example. Most people would skip all the steps and go straight to a prepared powdered mix. You've gotta put some time and effort into a meal if you want to eat well. Making things from scratch lets you control the quality of your ingredients and actually develop a life skill that everybody needs.

By exposing Flo and Aïla to the cooking process, everything I do in the kitchen becomes visual information that they can eventually apply. I hope in the future when they're at university and have apartments of their own, they won't buy Kraft Dinner and cans of ravioli. They'll have all these skills under their belts and know that it's possible to make good food on a good budget. They're going to buy a flank steak instead of a *côte de boeuf* that's five times the price, or maybe braise a chicken leg and put it on top of a rice pilaf, and they'll make a delicious meal with a little bit of salad that won't cost them $50.

See, that's the sad thing: people don't know anymore. Nobody cooks because everything is so available right away. The new generation have their phones and order some tacos when they have a craving—boom, done. How easy is that? They just want to eat something tasty and don't care about the cooking; they

might even be "foodies" and do their research for the best taco places online. But what about just cooking them yourself?

And more than developing a skill, by cooking with the girls, I'm building traditions too. For example, Dara is partial to El Paso hard taco shells. They're nostalgic for her because taco dinners are something that her family used to do when she was a kid. Me, I prefer making soft-shell tacos, but the whole spread of laying all the ingredients out on the table with those crunchy taco shells is sentimental for Dara. Preparing dishes that the kids like and doing it often creates memories. It becomes something that they'll probably end up doing with their loved ones when they get older.

Truite Amandine

Trout with Almonds

Yield: 2 PORTIONS
Preparation time: 20 MINUTES
Cooking time: 15 MINUTES

> When I was a teenager in New Brunswick, I used to fish for small rainbow trout. I would cook them whole, head on, in a cast-iron pan with lots of butter and a squeeze of lemon at the end. They didn't need anything more than that, and they tasted absolutely amazing. This dish takes me back to that idyllic time. It's a bit rustic, and will require a bit of work while eating it. But if you already know how to fillet a fish, you won't have a problem. The classic pairings of boiled potatoes and sautéed green beans are my favourite sides to serve with the trout.

What you'll need:

Large cast-iron or non-stick pan (at least 12 inches/30 cm in diameter)

2 whole rainbow trout (each about 9 ounces/250 g), cleaned and gutted (see tip)

Kosher salt and freshly cracked black pepper

¼ cup (40 g) all-purpose flour

2 tablespoons (30 mL) grapeseed oil

½ cup (115 g) unsalted butter, divided

⅔ cup (70 g) sliced roasted almonds, skin on

2 tablespoons (30 mL) finely chopped fresh flat-leaf parsley

Juice of 1 lemon

Season the trout inside and out with salt and pepper, and dust the skin side with the flour. Make sure they're well coated and shake off any excess flour. Transfer the trout to a large plate.

Warm up a large serving plate in the oven at 170°F (77°C). Heat a large cast-iron pan on medium-high heat. A large non-stick pan will also do the trick; just make sure it's big enough to hold both trout. Add the oil and about one-third of the butter. When the butter is foamy, place the trout in the pan on their sides. Lower the heat to medium and cook for 5 minutes on one side, constantly basting the flesh with the melted butter. Flip the fish onto the other side and cook for another 5 minutes, continuing to baste. Don't lift the fish or play with them too much—you'll break the skin, and they'll end up looking like a big mess.

Insert the tip of a paring knife into the flesh of the backbone for a few seconds and test it on your lower lip. It should feel warm—not cold and not piping hot, just warm. The internal temperature if taken with a thermometer should be 118°F (48°C) Take the pan off the heat and transfer the fish to the warm serving plate. Cover with foil to keep warm.

Discard the cooking fat from the pan. Add the remaining butter and a pinch of salt, return the pan to medium heat, and cook until the butter begins to brown. Add the almonds and shake the pan to brown them evenly to a rich golden colour. Stir in the parsley and lemon juice. Pour over the trout and serve immediately.

TIP *You can keep the trout heads on or take them off for this dish; it's your choice. Ask your fishmonger to butterfly and debone the trout for you; it'll make prepping this dish a bit easier. Keep in mind that butterflied trout will cook faster.*

IMAGE ON PAGE 92

Poulet Rôti du Dimanche

Sunday Roasted Chicken

Yield: SERVES 4 TO 6 LUCKY PEOPLE

Preparation time: 15 MINUTES + 24 TO 36 HOURS CURING + 2 HOURS TEMPERING

Cooking time: 1 HOUR + 30 TO 60 MINUTES RESTING

Roasted chicken is my absolute favourite Sunday dinner, and it has been since I was a little kid. When it's well seasoned and properly cooked, it's truly a thing of beauty. My mother used to make three meals out of one bird: roast chicken, then chicken sandwiches, and finally chicken soup with stock made from the bones. Stuffing it with Boursin cheese makes the meat even more moist, and gives you a nice condiment to serve with the bird. I usually serve the chicken with a green leafy salad with mustard vinaigrette to complement the dish. The key to success is to use a high-quality chicken. Spend money on it. Don't be cheap.

4.5-pound (2 kg) whole chicken

2 tablespoons (20 g) kosher salt (see tip, page 111)

Freshly cracked black pepper

16 fingerling potatoes, or 5 small Yukon Gold potatoes

2 tablespoons (30 mL) melted butter

½ small red onion

1 medium carrot, peeled

1 stalk celery

4 cloves garlic, chopped

3 sprigs thyme, leaves only

1 sprig rosemary, leaves only

2 tablespoons (30 g) unsalted butter

Drizzle of olive oil

5 ounces (150 g) Boursin cheese, garlic and herb or black pepper flavour

Rinse the chicken under cold running water and pat dry. Remove the wishbone with a butcher's knife or paring knife. Season every part of the chicken, including the cavity, with the salt and pepper. Place the bird on a wire rack atop a baking sheet and leave it in the fridge overnight for 24 hours, or up to 36 hours, until the skin looks dry—this will season the bird all the way through and help the skin become crispy as you're roasting it.

The next day, remove the chicken from the fridge and let stand at room temperature for 2 hours (putting a cold chicken in the oven is a bad idea).

Meanwhile, bring a large pot of heavily salted water to a boil (see tip, page 89). Add the potatoes and cook for about 30 minutes, until tender when pierced with the tip of a knife. Place the potatoes on a cutting board and smash them gently with the palm of your hand, then place them in a bowl and toss them with the melted butter. Set aside.

Preheat your oven to 425°F (220°C), with the rack in the lower position.

Cut the red onion, carrot, and celery into ½-inch (1 cm) chunks. In a medium sauté pan on high heat, melt the butter with the olive oil. Add the diced vegetables and the garlic, thyme, and rosemary to make a mirepoix. Season with a healthy pinch of salt. Cook for about 15 minutes, stirring and tossing until the vegetables are fully tender with light colouration. Transfer the mirepoix to a baking sheet to cool quickly.

Stuff the chicken with half of the cooled mirepoix, then the Boursin cheese, and finish with the remaining mirepoix. Tie the drumsticks together with butcher's twine to help the bird maintain a nice shape while roasting and to prevent the stuffing from escaping the cavity.

continued

You're now ready to cook the bird. But for how long? A roasted chicken of this size usually takes an hour—15 minutes per pound is a good rule of thumb (starting with a room temperature chicken), or until the leg meat reaches an internal temperature of 155°F (68°C). Line a baking sheet with a silicone mat, or use a baking dish large enough that the chicken and potatoes won't be crowded. Arrange the flattened potatoes on the pan (you won't be touching them again until the chicken is cooked, because you want them to be crispy). Place the chicken on the pan, breast side down, and roast for 15 minutes. Flip the chicken onto its side and roast for 15 minutes. Flip the chicken onto the opposite side and roast for 15 minutes. Finally, flip the chicken breast side up and roast for 15 minutes, totalling 1 hour of total cooking time.

When the chicken is ready and the skin is a beautiful golden brown, remove it from the oven and let it rest for at least 30 minutes, but 1 hour is better. This is a step you don't want to miss. The chicken continues to cook while resting, and all the juices will stay inside to keep it moist.

Carve the chicken and serve it with the Boursin cheese, mirepoix, crispy potatoes, and a fresh green salad.

⚜

Épaule d'Agneau Sept Heures

Seven-Hour Slow-Roasted Lamb Shoulder

Yield: 6 PORTIONS

Preparation time: 30 MINUTES + OVERNIGHT MARINATING + 2 HOURS TEMPERING

Cooking time: 7 HOURS

6.5-pound (3 kg) bone-in lamb shoulder (or leg of lamb)

3 tablespoons (30 g) kosher salt (see tip)

6 cloves garlic, chopped

2 sprigs rosemary, leaves stripped and chopped

1 teaspoon (2 g) freshly cracked black pepper

⅓ cup (75 mL) Dijon mustard

5 tablespoons (75 mL) olive oil, divided

2 small yellow onions, peeled and halved

1 bulb garlic, halved horizontally

1 cup (250 mL) white wine

2 to 2½ cups (500 to 625 mL) water

3 sprigs thyme

1 bay leaf

Most people default to leg of lamb as their go-to cut of meat for a lamb roast. But I'm here to make a case for lamb shoulder, a hardworking muscle that's high in both collagen and intramuscular fat. Seven hours of slow cooking makes it incredibly succulent and fall-off-the-bone tender—not to mention that your house will smell absolutely fantastic while it's cooking. This easy dish is a comfort-food favourite at my house all through the fall and winter. It's hearty and sticks to your ribs, and the leftovers are killer good.

TIP *For lamb, the perfect amount of salt is 1% of the meat's weight in grams. So, for a 6.5-pound (3 kg) lamb shoulder, I use 3 tablespoons (30 g) salt.*

Using a sharp knife, score the skin and flesh of the lamb to allow the salt and marinade to penetrate. Season evenly with the salt. In a small bowl, combine the chopped garlic, rosemary, pepper, mustard, and 2 tablespoons (30 mL) of the oil. Rub the mixture all over the lamb. Transfer the lamb to a baking sheet, and marinate overnight in the fridge.

The next day, remove the lamb from the fridge and let stand at room temperature for 2 hours. Meanwhile, preheat your oven to 450°F (230°C), with the rack in the lowest position.

Place the onions and halved garlic bulb in a large heavy-duty roasting pan and drizzle with the remaining oil. Rest the lamb on top. Roast for 30 minutes.

Meanwhile, in a small saucepan on medium-high heat, bring the wine to a boil. Boil for 1 minute, then stir in 2 cups (500 mL) water, along with the thyme and bay leaf, and bring back to a boil. Take the lamb out of the oven and pour the liquid and herbs into the roasting pan. Lower the oven temperature to 300°F (150°C), cover the meat tightly with foil, and return to the oven. Roast for another 6½ hours, basting with the pan juices every 30 minutes or so. If, toward the end, the pan juices are reduced to almost nothing, stir in another ½ cup (125 mL) water.

Remove the lamb from the oven and strain the juices back into the small saucepan. Skim the excess fat from the surface, then transfer the juices to a gravy boat. The lamb should be falling off the bones and tender enough to be portioned with a spoon.

Saucisses Toulouse et Lentilles en Vinaigrette

Toulouse Sausages and Lentil Vinaigrette

Yield: 4 PORTIONS

Preparation time: 30 MINUTES

Cooking time: 1 HOUR +
10 MINUTES RESTING

Toulouse sausage, from the south of France, has always been my favourite in terms of flavour profile. It's very simple, with a little garlic, white wine, and nutmeg to give the sausage some extra dimension, but the foundation of its flavour is very much about good-quality pork. It should be the first thing you taste in the sausage. Any good butcher should have decent mild pork sausages in their display case. They might not be called saucisses Toulouse, *but they should be similar. Whether they're grilled or pan-seared and finished in the oven, sausages are always a successful dinner at my house. Lentils and sausages are a match made in heaven, but french fries or mashed potatoes pair well too. Serve with Dijon mustard on the side, along with a green salad.*

What you'll need:

Large cast-iron pan

Vinaigrette:

1 tablespoon (15 mL) Dijon mustard

1 tablespoon (15 mL) red wine vinegar

¼ cup (60 mL) extra-virgin olive oil

Juice of ¼ lemon

1 clove garlic, grated

Kosher salt and freshly cracked black pepper, to taste

Lentils and Sausages:

⅓ cup (75 mL) extra-virgin olive oil

4 cloves garlic, finely sliced

2 medium shallots, finely diced

1 leek (white part only), finely diced

1 small bulb fennel, finely diced

1 stalk celery, finely diced

Kosher salt and freshly cracked black pepper

½ cup (125 mL) white wine

6 ounces (175 g) Puy lentils, rinsed under cold water

FOR THE VINAIGRETTE: In a small mixing bowl, combine the mustard and vinegar. Whisking constantly, slowly drizzle in the oil until fully emulsified. Whisk in the lemon juice, garlic, salt, and pepper.

FOR THE LENTILS AND SAUSAGES: In a large saucepan, heat the olive oil on medium heat. Sweat the garlic, shallots, leek, fennel, and celery, stirring often, until tender and sweet but without colouration, about 10 minutes. Season with a healthy pinch of salt and pepper. Add the wine and reduce by half. Stir in the lentils and enough stock to just cover the lentils. Bring to a gentle simmer, then lower the heat, cover halfway with a lid, and cook for 45 minutes, until the lentils are plump and tender but still retain their integrity. If the lentils absorb all the liquid before they're tender, stir in a little more stock or water. The fully cooked lentils should have soaked up all the liquid. Remove from the heat, cover fully with the lid, and let the lentils rest for 10 minutes.

Meanwhile, preheat your oven to 350°F (180°C), with the rack in the centre position.

In a large cast-iron pan on high heat, heat the grapeseed oil. Sear the sausages on one side until golden brown, about 3 minutes. Flip the sausages, transfer the pan to the oven, and bake for 8 to 10 minutes, until a meat thermometer inserted lengthwise into the centre of a sausage registers 160°F (71°C). Let rest in the pan while you finish the lentils.

continued

2 cups (500 mL) Chicken Stock
(page 308, or store-bought) or
water (approx.)

1 tablespoon (15 mL) grapeseed oil

8 mild pork sausages (preferably
Toulouse sausages)

½ cup (125 mL) fresh flat-leaf
parsley leaves

1 cup (250 mL) greens of your
choice, such as small kale, Swiss
chard, or spinach

Add a healthy splash of the vinaigrette to the lentils and stir to incorporate;
the lentils should have a nice acidity as a counterpoint to the richness. Fold
in the parsley and greens to add freshness. Taste and adjust with more salt,
pepper, and vinaigrette if required—bear in mind that adding salt and vinaigrette wakes up the lentils, so be generous.

Divide the lentils evenly onto four warm plates, and serve one or two sausages per person atop them.

❖

Poisson en Papillote et Rouille

Fish in Papillote with Rouille

Yield: 4 PORTIONS

Preparation time: 40 MINUTES + 30 MINUTES BRINING

Cooking time: 1 HOUR

Poisson en papillote is a beautiful cooking technique that I never get tired of. Not only does wrapping the fish in parchment paper mean that it cooks gently and perfectly, but the big bonus is how few dirty dishes there are. You can use any fish you like for this recipe, as long as you take the time to source the absolute freshest fish available. Poisson en papillote can be as simple as fish with white wine, lemon, and fresh herbs; this pared-back version is absolutely delicious. But I prefer to make the dish a bit more substantial by adding vegetables. My pro tip is to use precooked vegetables for a relatively quick cooking time. There's also great value in indulging here and there in "luxury" ingredients for your home kitchen, like great butter, good saffron, or really top-quality olive oil. It will elevate your cooking, I assure you. Even though the papillote *creates its own sauce, I like serving this dish with a* rouille*, a slight variation on aïoli, with saffron added to it. Some people like to add potato, bread, or tomato to a* rouille*; I prefer to leave it simple and make sure the saffron has space to sing.*

Fish:

4 cups (1 L) cold water, divided

¾ cup (100 g) kosher salt

1.3 pounds (600 g) fish of your choice (I like ling cod), skinned and deboned

12 fingerling potatoes

½ head savoy cabbage, cored and leaves separated

12 radishes

12 Tokyo turnips, or 2 medium turnips, cut into wedges

4 tablespoons (60 g) unsalted butter, softened

4 tablespoons (60 mL) white wine

4 teaspoons (20 mL) extra-virgin olive oil

Freshly cracked black pepper

4 slices lemon

4 teaspoons (20 mL) roughly chopped fresh dill

FOR THE FISH: In a small saucepan on high heat, bring 1 cup (250 mL) of the cold water and the salt to a simmer. Transfer to a large container, add the remaining cold water, and refrigerate until cold. Slice the fish into four equal portions, submerge in the brine, and refrigerate for 30 minutes.

Remove the fish from the brine, pat dry, and set aside at room temperature.

Preheat your oven to 375°F (190°C), with the rack in the centre position.

In a medium pot on medium-high heat, cook the potatoes in heavily cold salted water. Bring to a boil, lower the heat to medium, and simmer until tender when pierced with a paring knife, around 25 minutes. Drain and halve the potatoes lengthwise.

Prepare an ice bath. In a large pot of heavily salted boiling water on medium-high heat, blanch the cabbage leaves for 3 minutes, then transfer to the ice bath to stop the cooking. In the same pot of boiling water, blanch the radishes and turnips for 3 minutes, then transfer to the ice bath. Cut the cabbage into small strips, ¾ inch (2 cm) wide. Cut the radishes and turnips in half lengthwise.

continued

Pinch saffron

1 tablespoon (15 mL) hot water

2 oil-packed anchovy fillets

1 clove garlic, peeled

½ teaspoon (2 g) kosher salt

1 teaspoon (5 mL) Dijon mustard

2 egg yolks

¾ cup (175 mL) grapeseed oil

¼ cup (60 mL) extra-virgin olive oil

1 teaspoon (5 mL) lemon juice

Pinch cayenne pepper

Cut 4 sheets of parchment paper into 14-inch (35 cm) rounds. Brush each with 1 tablespoon (15 g) butter and fold them in half. Distribute the vegetables on the lower half of each round, leaving a 2-inch (5 cm) border. Lay one piece of fish atop each pile of vegetables, then drizzle it with 1 tablespoon (15 mL) wine and 1 teaspoon (5 mL) olive oil. Sprinkle each with pepper and a pinch of salt. Top each piece of fish with a slice of lemon and 1 teaspoon (5 mL) dill. Seal each *papillote* by folding the top half over the bottom, folding the edges over twice, and pinching them together to make an airtight seal, so that the package looks like an apple turnover. Transfer the *papillotes* to a baking sheet, taking care that they don't touch one another.

Bake for 15 to 20 minutes, depending on the thickness of the fish. I find that 15 minutes is plenty; by the time the *papillotes* are plated, presented, and opened in front of your guests, the fish will be cooked to perfection. But if you find this a bit stressful, just bake for 20 minutes—the fish will still be moist and lovely.

FOR THE ROUILLE: Meanwhile, in a small bowl, soak the saffron in the hot water until ready to use.

Using a mortar and pestle, crush the anchovies, garlic, and salt into a smooth paste, then incorporate the saffron water, mustard, and egg yolks. Combine the two oils and pour them into the mortar in a thin stream while stirring constantly with the pestle. As the sauce thickens and begins to resemble mayonnaise, add the lemon juice and cayenne. Taste for seasoning. Transfer the *rouille* to a gravy boat or bowl for your guests to serve themselves.

❧

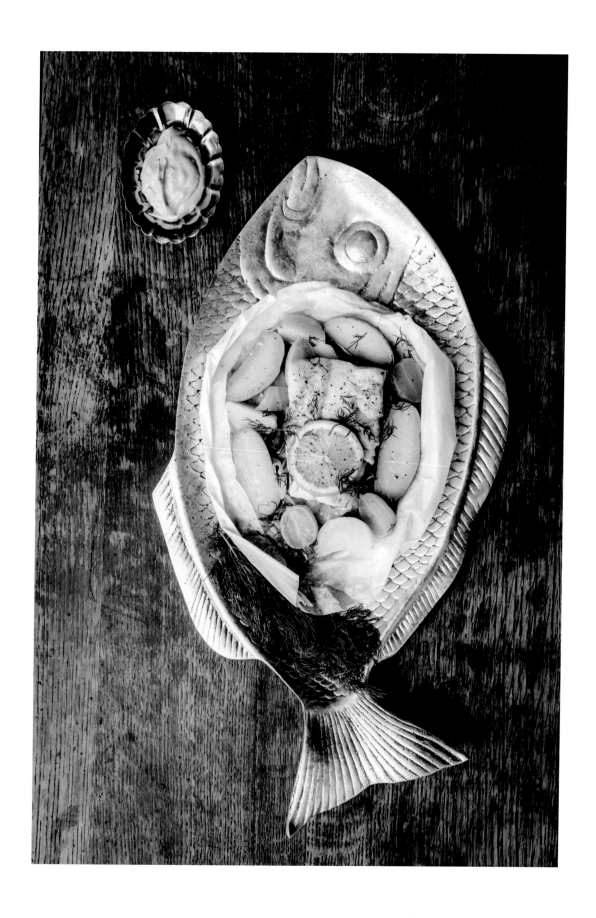

Steak aux Poivres

Steak with Peppercorn Cream Sauce

Yield: 4 PORTIONS

Preparation time: 20 MINUTES +
2 HOURS TEMPERING

Cooking time: 20 MINUTES

Why is steak frites *among the most popular dishes in the world? Because it's freaking delicious, that's why. I prefer a peppercorn sauce with my steak, rather than a* beurre maître d'hôtel; *the combined flavours of cream, peppercorn, and cognac are unbeatable. Many cooks crust one side of the steak in peppercorns and then sear it in a smoking pan, but I find the end result is usually a burned and bitter crust. Instead, I prefer toasting the peppercorns, crushing them with a mortar and pestle, and adding them directly to the sauce. This classic dish always pleases the family. Serve it with french fries (see Moules Marinière on page 250)—nothing else will do.*

Four 6-ounce (175 g) centre-cut beef tenderloin steaks

2 teaspoons (6 g) kosher salt

1 tablespoon (15 mL) black peppercorns

2 tablespoons (30 mL) grapeseed oil

3 tablespoons (45 g) unsalted butter, divided

2 sprigs thyme

1 large shallot, finely minced

1 clove garlic, finely chopped

¼ cup (60 mL) cognac

1 tablespoon (10 g) all-purpose flour

1 teaspoon (5 mL) Worcestershire sauce

1 tablespoon (15 mL) Dijon mustard

1 tablespoon (15 mL) brined green peppercorns

½ cup (125 mL) Veal Stock (page 309, or store-bought)

1 cup (250 mL) heavy or whipping cream (35% milk fat)

½ teaspoon (2 mL) fresh thyme leaves

Season the steaks on all sides with the salt. Place them on a large plate or baking sheet, cover with plastic wrap, and let stand at room temperature for 1 hour.

Meanwhile, in a small pan on medium-high heat, toast the black and green peppercorns, swirling them around for 1 to 2 minutes, until they start to become aromatic. Transfer the peppercorns to a mortar and use the pestle to coarsely grind them. Set aside.

In a large skillet on medium-high heat, heat the oil until very hot. Add the steaks and give them a good sear on one side for 4 minutes. Lower the heat to medium and add 2 tablespoons (30 g) of the butter and the thyme sprigs. Using a large spoon, baste the steaks with butter and thyme, and continue cooking until they're medium-rare; a meat thermometer inserted in the thickest part of the steak should read 125°F (52°C). Transfer the steaks to a plate and cover loosely with foil. Discard the thyme sprigs.

Add the shallot and garlic to the fat remaining in the skillet, and cook until tender, about 2 minutes. Add the cognac and, if desired, use a long match to light it and flambé to cook off the alcohol. Reduce the liquid to almost nothing. Whisk in the flour, Worcestershire sauce, mustard, and brined green and ground black peppercorns. Slowly whisk in the stock and cream, and cook until reduced by half. Whisk in the remaining butter and the thyme leaves.

Transfer the steaks and their accumulated juices to the skillet; you definitely don't want to waste these. Gently reheat the steaks for 2 minutes, while basting the steaks with the sauce. Transfer the steaks to serving plates and generously cover them with the sauce.

Chou-Fleur Rôti et Sauce Romesco

Roasted Cauliflower with Romesco Sauce

Yield: 4 PORTIONS
Preparation time: 20 MINUTES
Cooking time: 1 HOUR

Roasted Cauliflower:

1 large head cauliflower

2 tablespoons (30 mL) olive oil

Pinch Maldon salt

Freshly cracked black pepper, to taste

Romesco Sauce:

2 cups (500 mL) drained roasted red peppers (from a jar or you could roast them yourself)

⅔ cup (90 g) roasted Marcona almonds or regular toasted almonds

⅓ cup (35 g) finely grated Parmesan cheese

1 clove garlic, grated

⅓ cup (75 mL) extra-virgin olive oil

1½ tablespoons (7 g) smoked paprika

½ tablespoon (5 g) kosher salt

1 tablespoon (15 mL) sherry vinegar

Herb Salad:

½ cup (40 g) fresh mint leaves, packed

½ cup (30 g) fresh flat-leaf parsley leaves, packed

½ red onion, thinly sliced and rinsed under cold water

2 tablespoons (30 mL) extra-virgin olive oil

1 tablespoon (15 mL) lemon juice

Kosher salt and freshly cracked black pepper, to taste

½ lemon, for serving

〰 *Over the years, I've watched cauliflower, this underrated vegetable, become a star, gain popularity, and start appearing on restaurant menus. Most people still don't like it because they've only ever had it boiled and overcooked to mush. Roasting is a total game changer when it comes to the flavour of cauliflower—or any cruciferous vegetable, for that matter. And roasting a whole head of cauliflower is visually impressive for the people sitting at the dinner table. This is one of my wife's favourite dishes; she loves cauliflower, but she loves romesco sauce even more. No word of a lie, she'd put romesco on everything if she could. Yes, yes, I know it's from Spain, and decidedly not French. But because romesco sauce is so delicious, I think you should definitely have it in your repertoire.*

FOR THE ROASTED CAULIFLOWER: Preheat your oven to 450°F (230°C), with the rack in the centre position.

In a large stockpot on medium-high heat, bring heavily salted water to a boil. Remove the tough bottom leaves from the cauliflower but keep the smaller and most tender ones on the stem. Make a deep X incision with a paring knife on the base of the stem to help speed up the cooking time. Place the whole head of cauliflower into the boiling water and cook for 10 minutes. Drain the water and place the cauliflower on a roasting tray. Drizzle it with the olive oil, and season with the Maldon salt and black pepper. Bake in the oven for 45 to 50 minutes, until fully roasted and golden brown.

FOR THE ROMESCO SAUCE: Meanwhile, in a food processor, combine the roasted peppers, almonds, Parmesan, and garlic. Pulse until a paste develops. While still pulsing, slowly drizzle in the oil through the feed tube. Once the mixture is fully emulsified, add the paprika, salt, and vinegar, and pulse to combine. Taste for seasoning.

FOR THE HERB SALAD: In a small bowl, dress the mint, parsley, and red onion with the oil and lemon juice. Season with salt and pepper.

Cut the cauliflower into four wedges, or serve it whole on top of the romesco sauce with a knife for people to dig in. Serve the herb salad as a garnish, with the half lemon to squeeze over the dish, and more sauce on the side for everyone to scoop. Be generous!

Lapin Sauce Chasseur
Rabbit with Chasseur Sauce

Yield: 4 PORTIONS

Preparation time: 45 MINUTES + OVERNIGHT CURING + 1 HOUR TEMPERING

Cooking time: 70 TO 80 MINUTES

What you'll need:

Large cast-iron pan

1 large rabbit, legs separated and loin/saddle/breast cut into 4 pieces

Kosher salt (see tip)

Freshly cracked black pepper

3 tablespoons (30 g) all-purpose flour

4 tablespoons (60 g) unsalted butter

5 ounces (150 g) smoked bacon, cut into large lardons

1 pound (450 g) button mushrooms, halved (or quartered if large)

5 cloves garlic, finely chopped

2 shallots, finely chopped

2 tablespoons (30 mL) brandy

1½ cups (375 mL) Chicken Stock (page 308, or store-bought) or water

½ cup (125 mL) white wine

¾ cup (175 mL) tomato sauce or tomato *concassé* (diced fresh tomatoes)

2 tablespoons (30 mL) roughly chopped fresh flat-leaf parsley

1 tablespoon (15 mL) minced fresh chives

Sauce chasseur *was the first sauce I learned to make at culinary school. Step one was learning how to make proper stocks, followed by reducing them to a demi-glace. Once we had the demi-glace* en place, *the* sauce chasseur *came next. I loved the name, meaning the sauce was traditionally paired with game meat. But being a versatile sauce, we made the dish with a chicken leg, which was delicious (if rabbit isn't your thing, then that's the route you should go). For me, I've always liked the clean taste of rabbit that my mother used to prepare. She bought her fresh rabbit from a farmer when we lived in the small town of Ste-Croix. If you can find a quality rabbit at your butcher, give it a try—don't be afraid. Honestly, it tastes like a very good chicken. This dish tastes best when spooned over homemade egg noodles.*

TIP *For rabbit, the perfect amount of salt is 1% of the meat's weight in grams, or 10 grams of salt per kilogram of rabbit.*

Place a wire rack over a baking sheet. Season the rabbit with salt and pepper, place it on the rack, and refrigerate it overnight to cure slightly.

The next day, take the rabbit out of the fridge and let stand at room temperature for 1 hour.

Preheat your oven to 325°F (160°C), with the rack in the centre position.

Dredge the rabbit pieces in the flour until evenly coated. In a large cast-iron pan on medium-high heat, melt 3 tablespoons (45 g) of the butter. Working in batches as needed so you don't overcrowd the pan, sear the rabbit until golden brown on all sides, about 10 minutes. Transfer the rabbit to a cocotte or a baking dish.

In the same cast-iron pan on medium-high heat, sear the bacon until golden brown, about 4 minutes. Stir in the mushrooms and cook until caramelized, about 5 minutes. Add the garlic and shallots, and cook, stirring often, until they are soft and lightly browned. Add the brandy, use a long match to light it, and flambé to cook off the alcohol. When the flames die down, add the stock, wine, and tomato sauce, and bring to a simmer. Transfer the sauce to the cocotte with the rabbit.

continued

Cover and bake for about 45 minutes or until the meat just separates from the bone but isn't falling apart. Transfer the rabbit to a plate and tent with foil to keep warm.

If the sauce needs thickening (it may not), place the cocotte on medium heat and reduce until slightly thickened. Stir in the parsley, chives, and the remaining butter. Taste for seasoning. Return the rabbit pieces to the sauce and spoon the sauce over them to coat well.

Serve the rabbit from the cocotte and let people ladle sauce over their plates.

❧

Couscous Marocain

Moroccan Couscous

Yield: 8 PORTIONS
Preparation time: 1 HOUR
Cooking time: 2½ HOURS

1.6 pounds (750 g) boneless lamb shoulder, cut into 2-inch (5 cm) cubes

2 teaspoons (6 g) kosher salt

3 tablespoons (45 mL) grapeseed oil

5 cloves garlic, sliced

1 onion, roughly diced

8 cups (2 L) Chicken Stock (page 308 , or store-bought) or water, divided

2 tomatoes, diced

3 carrots, peeled and cut into 1-inch (2.5 cm) chunks

3 turnips, peeled and cut into small wedges

½ small head green cabbage, cut into 6 wedges

2 tablespoons (12 g) grated fresh ginger

2 star anise

1½ tablespoons (10 g) cumin seeds

1 tablespoon (5 g) coriander seeds, crushed

5 cardamom pods

Big pinch freshly grated nutmeg

Pinch saffron

Freshly cracked black pepper

8 merguez sausages (spicy lamb sausages)

1 large zucchini, cut into 1-inch (2.5 cm) chunks

1 cup (250 mL) drained canned chickpeas, rinsed

¼ cup (60 mL) extra-virgin olive oil

½ bunch fresh cilantro leaves (about ½ cup/10 g)

The French colonized Morocco in 1912, bringing with them a culinary culture of cafés, wine, ice cream, and pâtisseries. *For almost forty-five years, Morocco was a French protectorate, and the link between the two countries led to the introduction and popularization of Moroccan cuisine in France. Couscous is still hugely popular in France and is regularly served in school cafeterias and restaurants. I fell in love with couscous as a teenager when I was introduced to it by my parents' great friends from Morocco. Not only were the flavours totally new to me, but so was the way they served it in a giant round platter in the centre of the table that everyone ate from communally. There were no forks, which meant you had to use your fingers and a piece of torn French baguette to scoop up the food. I've since learned that eating with your hands is a time-honoured tradition in Morocco. The rule is to eat with your right hand only, using the thumb and first two fingers. Your left hand may only be used for picking up bread or passing dishes or to drink from your glass. That Moroccan dinner was forever implanted in my memory, and it was the inspiration for this recipe.*

Season the lamb with the salt. In a large braising pan or Dutch oven on high heat, heat the grapeseed oil. Working in batches so you don't overcrowd the pan, brown the lamb on all sides. Using a slotted spoon, transfer the lamb to a large bowl.

In the same pan on medium heat, sauté the garlic and onion until translucent, about 3 minutes. Add 6 cups (1.5 L) of the chicken stock and the tomatoes. Return the lamb and any accumulated juices to the pan and bring to a gentle simmer. Lower the heat to low, cover tightly, and cook for 1 hour.

Stir in the carrots, turnips, cabbage, ginger, star anise, cumin, coriander seeds, cardamom, nutmeg, and saffron to the pan, making sure they are well distributed. Season with a generous pinch of salt and pepper. Increase the heat to medium and bring to a simmer. Lower the heat to low, cover and continue simmering for 1 hour, checking the liquid level from time to time and adding water if it's too low.

Meanwhile, in a hot grill pan or on your barbecue, sear the merguez sausages to give them good grill marks, about 5 minutes.

continued

½ bunch fresh flat-leaf parsley
leaves (about ½ cup/30 g)

1 tablespoon (7 g) ground turmeric

3 tablespoons (45 g) unsalted butter

2 cups (500 mL) medium couscous

French baguette, for serving

Harissa, for serving

Add the sausages to the saucepan, along with the zucchini and chickpeas. Return to a simmer, cover with a lid, and cook for 20 minutes, until the sausages are cooked through and zucchini is tender but still holding its shape. Stir in the olive oil, cilantro, and parsley. Taste for seasoning.

Meanwhile, in a small saucepan, bring the remaining 2 cups (500 mL) of chicken stock, turmeric, and butter to a boil. Place the couscous in a medium bowl and pour the hot liquid over it. Cover the bowl with plastic wrap, making sure it's tight so the couscous can steam, and let stand for 15 minutes. Remove the plastic wrap and fluff the couscous with a fork.

To serve, spoon the couscous onto a large serving platter and cover with the vegetables, meats, and a little of the broth. Serve the remaining broth in a gravy boat. Place the baguette on the table, and serve some harissa in a bowl for those who like things spicy. Let your guests help themselves!

⚜

Mousse au Chocolat

Chocolate Mousse

Yield: 6 PORTIONS

Preparation time: 25 MINUTES +
3–12 HOURS CHILLING

❧ *This chocolate mousse recipe is so simple and so delicious that I can almost guarantee it will become your go-to. Chocolate mousse is, by far, my daughters' favourite dessert. I always get them to help whenever I make it—one melts the chocolate while the other separates the egg whites from the yolks to make the meringue. And you can bet that there are always two little sets of fingers in the bowl when we're done, scooping up all the tasty leftovers and licking the spatula. The chocolate mousse tastes best if you eat it when it's been refrigerated between 6 and 12 hours. After the 12-hour mark, the mousse becomes heavier and more dense.*

What you'll need:

Stand mixer fitted with the whisk attachment

1 cup (165 g) roughly chopped 65% chocolate

8 egg whites, at room temperature

¼ teaspoon (1 mL) fresh lemon juice

2 tablespoons (30 g) granulated sugar

In a large heat-resistant bowl set over a pan of simmering water, melt the chopped chocolate, stirring occasionally with a silicone spatula.

Meanwhile, wash and dry the bowl of your stand mixer so that it's spotlessly clean. Using the whisk attachment, whisk the egg whites and lemon juice on medium speed until they form soft peaks. Increase to high speed and gradually add the sugar, whisking until the egg whites form soft peaks (see tip on page 223).

Whisk one-third of the egg whites into the warm chocolate, then immediately use a silicone spatula to fold in the remaining egg whites. This step must be done quickly, since you're adding a cold mass to a hot mass and you don't want the chocolate to solidify, which would result in grainy mousse. That's why it's important that the egg whites are at room temperature. Be careful not to overmix, or the mousse will lose its lightness.

Spoon into six glasses or ramekins, or into one big bowl, and let set in the fridge for 3 to 12 hours before serving.

⚜

Pêche Melba

Poached Peaches with Raspberry Coulis and Vanilla Ice Cream

Yield: 4 PORTIONS
Preparation time: 1½ HOURS
Cooking time: 15 MINUTES

What you'll need:
Hand blender

Peaches:
4 peaches
4 cups (1 L) water
1½ cups (300 g) granulated sugar

Raspberry Coulis:
2 cups (250 g) fresh raspberries
(frozen works too)
1 cup (150 g) icing sugar
¾ cup (175 mL) water
Juice of 1 lemon

Crème Chantilly:
1⅔ cups (400 mL) heavy or
whipping cream (35% milk fat)
⅓ cup (50 g) icing sugar
1 vanilla bean, split and scraped

Vanilla Ice Cream:
4 cups (1 L) heavy or whipping
cream (35% milk fat)
2 vanilla beans, split and scraped
12 egg yolks (8 ounces/225 g)
¾ cup (150 g) granulated sugar

Serving:
A few extra raspberries, for garnish
Fresh mint leaves, for garnish

➤ *Doesn't get more old school than this—pêche Melba is a classic Escoffier recipe that he invented at the Savoy Hotel in honour of the Australian soprano Nellie Melba. This very simple dessert is made up of ripe, tender peaches served with a raspberry coulis, vanilla ice cream, and crème Chantilly. It's a great example that simplicity is best, and it's absolutely perfect the way it is. Don't try to be clever with variations that will ruin its delicate flavour balance; Escoffier might just roll over in his grave. I prefer to make my own vanilla ice cream, but to save some time you can just buy a good-quality store-bought ice cream.*

FOR THE PEACHES: Using a sharp paring knife, cut an X in the bottom of each peach. In a medium saucepan on medium-high heat, bring the water to a boil. Add the peaches for 30 seconds, then transfer to a plate. Let cool for a few minutes. When cool enough to handle, remove the skin with a paring knife, cut in halves, and remove the pit. Add the granulated sugar to the water, and bring back to a boil. Add the peach halves, lower the heat, and gently poach for 10 minutes or until tender when pierced with the tip of a knife. Remove from the heat and let cool in the syrup.

FOR THE RASPBERRY COULIS: In a medium saucepan, combine the raspberries, icing sugar, and water. Bring to a boil on medium-high heat, cover, and boil for 2 minutes. Using a hand blender, purée the raspberry mixture, then strain it through a fine tamis to remove all the seeds. Let cool, then stir in the lemon juice. Set aside.

FOR THE CRÈME CHANTILLY: In a medium bowl, using a balloon whisk, whip the cream, icing sugar, and vanilla seeds for 4 minutes; little by little, the cream will double in volume and resemble an airy cloud. You want to form soft peaks on the whisk, and the whipped cream should stick between the wires. Transfer the crème Chantilly to a container of your choice and refrigerate until needed. (The finished cream will maintain its consistency for 6 to 12 hours in the fridge. If it starts to lose its airiness, a few turns of the whisk will restore it.)

FOR THE VANILLA ICE CREAM: In a medium saucepan on medium heat, bring the cream and vanilla beans (skins and seeds) to a gentle simmer. Remove from the heat and discard the vanilla skins.

continued

In a mixing bowl, beat the egg yolks and granulated sugar for 1 minute. While whisking constantly, very slowly pour in the hot cream to temper the eggs, making *crème anglaise*. Pour the *crème anglaise* back into the pan. Using a silicone spatula to gently stir it, bring the *crème anglaise* to 185°F (85°C) on medium heat.

Remove from the heat and strain the *crème anglaise* through a tamis into a bowl to remove any pieces of cooked egg yolk. Let cool completely on ice before adding it to your home ice cream maker and proceeding according to the manufacturer's instructions.

TO SERVE: For each serving, place a scoop of vanilla ice cream in the centre of a glass or an elegant vintage cup. Add half a poached peach and drizzle with raspberry coulis. Top with a generous spoonful of crème Chantilly, a small handful of fresh raspberries, and mint to decorate.

⚜

Tarte aux Framboises

Raspberry Tart

Yield: ONE 9-INCH (23 CM) TART, 8 PORTIONS

Preparation time: 45 MINUTES + 1 TO 1¼ HOURS CHILLING

Cooking time: 1 HOUR

✥⟶ I like making this tart in summertime, when all the fruits are in season. It's a fairly easy recipe for a simple go-to dessert you'll want to have in your repertoire. All you have to do is prebake the shell, fill it with crème pâtissière, *and top it with your favourite fruit. The tart is fantastic with raspberries, as I'm suggesting here, or strawberries, blueberries, peaches, apricots, cherries . . . the possibilities are never-ending. A slice can even stand on its own because of the pastry cream's smooth richness. You don't need anything else, really.*

What you'll need:

Stand mixer fitted with the paddle attachment

9-inch (23 cm) round tart ring, 1 inch (2.5 cm) deep

Piping bag with a plain tip

Tart Shell:

½ cup + 1 tablespoon (80 g) icing sugar

½ cup + 1 tablespoon (130 g) unsalted butter, softened

1 large egg

1¼ cups (200 g) all-purpose flour

⅓ cup + 1 tablespoon (50 g) cornstarch

¼ teaspoon (1 g) kosher salt

Crème Pâtissière:

2¼ cups (550 mL) homogenized milk (3.25% milk fat)

½ cup (110 g) granulated sugar, divided

1 vanilla bean, split and scraped (or a splash of vanilla extract)

7 egg yolks

⅓ cup + 1 tablespoon (50 g) cornstarch

¼ cup (60 g) unsalted butter, softened and cubed

FOR THE TART SHELL: In a stand mixer fitted with the paddle, cream the icing sugar and butter for 30 seconds on low speed. Add the egg, scrape down the sides of the bowl with a rubber spatula, and mix on medium speed until evenly combined.

In a medium bowl, combine the flour, cornstarch, and salt. With the mixer on low speed, stir in the flour mixture until just combined, about 10 seconds. Finish mixing the dough by hand to ensure it isn't overmixed. The dough should be creamy and smooth, and should have the consistency of cookie dough. Flatten it into a 1-inch-thick (2.5 cm) disc, wrap it in plastic wrap, and refrigerate until firm, 30 to 45 minutes.

Liberally flour your work surface and a rolling pin. Unwrap the dough and roll it out to about ⅛ inch (3 mm) thick. Using the tart ring as a guide, cut a circle 1 inch (2.5 cm) wider than the outside of the ring, so that the dough will reach up the sides of the ring.

Place the tart ring on a baking sheet lined with a silicone mat. Place the dough round on top of the tart ring and push down gently with your fingers, pressing the dough along the inside of the ring and making sure to get into the inside edges. Use a paring knife to trim off excess dough hanging over the edge of the ring. Chill in the fridge for 30 minutes.

Meanwhile, preheat your oven to 350°F (180°C), with the rack in the centre position.

Line the tart shell with parchment paper so the surface of the dough is completely covered. Press the parchment against the sides of the dough. Fill the shell completely with dried beans to weigh it down and prevent it

continued

Finishing:

1 pound (450 g) of the best-tasting raspberries that you can find (or the fruit of your preference)

Icing sugar, for dusting

from rising while baking. Blind-bake for 25 minutes. Remove from the oven and remove the beans from the tart shell, then bake for another 10 to 15 minutes, until it's a sandy light-golden colour and you don't see any wet spots. Unmould the tart shell while it's still warm and let cool completely on a wire rack.

FOR THE CRÈME PÂTISSIÈRE: In a medium pot on medium heat, combine the milk, half the sugar, and the vanilla seeds, and bring to a boil.

In a bowl, whisk together the remaining sugar with the egg yolks. Stir in the cornstarch until smooth. While whisking constantly, slowly pour in ½ cup (125 mL) of the warm milk mixture, whisking until combined. (This process is called tempering.) While stirring constantly, pour the egg mixture into the pot. Heat on low to medium heat, stirring constantly, until the mixture thickens noticeably. It takes about 3 minutes to thicken and, once thickened, another minute to cook out the raw taste from the cornstarch.

Remove from the heat and whisk in the cubed butter until fully incorporated. To help remove any lumps, strain through a fine-mesh sieve into a bowl. Press plastic wrap directly onto the surface of the *crème pâtissière* and let cool completely in the fridge until needed.

TO FINISH: Transfer the *crème pâtissière* to a piping bag with a plain tip and pipe it into the tart shell in a spiral pattern. Arrange the raspberries beautifully atop the *crème pâtissière*, pointed end up and tight together. Let the tart set in the fridge for 2 hours. Dust with icing sugar, and your tart is ready to slice and eat.

⚜

282   Where the River Narrows

Cygnes Profitéroles et Sauce au Chocolat

Swan Cream Puffs with Chocolate Sauce

Yield: 8 PORTIONS
Preparation time: 1½ HOURS
Cooking time: 30 MINUTES

What you'll need:

Piping bag with a plain ⅔-inch (1.5-cm) nozzle, a plain ¼-inch (5-mm) nozzle, and a star-tip nozzle

Swans:

1 batch Pâte à Choux (page 297)

Chocolate Sauce:

½ cup (350 mL) water

¾ cup (150 g) granulated sugar

1 cup (85 g) cocoa powder

2 tablespoons (30 g) unsalted butter

Crème Chantilly:

1⅔ cups (400 g) heavy or whipping cream (35% milkfat)

⅓ cup (50 g) icing sugar

1 vanilla bean, split and scraped

Assembly and Serving:

2 cups (500 mL) Vanilla Ice Cream (page 279, or good-quality store-bought)

🦢 *Jacques Pépin's* La Technique *cookbook is, to me, a masterpiece. It's a book that any respectable professional cook should have and should reference from time to time because it has all the basic techniques that you need to master before you can call yourself a decent cook. While leafing through it one day to find more information about eclairs, I saw that Jacques Pépin was making swans out of the choux pastry. The dough was shaped, baked, cut, and filled with cream so that the pastry looked like a swan swimming in chocolate sauce. Sure it sounds a bit cheesy, but you'll probably think differently if you're the parent of young kids; for me, it felt like I had just found the Holy Grail of ideas. I make this dessert regularly for my daughters and, believe me, it never fails to impress.*

FOR THE SWANS: Preheat your oven to 425°F (220°C), with the rack in the centre position, and have a wire cooling rack at the ready.

Fit a piping bag with a plain ⅔-inch (1.5 cm) nozzle, and use a spatula to fill the bag with choux pastry dough. On a large baking sheet lined with a silicone mat or parchment paper, pipe the dough into a large puff about 2 inches (5 cm) wide at one end and narrowing gradually to finish in a point at the other end (that will be the tail). The swan's body should be around 3 inches (7 to 8 cm) long. Pipe out 7 more bodies in this way to make a total of 8.

Change the nozzle to a plain ¼-inch (5 mm) tip and pipe eight S-shapes (the necks and heads of the swans) that are 2.5 inches (6 to 7 cm) long.

Bake in the oven for 6 minutes, then lower the heat to 375°F (190°C) and bake for 6 more minutes. Take the tray out of the oven and use a silicone spatula to transfer S-shapes (the heads and necks) to the wire cooling rack. Then return the baking tray to the oven to bake the bodies for a further 20 minutes, keeping the handle of a wooden spoon wedged in the oven door so there's a little opening for the steam to escape. This will prevent the choux from collapsing.

Shut off the oven and open the oven door halfway. Let the puffs sit in the oven for 10 minutes, then remove them from the oven and transfer the puffs to the wire rack to cool.

continued

FOR THE CHOCOLATE SAUCE: In a small pot on medium-high heat, whisk the water, sugar, and cocoa powder together until smooth, and bring to a boil while whisking constantly. Lower the heat to medium-low and simmer for 3 minutes. Add the butter and simmer for 4 minutes, whisking constantly. Remove from the heat, transfer the sauce to a small pouring container, and let cool at room temperature.

FOR THE CRÈME CHANTILLY: In a medium bowl, use a whisk to whip the cream, icing sugar, and vanilla seeds to a thick ribbon consistency. Using a spatula, transfer to a piping bag with a star-tip nozzle.

FOR ASSEMBLY AND SERVING: Holding a swan body on its side, slice through the centre with a serrated knife to remove the top. Then slice the top half vertically and lengthwise to make the wings. Repeat for each swan body.

Place a spoonful of vanilla ice cream into each body, then beautifully cover the ice cream with the crème Chantilly. Place the S-shaped necks and heads at the front of the bodies and attach both pieces of the wings onto the cream. Sprinkle the swans with a little icing sugar.

Fill the bottom of individual serving plates with the slightly warm chocolate sauce, and carefully place a swan in the centre of each plate. Place the remaining chocolate sauce in a sauce boat, and serve the swans immediately.

⚜

Gâteau Mille-Crêpes au Nutella

Crêpe Cake with Nutella Custard

Yield: 8 PORTIONS

Preparation time: 1 HOUR +
2 HOURS TO OVERNIGHT
RESTING

Cooking time: 45 MINUTES

What you'll need:

One 9-inch (23-cm) crêpe pan or
non-stick skillet

Piping bag with small plain tip
(optional)

Stand mixer with the whisk
attachment

Crêpes (makes 2 dozen):

½ cup (115 g) unsalted butter

1¾ cup (250 g) all-purpose flour

⅓ cup (65 g) granulated sugar

3 eggs

2 egg yolks

2½ cups (625 mL) homogenized
milk (3.25% milkfat), divided

Good pinch kosher salt

Nutella Crème Pâtissière:

2 sheets gelatin

2¼ cups (565 mL) homogenized
milk (3.25% milkfat)

¼ cup (50 g) granulated sugar

7 egg yolks

⅓ cup + 1 tablespoon (50 g)
cornstarch

¼ cup (55 g) unsalted butter,
softened and cubed

½ cup (150 g) Nutella

Swiss Meringue:

7 egg whites

1 cup (220 g) granulated sugar

Few drops of lemon juice

Mille-crêpes *literally translates to "a thousand crêpes." There's obviously no such thing as a thousand-layer cake, and the name symbolizes the artistry that goes into making this cake. It has no less than 24 delicate, paper-thin crêpes layered with pastry cream; even a* crème pâtissière *as simply flavoured as vanilla would be perfect for* mille-crêpes. *For this recipe, I decided to play around with an absolute favourite of my kids' (or any kids I know, for that matter), the famous Nutella. The chocolate-hazelnut spread is a match made in heaven for crêpes; I'm sure you already knew that. Nothing super innovative here, just comforting deliciousness.*

FOR THE CRÊPE BATTER: In a small saucepan on medium-high heat, melt the butter, then turn the heat down to medium and cook until it becomes brown butter (*beurre noisette*, page 307). Prepare a bowl of ice atop which you'll put the saucepan (this will stop the butter's cooking process).

Meanwhile, you should have enough time to whip the crêpe batter. In a medium mixing bowl, combine the flour and sugar. Make a well in the centre and pour in the eggs, egg yolks, and ¾ cup (200 mL) of the milk (about one-third). Whisk in the eggs and milk, then begin incorporating the flour a little at a time. Continue whisking energetically until the batter is homogeneous, thick, and without any lumps of flour. Gradually whisk in the rest of the milk and throw in the salt. You should now have a thin batter with a consistency similar to thick cream.

By this time, your brown butter should be ready and slightly cooled down with the help of the ice. Gradually whisk the brown butter into the crêpe batter. Let the batter rest in the fridge for 1 hour or up to the next day.

FOR THE NUTELLA CRÈME PÂTISSIÈRE: Soak the sheets of gelatin in a bowl filled with very cold water.

Meanwhile, in a medium pot on medium heat, bring the milk to a boil. In a medium bowl, whisk together the sugar with the egg yolks. Stir in the cornstarch until smooth, then slowly whisk in ½ cup of the warm milk, stirring until combined (this process is called tempering). Stirring continuously, pour the tempered egg mixture back into the pot of milk.

continued

Lower the heat to medium and cook the egg and milk mixture, stirring constantly until it thickens noticeably, about 3 minutes. Lower the heat to low and, stirring continuously, cook for 1 minute to cook out the raw taste from the cornstarch. Remove from heat and whisk in the cubed butter and Nutella until evenly combined.

Squeeze out the soaked gelatin sheets with your hands to remove all the water, then add to the hot custard and dissolve. Strain through a fine mesh sieve to remove any lumps. Cover with plastic wrap directly pressed onto the custard's surface and let cool at room temperature while you are making the crêpes.

FOR ASSEMBLY: Start making the crêpes. Line a baking sheet with parchment paper. Heat the crêpe pan or non-stick skillet on medium heat. When the pan is hot, brush with a little softened butter. For each crêpe, ladle about 1½ ounces (3 tablespoons/45 mL) of batter onto the edge of the skillet. Tilt the skillet to spread the batter evenly until it covers the bottom of the skillet. When the edges peel off easily and begin to brown, it's time to flip the crêpe with a silicone spatula. Continue cooking for 10 seconds, until the crêpe is cooked through, and remove from the skillet. Keep in mind that the first crêpe always looks like garbage—you can discard that one. Place the cooked crêpes onto the lined baking sheet as you go, and cover them with plastic wrap once they are cool to keep them from drying out. You'll need about 24 crêpes.

Time to assemble your *mille-crêpes* cake. Using a spatula, transfer the Nutella *crème pâtissière* to a piping bag fitted with a small plain tip; this is optional, but it will definitely make your life easier. Place one crêpe on a serving plate and pipe the custard mixture in a circle around the edge of the crêpe. With a spatula, spread the custard evenly, gradually moving it towards the centre and spreading it into a thin layer. Keep in mind that you'll need custard for all the layers. Cover with another crêpe and repeat the sequence with the remaining ingredients to create 24 layers of crêpes, ending up with a crêpe as the top layer. Refrigerate for 2 hours before serving.

FOR THE SWISS MERINGUE: When your *mille-crêpes* has rested for 2 hours, fill a medium pot one-quarter full with water and bring it to a simmer on medium-high heat.

Combine the egg whites, sugar, and lemon juice in a medium heat-proof mixing bowl and place it over the pot. Whisk constantly for about 5 minutes until the sugar is dissolved and the whites are quite hot to the touch,

continued

around 113°F (45°C). You can test it by rubbing the meringue between your fingers and making sure that you don't feel any grains of sugar. Transfer the mixture to the bowl of your stand mixer fitted with the whisk attachment, and whip on medium speed until glossy peaks form, about 5 minutes.

When ready to serve, use a rubber spatula to cover the sides and top of your *mille-crêpes* with the Swiss meringue. Try to create random peaks here and there for presentation. Using a blowtorch, caramelize the Swiss meringue, the same way you'd torch marshmallows. With a sharp serrated knife, cut the *mille-crêpes* into slices, just like you'd cut a cake.

TIP *Whenever you're whipping egg whites, use a glass, stainless-steel, glazed ceramic, or copper mixing bowl—not plastic. Make sure that your mixing bowl and whisk are spotlessly clean and impeccably dry.*

CHEF'S ESSENTIALS

PEOPLE ARE OFTEN INTIMIDATED by how long many dishes take to cook. But if you want to make good food, you need to allow time and patience for assembling and creating your main ingredients.

Chicken Stock (page 308), Vegetable Stock (page 313), and Veal Stock (page 309) are three key items in a well-stocked freezer for people who love to cook French food. Sauce is one of the cornerstones of French cuisine, and having stock readily available in your kitchen saves you a lot of time when prepping your mise en place. And making it at home instead of buying it off the grocery store shelf in a Tetra Pak container makes a world of difference to the flavour of any finished dish. It's not as hard as you might think to carve out the time to simmer stock: just throw Sunday dinner's roasted chicken carcass into a pressure cooker while you're doing the dishes. Add some carrots and celery, along with dried shiitakes and maybe a little bit of kelp for umami. One whole star anise contributes depth of flavour without being overwhelming, as does a tablespoon of fish sauce. After just 30 minutes in the pressure cooker, you have a clean well-balanced broth that tastes of roasted chicken rather than the ingredients you're simmering it with.

Pâte Brisée (page 299) and *Pâte Sucrée* (page 302) are also good items to have on hand. When you're at the market and see some really nice rhubarb, all you have to do is defrost your pastry, poach your rhubarb, and make some *crème pâtissière* (see Tarte aux Framboises, page 281) and you can assemble a beautiful tart for dessert in relatively little time.

Épices à Pâté

Pâté Spice

Yield: 3 TABLESPOONS (30 G)   *Preparation time:* 5 MINUTES

1 teaspoon (3 g) ground cloves

1 teaspoon (3 g) ground nutmeg

1 teaspoon (3 g) ground ginger

1½ teaspoons (4 g) ground cinnamon

1 tablespoon (12 g) freshly cracked black pepper

In a small bowl, mix all the ingredients together. Store at room temperature in an airtight container. This will keep for 6 months in your pantry; after that, the spices will start to lose their potency of flavour. You can also use these spices to season terrines, rillettes, and sausages.

⚜

Saumure Rouge

Basic Red Pickling Liquid

Yield: 3 CUPS (750 ML)   *Preparation time:* 10 MINUTES

1½ cups (375 mL) water

1½ cups (375 mL) red wine vinegar

5 tablespoons (80 g) granulated sugar

2 tablespoons (20 g) kosher salt

In a small saucepan on medium-high heat, stir together the water, vinegar, sugar, and salt, and bring to a simmer.

While the liquid is hot, pour it over the ingredient you'd like to pickle. I suggest shallots, onions, or cooked red beets.

⚜

Saumure Blanche

Basic White Pickling Liquid

Yield: 3 CUPS (750 ML)   *Preparation time:* 10 MINUTES + 1 HOUR COOLING AND CHILLING

1½ cups (375 mL) water

1½ cups (375 mL) apple cider vinegar

¼ cup + 1 teaspoon (60 g) granulated sugar

2 tablespoons (20 g) kosher salt

In a small saucepan on medium-high heat, stir together the water, vinegar, sugar, and salt, and bring to a simmer. Remove from the heat and let cool completely, then transfer to a bowl and refrigerate until chilled.

Once the pickling liquid is cold, it's ready to use. You can use it to pickle apples, celery, or cucumbers, just to mention a few ideas.

⚜

Aïoli

Garlic Mayonnaise

Yield: 1½ CUPS (375 ML)   *Preparation time:* 10 MINUTES

2 cloves garlic

½ teaspoon (2 g) kosher salt

2 egg yolks

2 teaspoons (10 mL) Dijon mustard

½ cup (125 mL) grapeseed oil

½ cup (125 mL) extra-virgin olive oil

Juice of ¼ lemon

Using a mortar and pestle, smash the garlic cloves into a paste, using the salt as an abrasive. Add the egg yolks and mustard, stirring to combine.

In a small pitcher or measuring cup, mix together the grapeseed oil and olive oil. Drop by drop, drizzle the oil into the mortar while stirring quickly with the pestle until an emulsion forms. Continue until you've incorporated all the oil. Stir in the lemon juice.

The aïoli will keep in an airtight container in the fridge for up to 3 days, but it's best when used right away at room temperature.

❖

Crème Fraîche

Yield: 1¾ CUPS (425 ML) *Preparation time:* 2 MINUTES + 1 TO 3 DAYS RESTING

2 cups (500 mL) heavy or whipping cream (35% milk fat)

3 tablespoons (45 mL) buttermilk

In a small bowl, combine the cream and buttermilk. Partially cover with a towel and let stand in a warmer spot of your kitchen until the cream tastes slightly sour and has thickened to a pudding-like consistency, anywhere from 1 to 3 days depending on the temperature of your kitchen.

Line a tamis with cheesecloth and rest it over a mixing bowl. Place the cream in the tamis to drain. The whey will drip into the bowl (you can reserve it for other uses, such as marinade), and the crème fraîche will remain in the tamis.

Store the crème fraîche in an airtight container in the fridge for up to 2 weeks.

⚜

Mayonnaise St. Lawrence

Yield: 2 CUPS (500 ML) *Preparation time:* 10 MINUTES

2 egg yolks

1 tablespoon (15 mL) Dijon mustard

1 teaspoon (3 g) kosher salt

½ teaspoon (2 g) granulated sugar

1½ cups (375 mL) grapeseed oil

2 tablespoons (30 mL) lemon juice

A few drops of water, if needed

Place a mixing bowl on top of a damp dishtowel; the towel will keep the bowl stable while you're whisking. Place the egg yolks, mustard, salt, and sugar in the bowl. While whisking constantly, slowly add half the grapeseed oil to create an emulsion. Whisk in half the lemon juice, then whisk constantly while drizzling in the rest of the oil. Whisk in the remaining lemon juice and taste for seasoning and acidity. Add a few drops of water if you find the mayonnaise too thick.

Store the mayonnaise in an airtight container in the fridge for up to 3 days.

⚜

Pâte à Choux

Choux Pastry

Yield: 1.7 POUNDS (750 G), ENOUGH FOR 22 TO 25 PUFFS OR ECLAIRS *Preparation time:* 30 MINUTES
Cooking time: 30 MINUTES

What you'll need:

Piping bag fitted with an appropriate tip for your chosen shape

1 cup (250 mL) homogenized milk (3.25% milk fat)

½ cup (115 g) unsalted butter, diced

1 teaspoon (4 g) granulated sugar

½ teaspoon (2 g) kosher salt

1 cup + 2 tablespoons (170 g) all-purpose flour

4 large eggs

FOR THE CHOUX PASTE: In a saucepan, combine the milk, butter, sugar, and salt. Bring to a boil on high heat, and boil for 1 minute, stirring constantly with a wooden spoon. Remove from the heat and, while stirring constantly, add all the flour at once. Continue stirring until the dough begins to form a ball or come away from the sides of the pan and is very smooth.

The next "drying out" step is important. Return the pan to low heat and stir vigorously for 2 minutes. Some of the water will evaporate and dry out the dough a little. Transfer to a bowl and continue to let the mixture dry out for 1 to 2 minutes, so more steam can escape.

While the mixture is still warm, using a wooden spoon, beat in the eggs, one at a time. Work fast so you don't cook the eggs and, most importantly, don't panic: the pastry will look separated at first, but keep going—it will all come together. Continue stirring until it is perfectly smooth and has a sheen to it.

At this point, the choux paste is best used immediately, but can be kept in the fridge in an airtight container for up to 2 days.

Use as directed in your recipe or continue with the baking steps below.

TO BAKE: Preheat your oven to 425°F (220°C), with the rack in the centre position. Line a baking sheet with parchment paper or a silicone mat.

Transfer the choux paste to a piping bag fitted with an appropriate tip to pipe out your chosen shape, whether it's small or large choux buns, éclairs, Hazelnut Paris-Brest (page 127), or even swans (page 285). Pipe out the choux paste onto the lined baking sheet.

Bake for 10 minutes, then lower the temperature to 350°F (175°C) and leave the oven door slightly ajar by wedging it open with the handle of a wooden spoon. This allows steam to escape and prevents the choux pastry from collapsing. Bake for another 20 minutes. Transfer to a wire rack and let cool completely.

Pâte à Pâté

Pâté en Croûte Dough

Yield: 3.3 POUNDS (1.5 KG), ENOUGH FOR A 16-INCH (40 CM) TERRINE MOULD   *Preparation time:* 15 MINUTES

What you'll need:

Stand mixer fitted with the paddle attachment

4¾ cups (700 g) all-purpose flour

½ cup + 2 tablespoons (80 g) cornstarch

1¾ cups (395 g) unsalted butter, softened

7 egg yolks (3.5 ounces/100 g)

¾ cup (175 mL) cold water

1 tablespoon + 2 teaspoons (16 g) kosher salt

In a medium bowl, mix together the flour and cornstarch.

Using a stand mixer fitted with the paddle, begin mixing the butter on medium speed, then incorporate the egg yolks, followed by the water and salt. Add the flour mixture in two batches, mixing until just combined, taking care not to overwork the pastry.

Wrap the pastry in plastic wrap and refrigerate for up to 3 days. Use as directed in your recipe.

⚜

Pâte Brisée

Pie Dough

Yield: 2 POUNDS (900 G), ENOUGH FOR TWO 9-INCH (23 CM) SINGLE-CRUST PIES OR ONE 9-INCH (23 CM) DOUBLE-CRUST PIE   *Preparation time:* 15 MINUTES + 30 MINUTES CHILLING

3 cups (450 g) all-purpose flour

1 teaspoon (3 g) kosher salt

1⅓ cups (300 g) cold butter, diced

¼ to ½ cup (75 to 125 mL) ice water

In a large mixing bowl, combine the flour and salt. Using a pastry cutter, cut in half the butter until the mixture resembles coarse cornmeal. Cut in the remaining butter just until the biggest pieces are the size of green peas. Gradually dribble in ice water, tossing and mixing until the dough just holds together. Don't overwork it, as this will make it tough. If it looks like there are dry patches, add another 1 tablespoon (15 mL) water and mix until the dough comes together.

Divide the dough in half. Firmly press each half into a 4-inch (10 cm) disc and wrap tightly in plastic wrap. Refrigerate for at least 30 minutes before rolling out.

When you're ready to roll out the dough, remove one disc from the fridge at a time. Let it soften slightly so that it's malleable but still cold. Unwrap the dough and press the edges of the disc so that there are no cracks. On a lightly floured work surface, roll out the dough as directed in your recipe. Brush off any excess flour from both sides with a dry pastry brush. Line a baking sheet with parchment paper, transfer the dough to the pan, and refrigerate for at least 1 hour before use.

VARIATION   *You can also use a food processor to make the dough. Place the flour, salt, and butter in the food processor and pulse about ten times, until the butter is incorporated—don't overmix. It should look like wet sand, and a few little pieces of butter here and there is okay. With the motor running, through the feed tube, slowly add ice water until the dough forms a ball—again don't overmix. Wrap, chill, and roll out as directed above.*

❖

Pâte Feuilleté Rapide

Quick Puff Pastry

Yield: 2.8 POUNDS (1.3 KG) DOUGH   *Preparation time:* 25 MINUTES + 1 HOUR AND 40 MINUTES CHILLING
Cooking time: 25 TO 30 MINUTES

1.1 pounds (500 g) all-purpose flour

1.1 pounds (500 g) unsalted butter, firm but not too hard, diced into ½-inch (1 cm) cubes

1 tablespoon (10 g) kosher salt

1 cup (250 mL) ice water

1 egg yolk (optional)

1 tablespoon (15 mL) homogenized milk (3.25% milkfat) (optional)

FOR THE DOUGH: Pour the flour onto a clean work surface and make a well in the centre. Place the cubed butter and the salt in the well. Using your fingertips, work the butter and salt together with the flour. When the butter chunks become very small and half of the mixture is grainy, pour the ice water into the centre and incorporate it into the dough. It's very important not to knead the dough at this stage and to stop working it as soon as it becomes homogeneous, with flakes of butter here and there. Wrap the dough in plastic wrap and refrigerate it for 10 minutes while you clean your work station.

On a lightly floured work surface, roll out the dough into a 12 by 6-inch (30 by 15 cm) rectangle. Brush off the excess flour from the surface of the dough. Fold one end into the centre and fold the other end over top, creating a smaller rectangle with three layers. This is your first turn. Wrap the dough in plastic wrap and refrigerate for 20 minutes. Repeat the process of rolling out, folding, and chilling twice more, for a total of three turns.

At this point, the dough can be kept in the fridge for up to 3 days, or in the freezer for up to 1 month. Thaw the dough completely before continuing with baking steps.

Use as directed in your recipe or continue with the baking steps below.

TO BAKE: Roll out the dough to your desired shape and thickness, place it on a baking sheet lined with a silicone mat or parchment paper, and refrigerate it for 30 minutes before baking. You must let it chill before baking, or it will shrink and not hold its shape.

Meanwhile, preheat your oven to 425°F (220°C), with the rack in the centre position.

If you wish to use an egg wash, in a small bowl, lightly beat the egg yolk with the milk and brush it over the pastry.

Bake for 25 to 30 minutes or until golden brown; timing depends on your pastry shapes. Bear in mind that the *pâte feuilleté rapide* will rise about 30% less than a classic puff-pastry dough. Bake your dough the same day you make it, or freeze for up to 3 days.

TIP *Puff pastry* fleurons *are an ideal way to use up leftover pastry, and they look great as a garnish on any plate. To make them, cut the pastry scraps into interesting shapes, bake them for 20 minutes, and use them as a textural accent for your dishes, particularly in place of croutons.*

❖

Pâte Sucrée

Sweet Pastry

Yield: 1.2 POUNDS (550 G) DOUGH, ENOUGH FOR ONE 9-INCH (23 CM) TART SHELL
Preparation time: 15 MINUTES + 60 TO 75 MINUTES CHILLING
Cooking time: 35 MINUTES + 30 MINUTES COOLING

What you'll need:

9-inch (23 cm) tart ring, 1 inch (2.5 cm) deep

1⅓ cups (200 g) all-purpose flour

½ cup + 1 tablespoon (130 g) cold unsalted butter, diced into ¼-inch (5 mm) cubes

½ cup + 1 tablespoon (80 g) icing sugar

⅓ cup + 1 tablespoon (50 g) cornstarch

Pinch kosher salt

1 large egg, beaten

FOR THE DOUGH: Pour the flour onto a clean work surface and make a well in the centre. Place the cubed butter in the well. Using your fingertips, work the flour and butter together until the butter is softened. Make another well, add the icing sugar, cornstarch, and salt to it, and mix well with your fingers. Make another well, add the egg, and mix with your fingers until well incorporated.

Work the dough once or twice with the palm of your hand until it's very smooth and the butter is fully incorporated. It's important not to overwork it at this stage or your pastry will shrink as it bakes. Roll the dough into a ball, flatten it, and wrap it in plastic wrap. Refrigerate until firm, about 30 to 45 minutes, or for up to 3 days.

Use as directed in your recipe or continue with the steps for making a tart shell below.

FOR A TART SHELL: Liberally flour your work surface and a rolling pin. Unwrap the dough and roll it out into a 12-inch (30 cm) circle about ⅛ inch (3 mm) thick. Make sure to work quickly so the dough doesn't get too warm.

Place the tart ring on a baking sheet lined with a silicone mat. Place the dough circle on top of the tart ring and push down gently with your fingers, pressing the dough along the inside of the ring and making sure to get into the inside edges. It's important not to press too hard and to keep the tart shell an even thickness so that it doesn't bake unevenly. Use a paring knife to trim off any excess dough hanging over the edge of the ring. Using a fork, poke holes in the dough on the bottom only; this helps prevent the pastry from rising during baking. Chill in the fridge for 30 minutes.

Meanwhile, preheat your oven to 350°F (180°C), with the rack in the centre position.

Line the tart shell with parchment paper so the surface of the pastry is completely covered. Press the parchment against the sides of the pastry. Fill the shell completely with dried beans to weigh it down and prevent

it from rising while baking. Blind-bake for 25 minutes, until it's a sandy light-golden colour and you don't see any wet spots.

Remove the tart shell from the oven. Remove the parchment paper and dried beans. Return to the oven for another 10 minutes. Remove from the oven and let the tart shell cool enough to remove the ring, about 15 minutes. Transfer to a cooling rack and let cool for 15 minutes before filling. Tart shells can be baked in advance and stored in airtight container for up to 2 days, but they taste best when enjoyed fresh the same day. Ideally speaking, fill your tart shell with creams and fillings and serve right away so that it stays nice and crispy.

❧

Vol-au-Vents

Puff Pastry Cases

Yield: 6 MEDIUM CASES OR 12 SMALL CASES *Preparation time:* 30 MINUTES + 1 HOUR OR OVERNIGHT CHILLING *Cooking time:* 30 MINUTES

What you'll need:

3-inch (7.5 cm) round pastry cutter (or fluted for a decorative touch)

2-inch (5 cm) round pastry cutter

Four 2-inch-high (5 cm) ring moulds

1.1 pounds (500 g) Pâte Feuilleté Rapide (page 300, or store-bought)

1 egg yolk + 1 tablespoon (15 mL) heavy or whipping cream (35% milkfat), for egg wash

On a floured work surface, roll out the puff pastry dough to ⅛ inch (3 mm) thick. Using the larger pastry cutter, cut the pastry into twelve discs, slightly twisting the cutter to ensure that the edges detach neatly from the puff pastry sheet.

In a small bowl, lightly beat the egg yolk with the cream to make an egg wash.

Line a baking sheet with a silicone baking mat. Arrange six dough discs on the mat and, using a pastry brush, glaze them lightly with egg wash.

Using the smaller pastry cutter, cut a hole in the centre of each of the discs remaining on your worktop, creating six pastry rings. Carefully place one ring on top of each disc, making sure to line up the edges. Brush the rings with egg wash and refrigerate for at least 1 hour or overnight to prevent them from shrinking during baking. Reserve the remaining egg wash.

Preheat your oven to 425°F (220°C), with the rack in the centre position.

Remove the pastry dough from the fridge and brush with more egg wash. Place a ring mould in each corner of the baking sheet and rest a second baking sheet on top of the ring moulds. (This will help control how much the puff pastry cases rise during baking.)

Bake for 10 minutes, then lower the heat to 350°F (175°C) and bake for 15 minutes. Remove the baking sheet on top, and bake for a further 10 minutes. Make sure the base of the pastry shells is well cooked, remove from the oven, and let cool completely before adding your savoury or sweet filling of choice.

VARIATION *To make twelve small puff pastry cases, use a 2-inch (5 cm) round (or fluted) pastry cutter for the discs and a 1½-inch (4 cm) round pastry cutter for the hole in the middle.*

Sauce Béarnaise

Béarnaise Sauce

Yield: 1 CUP (250 ML)   *Preparation time:* 15 MINUTES   *Cooking time:* 20 MINUTES

3 sprigs tarragon

1 shallot, finely chopped

½ cup (125 mL) + 3 tablespoons (45 mL) water, divided

3 tablespoons (45 mL) white wine vinegar

1 teaspoon (5 mL) crushed black peppercorns

5 egg yolks

¾ cup (175 mL) clarified butter (see tip, page 125)

½ teaspoon (2 g) kosher salt

2 tablespoons (30 mL) chopped fresh tarragon leaves

Fresh lemon juice, to taste

> *Sauce Béarnaise has traditionally been paired with grilled beef, especially* côte de boeuf. *When you see* côte de boeuf *for two on a menu or as a feature, the chances are pretty high that it comes with Béarnaise. However, Béarnaise also goes well with fish; Sauce Choron, a variant of Béarnaise, is a classic Paul Bocuse pairing with fish in pastry. I've given you two other variations as well: Sauce Paloise is perfect with lamb, while Sauce Foyot would be great with game meat, such as venison, moose, or elk.*

In a small saucepan, stir together the tarragon sprigs, shallot, ½ cup (125 mL) water, vinegar, and peppercorns. Bring to a simmer on medium heat, and simmer until reduced to about 1 tablespoon (15 mL) of liquid. Remove from the heat and let cool. Discard the tarragon sprigs.

Pour the 3 tablespoons (45 mL) water into a heat-resistant bowl set over a pot of simmering water on medium-high heat. Whisk in the egg yolks and continue whisking until light and creamy, 5 to 8 minutes. Don't let the temperature get any hotter than 150°F (66°C), or you'll end up with scrambled eggs.

Remove the bowl from the heat and, while whisking constantly, slowly pour in the clarified butter. Season with the salt and stir in the shallot reduction, along with the chopped tarragon. Add some lemon juice to taste for extra acidity. The sauce can be kept warm for 30 minutes in a warm *bain-marie*.

Other sauces you can make from Béarnaise:

SAUCE CHORON   Whisk 2 tablespoons (30 mL) tomato paste into the sauce with the lemon juice.

SAUCE FOYOT   Whisk in 3 tablespoons (45 mL) of *glace de viande*, meaning very strong (reduced) veal jus, with the lemon juice.

SAUCE PALOISE   Replace the tarragon sprigs and leaves with mint.

Sauce Béchamel

Béchamel Sauce

Yield: 4 CUPS (1 L) *Preparation time:* 15 MINUTES *Cooking time:* 15 MINUTES

⅓ cup (75 g) unsalted butter

½ cup (75 g) all-purpose flour

2 cups (500 mL) homogenized milk (3.25% milk fat)

2 cups (500 mL) heavy or whipping cream (35% milk fat)

1 small onion, peeled and studded with 2 whole cloves

1 tablespoon (10 g) kosher salt

1 bay leaf

Pinch freshly grated nutmeg

In a small pot on medium heat, heat the butter until foamy. Whisk in the flour and cook, whisking constantly, for 2 minutes. (This process is called making a roux.) Mix the milk and cream together in a small pitcher. Pour in a little of the milk-cream mixture, whisking until a thick paste forms. Lower the heat to low and gradually whisk in the remaining liquid little by little.

Add the studded onion and stir in the salt, bay leaf, and nutmeg. Simmer very gently for 10 minutes. Stir it often, as you don't want the sauce to burn onto the bottom of the pot—that would be devastating. Strain the sauce through a tamis and transfer to a blender. Blend until smooth.

The sauce can be used immediately or stored in an airtight container in the fridge for up to 3 days. If you must cook your béchamel in advance, cover the surface with plastic wrap laid directly on the surface of the sauce to prevent a skin from forming. Always reheat béchamel sauce by starting with a little bit of fresh milk in your pot.

⚜

SAUCE MORNAY

Mornay Sauce

Yield: 5 CUPS (1.25 L)

4 cups (1 L) warm sauce béchamel

1 cup (115 g) grated Gruyère cheese

1 cup + 2 tablespoons (115 g) freshly grated Parmesan cheese

3 egg yolks (optional)

Stir the Gruyère and Parmesan cheeses into the warm béchamel until fully incorporated. Whisk in the egg yolks, making sure you don't simmer the sauce.

⚜

Sauce Hollandaise

Hollandaise Sauce

Yield: 1 CUP (250 ML)   *Preparation time:* 20 MINUTES   *Cooking time:* 20 MINUTES

1 small shallot, minced

3 tablespoons (45 mL) white wine vinegar

½ teaspoon (2 g) kosher salt, plus more to taste

2 tablespoons (30 mL) water

5 egg yolks

¾ cup (175 mL) clarified butter (see tip, page 125)

Pinch cayenne pepper

Fresh lemon juice, to taste

In a small pan, combine the shallot, vinegar, and salt. Bring to a boil and reduce by two-thirds, or until you have about 1 tablespoon (15 mL) liquid, then remove from the heat. Strain through a fine-mesh sieve and discard the shallot.

In a heat-resistant bowl set over a pan of simmering water, whisk the water and egg yolks together and continue whisking, until the yolks are light and creamy, 5 to 8 minutes. Don't let the temperature get any hotter than 150°F (66°C), or you'll end up with scrambled eggs.

Remove the bowl from the heat and, while whisking constantly, slowly pour in the clarified butter. Season with the reduced vinegar, cayenne, and salt to taste. Add some lemon juice for extra acidity. Serve immediately or keep warm for no longer than 30 minutes in a warm *bain-marie*.

Other sauces you can make from hollandaise:

SAUCE MOUSSELINE   Whisk ¼ cup (60 mL) whipped cream into the finished hollandaise.

SAUCE NOISETTE   Instead of using clarified butter, make *beurre noisette* by placing 1 cup (225 g) unsalted butter in a small pot on high heat and cooking it a little past the melting point, browning the milk solids in the butter and creating a wonderfully nutty aroma. Proceed with making the hollandaise.

SAUCE MALTAISE   Whisk the grated zest and juice of 1 blood orange into the Hollandaise along with the lemon juice at the end of the process.

SAUCE MOUTARDE   Whisk ¼ cup (60 mL) heavy or whipping cream (35% milk fat) and 1 tablespoon (15 mL) Dijon mustard into the finished hollandaise.

Bouillons

Stocks

꧁ *So many cooks don't take making stock seriously. They use their stockpot as a place to throw all their scraps, not taking into account the amount of, say, carrots or parsley stems they put in, or throwing in vegetables that don't belong, like turnips or peppers. It's only logical that if you put too much of an ingredient in your stock, or maybe roast the bones too long and burn the tomato paste in the process, your finished stock will end up being . . . well, shit. Stock must be made with care.*

One of the key things to remember is that you should never boil stock. Always cook it at a gentle simmer so that any impurities rise to the surface for you to skim off and don't end up mixing into the stock.

Each of these stocks can be stored in the fridge for up to 3 days, or frozen for up to 3 months.

BOUILLON DE POULET

Chicken Stock

Yield: 8 CUPS (2 L) STOCK OR 1 CUP (250 ML) JUS   *Preparation time:* 20 MINUTES   *Cooking time:* 2½ HOURS

What you'll need:
Large cast-iron pan

1 large onion
4.5 pounds (2 kg) chicken bones (neck, wings, and feet preferred)
3 cloves garlic (unpeeled), smashed
1 stalk celery, cut into large pieces
3 parsley stems
1 sprig thyme
¼ sheet kombu (optional)
16 cups (4 L) cold water

Peel the onion and cut it in half through the root end. Heat a large cast-iron pan on high heat, and char the onion halves, flat side down. (This step is optional but will give your stock a lot of depth of flavour.)

In a large stockpot, combine the chicken bones, onion, garlic, celery, parsley, thyme, and kombu. Cover with the cold water, bring to a simmer on low heat, and simmer gently for 2½ hours, skimming off any impurities that rise to the surface.

Strain the stock carefully through a chinois or tamis; you should have around 8 cups (2 L).

To make jus, return the stock to the pot and cook on medium heat until reduced to 1 cup (250 mL).

⚜

BOUILLON DE VEAU

Veal Stock

Yield: 8 CUPS (2 L) STOCK OR 1 CUP (250 ML) DEMI-GLACE   *Preparation time:* 20 MINUTES
Cooking time: 5 HOURS

4.5 pounds (2 kg) veal bones

3 tablespoons (45 mL) grapeseed oil

1 pig trotter, halved, optional

5 cloves garlic (unpeeled), smashed

3 medium onions, peeled and quartered

2 large carrots, peeled and cut into 1-inch (2.5 cm) chunks

1 stalk celery, cut into 1-inch (2.5 cm) chunks

2 tablespoons (30 mL) tomato paste

5 parsley stems

3 sprigs thyme

1 teaspoon (5 mL) black peppercorns

1 bay leaf

20 cups (5 L) cold water

Preheat your oven to 400°F (200°C), with the rack in the centre position.

In a mixing bowl, toss the veal bones with the oil. Transfer to a baking sheet and roast for 30 minutes. Add the pig trotter, garlic, onions, carrots, and celery, and roast for 25 minutes. Toss the veal bones and vegetables with the tomato paste, parsley, thyme, peppercorns, and bay leaf. Roast for 5 more minutes.

Transfer all the ingredients to a large stockpot, cover with the cold water, bring to a simmer on low heat, and simmer gently for 4 hours, skimming off any impurities that rise to the surface.

Strain the stock carefully through a chinois or tamis; you should have around 12 cups (3 L).

Return the stock to the pot and cook on medium heat until reduced to 8 cups (2 L). To make demi-glace, continue reducing to 1 cup (250 mL).

✤

BOUILLON DE PORC

Pork Stock

Yield: 8 CUPS (2 L) STOCK OR 1 CUP (250 ML) DEMI-GLACE *Preparation time:* 20 MINUTES
Cooking time: 4 HOURS

4.5 pounds (2 kg) pork bones

3 tablespoons (45 mL) grapeseed oil

4 cloves garlic (unpeeled), smashed

3 medium onions, peeled and quartered

2 shallots, peeled and quartered

2 large carrots, peeled and cut into 1-inch (2.5 cm) chunks

1 leek (white and green parts), cut into 1-inch (2.5 cm) chunks

5 parsley stems

1 sprig thyme

20 cups (5 L) cold water

Preheat your oven to 400°F (200°C), with the rack in the centre position.

In a mixing bowl, toss the pork bones with the oil. Transfer to a baking sheet and roast for 30 minutes. Add the garlic, onions, shallots, carrots, leek, parsley, and thyme, and roast for 25 minutes.

Transfer all the ingredients to a large stockpot, cover with the cold water, bring to a simmer on low heat, and simmer gently for 3 hours, skimming off any impurities that rise to the surface.

Strain the stock carefully through a chinois or tamis; you should have around 12 cups (3 L).

Return the stock to the pot and cook on medium heat until reduced to 8 cups (2 L). To make demi-glace, continue reducing to 1 cup (250 mL).

⚜

BOUILLON DE CANARD

Duck Stock

Yield: 3 CUPS (750 ML) STOCK OR ½ CUP (125 ML) DEMI-GLACE *Preparation time:* 20 MINUTES
Cooking time: 2 HOURS

Bones from 1 duck

3 tablespoons (45 mL) grapeseed oil

2 shallots, sliced

2 cloves garlic (unpeeled), smashed

1 medium onion, sliced

1 small carrot, peeled and sliced

4 cups (1 L) cold water

1 bay leaf

2 sprigs thyme

Using a cleaver, chop the duck bones into small pieces. In a large pot on high heat, heat the oil and sear the duck bones. Remove the bones from the pot and sauté the shallots, garlic, onion, and carrot for 10 minutes, or until brown. Return the duck bones to the pot and stir in the cold water, bay leaf, and thyme. Bring to a simmer on low heat, and simmer gently for 1¾ hours, skimming off any impurities that rise to the surface.

Strain the stock carefully through a sieve.

To make demi-glace, return the stock to the pot and cook on medium heat until reduced to ½ cup (125 mL).

⚜

FUMET DE POISSON

Fish Stock

Yield: 4 CUPS (1 L) *Preparation time:* 20 MINUTES *Cooking time:* 1 HOUR + 5 MINUTES RESTING

4.5 pounds (2 kg) fish bones

3 tablespoons (45 mL) grapeseed oil

2 medium shallots, sliced

1 bulb fennel, sliced

1 leek (white and green parts), sliced

1 onion, sliced

1 bay leaf

1 cup (250 mL) white wine

1 small bunch fresh flat-leaf parsley

1 sprig thyme

Place the fish bones in a large bowl, rinse with cold water, and discard the water. Chop the bones into small pieces.

In a large pot on medium heat, heat the oil. Sweat the shallots, fennel, leek, onion, and bay leaf for 10 minutes, ensuring they don't pick up any colouration. Stir in the fish bones and sweat for 5 minutes. Stir in the wine and cook until reduced by half. Stir in the parsley, thyme, and 8 cups (2 L) cold water. Bring to a gentle simmer—whatever you do, don't boil the stock—and partially cover the pot, leaving the lid ajar. Lower the heat to low and simmer gently for 45 minutes, skimming off any impurities that rise to the surface. Remove from the heat and let rest for 5 minutes.

Strain the stock carefully through a chinois or a tamis; you should have around 6 cups (1.5 L).

Return the stock to the pot and cook on medium heat until reduced to 4 cups (1 L).

⚜

BOUILLON DE LÉGUMES

Vegetable Stock

Yield: 2 CUPS (500 ML)   *Preparation time:* 20 MINUTES   *Cooking time:* 30 MINUTES + 10 MINUTES RESTING

4 cups (2 L) water

1 tablespoon (10 g) kosher salt

8 button mushrooms, diced

2 stalks celery, diced

1 medium onion, diced

1 large carrot, peeled and diced

1 large tomato, diced

5 parsley stems

1 sprig thyme

1 bay leaf

1 sprig tarragon

1 star anise pod

In a large stockpot on medium-high heat, combine all the ingredients and bring to a simmer. Lower the heat to low and simmer gently for 30 minutes. Remove from the heat and let rest for 10 minutes.

Strain the stock carefully through a sieve; you should have around 4 cups (1 L).

Return the stock to the pot and cook on medium heat until reduced to 2 cups (500 mL).

⚜

MENUS

HOW TO PREPARE A SUCCESSFUL MEAL My first rule of thumb is to never—and I really mean never—test new dishes on my guests, either in the restaurant or when I throw a dinner party at home. I let my kitchen team, family, or most trusted friends bite the bullet and help with the honest criticism first. Family and close friends will easily forget a mistake, but customers or guests probably won't let it go.

When figuring out which dishes to tackle, start with easy recipes first. Or, if the main course is time-consuming, pair it with a simple starter and an easy dessert. And it's absolutely key to fully read through each of your chosen recipes before you even start your shopping and preparation.

There are a few things that determine a great meal, such as the skill of the cook, the quality of the ingredients, the temperature of the dishes (meaning hot food should be hot), and the portioning of the dishes. Of equal importance is setting the mood of your dining space. Think about elements like light quality (Is it too cool? Would candlelight be better, to soften the vibe?), choice of tableware, background music . . . you catch my drift. All of these elements should complement each other, and should always be in balance.

No matter what, don't panic. All you need is proper planning and a methodical approach. Read through your recipes at least twice and look for steps that can be done in advance without affecting the quality of the dish—that's how we work in the restaurant. Weigh and prepare (wash, peel, and cut) your ingredients ahead of time; well-organized mise en place will save you countless headaches.

Remember that the whole process should be easy and fun, from mapping out your menu to shopping and cooking. Your efforts will be well rewarded by the smiles and admiration on the faces of your guests.

THOUGHTS ON WINE

BY LISA HALEY

I WANTED TO get my hands on the St. Lawrence wine list from the first time I dined there, mere weeks after its opening. Really, it's my dream list. French wine is my first love, and I've always wanted to work with a small regional *carte de vin*.

J-C's menu feels like home to me. Though I grew up in Ontario, my family is from the Gaspé Peninsula, and many of J-C's dishes and food traditions are in my DNA too: eating sugar pie during the holidays, stopping at *casse-croûtes* on road trips, and watching my father stock up on *cretons* every time we took a trip east. The real game-changer was moving to Montréal for university when I was 19—I ended up staying for 13 years, immersing myself in the city's vibrant food culture. I'd spend hours shopping at Atwater Market, which was just steps from where I lived, indulged in countless meals at classic favourites L'Express and Leméac, and learned all about wine. Of course, in Montréal, that meant French wine.

The wine list at St. Lawrence isn't long. Today it comes in at just half a page. I'd been longing to curate a list as strict as this one after working on big international wine lists for years, and when I heard that J-C and his team were looking for a sommelier, I jumped at the chance. Building a complete wine program from only one country when we are so spoiled for choice here in Vancouver was both challenging and freeing. I could focus on the task at hand without having to consider every varietal, every region, every style. Just France. And what a country it is to work with. If a complementary wine list needed to have a range of style and value, there isn't an easier place to find it than France. The home of both Champagne and its much less expensive ancestor Crémant de Limoux. Bordeaux and Cahors. Bourgogne and Côtes de Jura. France has everything we could need. Some things have changed at St. Lawrence. We offer British Columbian wines now and rotate the wines by the glass on a whim. But the idea is the same: you don't need to have much to have what you need.

Much is made of the challenge of pairing wines with food, and it's true that you can deep dive into achieving the "perfect" pairing, but the true joy in wine comes from sharing a good bottle with a good meal with good friends and family. I stick to a few basic rules.

First, only drink wines you like. This doesn't mean you should never try new wines—that wouldn't be living—but it doesn't matter how perfect the pairing is if you don't like the wine. If you don't like light white wines like those of the Loire Valley, don't drink them. There's always something else that will work.

Second, neither the wine nor the food should steal the show. They are there to work together. Big, bold red will usually overpower a delicately seasoned poultry dish, and richly spiced *tourtière* will obliterate a Provence rosé. But a peppery syrah from the Rhône will sing with red meat like *pot-au-feu*.

Third—and definitely not least—nearly every sommelier will tell you the same thing. When in doubt, Champagne will work. Truly.

Québec

SOUPE AUX PETITS POIS
Yellow Pea Soup

※

TOURTIÈRE DU LAC ST-JEAN
Rustic Meat Pie

※

LES FÈVES AU LARD
Baked Beans with Maple Syrup

※

POUDING CHÔMEUR ET
CRÈME GLACÉE VANILLE
Poor Man's Pudding with Vanilla Ice Cream

I can 100% guarantee that all four of these dishes were on the table for our huge family dinners at my grandfather's cabane à sucre. *It was always potluck, because there's no way that any one person could prepare such a massive amount of food on their own. Mom would be in charge of the* soupe aux petits pois, *my grandmother would do the* pouding chômeur, *my father's sister would bring the* fèves au lard, *and someone else would bring* tourtière. *Everyone would throw down what they did best, and it was always interesting to taste how everyone put their individual touches on these traditional Québécois recipes from household to household. And there was inevitably a healthy sense of competition with everyone sharing their opinions on their favourites. If everybody declared my grandmother's* pouding chômeur *unbeatably the best, then hers would remain a staple. But if someone else thought they could do a particular dish better, then they'd step up and volunteer to bring it the following year—game on. It's all part of what made these meals some of my most cherished memories—not just for the food that was on the table, but for the love that brought us together to share it.*

Classic French

FEUILLETÉ D'ASPERGES
AU BEURRE DE CERFEUIL
Asparagus with Chervil Butter Sauce and Puff Pastry

⚜

POULET À LA CRÈME
Braised Chicken in Cream Sauce

⚜

ÎLES FLOTTANTES ET CRÈME ANGLAISE
Poached Meringues and Crème Anglaise

If chef Rob Feenie and I were to sit down together over a home-cooked meal, it's pretty much a given that the star of the show would be poulet à la crème—*apropos, given his classical French culinary background. He worked with iconic Vancouver chef Michel Jacob at Le Crocodile before a stint in Alsace, which is where his lifelong love affair with* poulet à la crème *began. Every time he talks about one particular restaurant in Strasbourg, his eyes always light up. It's been open for over 100 years, and the traditional* poulet à la crème *on their menu is even better than the transformed modern iteration Rob had at Alain Ducasse. He loves the recipe so much that he taught his own kids how to prepare it, offering a little insight into the classic French techniques that form the foundation for his creative culinary explorations, which also weave in threads of Asian influence. My time with Rob at Lumière was incredibly inspirational; after my years in Toqué!'s avant-garde kitchen, it really put me back on track to pursue classically grounded dishes.*

St. Lawrence

ESCARGÔTS AU BEURRE À L'AIL
Snails in Garlic Butter

⚜

SALADE D'ENDIVES, PACANES, POMMES, ET BLEU ÉLIZABETH
Endive Salad with Pecans, Apples, and Blue Elizabeth Cheese

⚜

CÔTE DE PORC, POMME PURÉE, ET SAUCE CHARCUTIÈRE
Pork Chops with Potato Purée and Charcutière Sauce

⚜

TARTE AU CITRON FLAMBÉE AU PASTIS
Lemon Tart Flambéed with Pastis

In developing the St. Lawrence menu, I had to take a few steps back before I could move forward. Back to the classical French beginnings of my culinary career. Back to rich and rustic family meals. And somehow meshing these two disparate food experiences to compile a slate of dishes grounded in tradition, memory, and love. Sure, presentation is important—our Cailles en Sarcophage *(page 203) and* Pâté en Croûte *(page 151) are two perfect examples—but what we create isn't precious tweezer food. Instead, it's cooking that grabs people by the heart and prompts soulful, visceral reactions. Flavour comes first, but it goes hand in hand with emotion and comfort.*

Home Cooking

CERVELLE DE CANUT
Fresh Cheese with Herbs

⚜

STEAK AUX POIVRES
Steak with Peppercorn Cream Sauce

⚜

MOUSSE AU CHOCOLAT
Chocolate Mousse

My neighbourhood here in Vancouver has a long-standing tradition of holding annual block parties. We close off the street so that the kids, both big and little, can run around and play freely. All the neighbours contribute: everything from Steph and Steph's chicken wings to Holly and Kathy's GDD (God-Damned Dip!) to Joie's pandesal bread pudding with rum-macerated mangoes. Our 94-year-old Italian neighbour, Mike, pours his homemade red wine and grappa with his wife Lydia's encouragement. Another neighbour, Bruce, is the bassist for a cover band, and they peel off a few songs before heading off to their gig for the evening. It's definitely a unique, diverse neighbourhood, warm and welcoming. One generation of kids has grown up into their university years, while the next generation of toddlers moves up to take their place with a whole new crop of sidewalk chalk drawings and backyard wading-pool parties.

Pulling It All Together

PÂTÉ DE FAISAN
Pheasant Terrine
(CLASSIC FRENCH)

⚜

BISQUE DE HOMARD THERMIDOR
Lobster Bisque Thermidor
(QUÉBEC)

⚜

POISSON EN PAPILLOTE ET ROUILLE
Fish in Papillote with Rouille
(HOME COOKING)

⚜

SOUFFLÉ GLACÉ À L'ORANGE
ET GRAND MARNIER
Frozen Orange Soufflé with Grand Marnier
(ST. LAWRENCE)

People who never cook think that cooking is complicated. But when you start cooking, you quickly realize that it isn't that complicated after all. The trick is to live it, with emotion, to feel it. Creativity in cooking shouldn't be all about provoking the palate or showcasing difficult techniques, but being yourself in the process of it, being authentic, sharing a piece of yourself with your guests, and bringing your cooking to life. The only difficulty is your fear—you've gotta put your fear away in the pantry and close the door. A recipe is just a recipe, so don't be intimidated. It gives you direction, like a highway, but this highway isn't always straight. You have to put a little bit of your own touch and thoughts into it. This is why we are mixing and matching recipes from different chapters here, pairing them to create a very classy, elegant dinner that will make you look like a great chef in the eyes of your guests. The beauty of this particular menu is that most of the dishes can be prepared and assembled in advance so you'll be in control and organized while hosting and enjoying the evening with your guests.

JEAN-CHRISTOPHE POIRIER & JOIE ALVARO KENT

ACKNOWLEDGEMENTS

J-C POIRIER

There are many people who helped me along the way to make this journey possible. Among them, Joie Alvaro Kent, who put her heart and soul into the writing of this book and the food and photo shoot styling, who introduced me to our publisher, and who believed that I could write in English (thank God for the auto-correct function!).

My gratitude to my team: Colin Johnson, Ashley Kurtz, Landen Swick, Margaux Herder, Jacob Isaak, Jul Bradley, Taejun Kim, Sri Rodwell, Danielle McAlpine, Julie Sopuck, Christophe Retru, Sarah Hawkins, David Lawson, Vivien Laforest, Lisa Haley for her thoughts on wine pairings, and all past and present employees at St. Lawrence. *Merci beaucoup* for your continuous collaboration and help.

My sympathy and thanks to all our long-suffering recipe testers: Elizabeth Li, Sarah Westwood, Jonathan Yuen, Lee Gibson, Quentina Siah, Brian Chan, and Rachelle Radiuk.

Many thanks to the team at Appetite by Random House: Robert McCullough, Zoe Maslow, and Jennifer Griffiths. Thank you to my friend and photographer Brit Gill whose talent and brilliant professional skills made my food magical.

To the chefs with whom I've spent numerous hours going through hard services and who made me a better person and a better cook, thank you to Normand Laprise, Rob Feenie, Charles-Antoine Crête, Cameron Smith, Dana Ewart, Aimée Wimbush-Bourque, Angus An, Cheryl Johnson, Marc-André Choquette, Jérémie Bastien, Cameron Picek, Vincent Fraissange, Paul Croteau, Dominic Aubin, and Guillaume St-Pierre.

Many thanks to my close friends Christian Quintal (CQ), Camille Belisle (Bill), Mathieu Larivière (Ti-Jus), Patrick Desoniers (Deso), and Stephane Champagne (Le Gros Steph), who pushed me into this profession with their tremendous support, appetite, and large *joie de vivre*.

Thank you to my mother and father for bringing me into this world. Even though most of the time you didn't know what was going through my head, you so patiently dealt with my silence and somehow understood me, trusting all along that I would come out on top in whatever I decided to do.

And my most special thanks to my beautiful wife, Dara Dammann, who gave me help with the creative styling of the photos with all her stunning linens and her natural instinct for hosting and setting up the perfect dinner table, along with her moral support, positive vibes, and love throughout the long process of making this book.

JOIE ALVARO KENT

The creative process for bringing this book to fruition has been a joyful, magical journey. J-C Poirier, thank you for doing the deep dive with me, for always wearing your heart on your sleeve, and for pouring your creativity and fire into St. Lawrence—your passion project resonated with me from the word go. I'm grateful beyond words for your confidence and trust in me to tell your story. Writing this book with you has forever changed me and how I approach my craft.

My wonderful husband, Ian Kent—it was your gentle nudge that kickstarted me on my professional writing path. Your support and unwavering belief in me challenge me to step outside my comfort zone and choose the projects that scare me a little. Thank you for your love and for always being my safe place.

Noah Kent, my remarkable son, you are my life's most miraculous gift. You amaze and inspire me every day with your boundless creative vision, intellect, and wisdom beyond your years. It fills my heart to know that all the time we've spent together in the kitchen since you could stand on a chair at the counter has turned into a shared lifelong passion for food. However near or far apart we are, know that my heart remembers your heartbeat and will forever hold you there. Love you forever and ever, sweet lad.

Mom, how I wish you were alive today to read this book. By persevering through my picky-eating years and taking me on all kinds of food adventures, you laid the groundwork for my culinary explorations. You moved through life with such incomparable grace, faith, and courage; your extraordinary strength and unconditional love inspire me to this day. I dearly love and miss you.

For treasured friends who are the touchstones that nurture my soul, I am immensely grateful. Barrett Jones, thank you a million for countless drives to nowhere, late-night philosophical chats and Frosty runs, and screwing my head back on straight when I need it most. Words don't even begin to cover it. Sarah Westwood, my long-distance sounding board and confidante, sharer of giggle fits that leave us in tears, you're so often the lynch pin that helps keep my sanity intact. Jonathan Yuen, the stalwart buffer who keeps Sarah's and my irreverent asses from getting hit in public, you're not half-bad yourself. My go-to source for second opinions and number one recipient of drive-time calls, Sophia Cheng. To Anya Levykh, Quentina Siah, Katharine Manson, and Nicole Holoboff, strong warrior women who distract me with silliness, commiserate over my greatest challenges, and celebrate my deepest joys. Hamid Salimian, your friendship and unfailing support are precious gifts—you are family to me. To Barbara Faugno, Maggie Chow, Callula Voogd, and Lee Man for your loving encouragement. I'm blessed beyond measure to have such remarkably kind, dynamic human beings in my corner.

To the special women in J-C's life who are now a wonderful part of mine: Dara Dammann, Aïla, and Florence. I can't thank you enough for warmly welcoming me into your home, for wine and popsicles and sidewalk-chalk drawings. For your love and laughter. I'm grateful.

Massive gratitude to the dream team at Appetite Random House, especially Robert McCullough for your friendship and faith, editing goddess Zoe Maslow for being so sympatico right from square one, and Jennifer Griffiths for your graphic prowess in making our words come alive on the page. Brit Gill, your talent for capturing emotion and an incomparable softness in your photos is so special—thank you for being an integral part of this project.

Colin Johnson, I have boundless respect for your incredible culinary talent, your unswerving dedication to precision (details matter!), and the passion you pour into pursuing your craft. It was a pleasure and an honour to collaborate with you on immortalizing your *pâté en croûte* recipe in print. I'm hugely thankful for the gift of your friendship—big love your way.

To the entire St. Lawrence crew, both past and present, this book wouldn't exist without all of you collectively kicking serious culinary ass every single day. I'm thankful for the restaurant magic that you as an inspired and talented team consistently create together. And thank you, Lisa Haley, for contributing your words on wine.

Giant high five to our intrepid recipe testers: Sarah Westwood, Jonathan Yuen, Elizabeth Li, Quentina Siah, Lee Gibson, Brian Chan, and Rachelle Radiuk. Thank you all for blowing a disproportionate amount of your grocery bills on butter and jeopardizing your cholesterol counts to lend us a hand.

And Donna Bellavance, once upon a time in Grade 11 English Lit, you asked us to put our heads down on our desks and close our eyes as you dropped the needle on a record. The classroom was soon filled with the wonderful sonorous voice of Dylan Thomas reading his poem "A Child's Christmas in Wales," and I was mesmerized. You instilled in me a deep love for thoughtfully written words and an understanding that these same words have so much more beauty when they're spoken aloud, not just read in silence. I cannot thank you enough.

INDEX